Gender and International
Aid in Afghanistan

M000206902

Gender and International Aid in Afghanistan

The Politics and Effects of Intervention

LINA ABIRAFEH

McFarland & Company, Inc., Publishers
Jefferson, North Carolina, and London

All photographs are by the author.

LIBRARY OF CONGRESS CATALOGUING-IN-PUBLICATION DATA

Abirafeh, Lina, 1974–
    Gender and international aid in Afghanistan : the politics and
effects of intervention / Lina Abirafeh.
        p.   cm.
    Includes bibliographical references and index.

    ISBN 978-0-7864-4519-6
    softcover : 50# alkaline paper ∞

    1. Women's rights — Afghanistan.   2. Women — Afghanistan —
Social conditions.   3. Economic assistance — Social aspects —
Afghanistan.   4. Economic development — Social aspects —
Afghanistan.   5. Afghanistan — Social policy.   6. Afghanistan —
Politics and government.   I. Title.
HQ1236.5.A3A25   2009
305.4209581 — dc22   2009028951

British Library cataloguing data are available

©2009 Lina Abirafeh. All rights reserved

*No part of this book may be reproduced or transmitted in any form
or by any means, electronic or mechanical, including photocopying
or recording, or by any information storage and retrieval system,
without permission in writing from the publisher.*

On the cover: A door in Baagh-i-Babur (Babur's Garden), Kabul

Manufactured in the United States of America

McFarland & Company, Inc., Publishers
   Box 611, Jefferson, North Carolina 28640
      www.mcfarlandpub.com

Table of Contents

Acknowledgments   vii

Preface   1

1 — An Agenda for Social Change   9

2 — Discourses on *Chaddari* Politics   32

3 — Gender and the Aid Apparatus   50

4 — Transplanting Democracy   69

5 — *Afghaniyat* and the Gender Order   85

6 — *Maida, Maida*   106

7 — This Is Afghanistan   122

8 — Violence in the Aftermath   141

9 — Insecurities and Ideological Occupations   163

Dari Terminology   189

Acronyms and Abbreviations   191

Chapter Notes   193

Bibliography   207

Index   221

for ru,
who helps me find balance —
and my way home.

Acknowledgments

A series of happy accidents contributed to my interest in Afghanistan, but my first taste of the country would not have been possible without Zainab Salbi of Women for Women International, who trusted me to "take it to the moon"—and handed me a ticket. I do not know how to begin thanking all those who opened doors for me on this journey. I find this harder than writing the book itself. I hope I can convey the gratitude I feel and the growth I have experienced on this adventure.

Above all else, I receive limitless support from my family—broadly defined—who indulge my nomadic fantasies. My work is fueled by you, Salwa and Souhail, on whose shoulders I stand even when I am oceans away.

My energy is nourished by my Shami family: home is where you are. *Doorik Doctora Muna!* Meghdessians: I follow in your wandering footsteps. Lena and Lilly, my solid sister lifelines: you wake me up—and shake me up! Shel and Julie-jan: you inspire me, counsel me, and shower me with care (packages!). And Bruno knows that I only work in pajamas.

An array of brilliant minds helped bring this research to life. Almut Wieland-Karimi gave me a good German kick in the *patlun* to get this going. Lynel Long kept after me to get it done. Gretchen Bloom kept me thinking—and talking. Jo Beall guided me gently to the finish line. Elaheh Rostami-Povey and Donna Pankhurst envisaged the book from the start. Rosemarie Skaine found me, planted the idea, and cultivated it with encouraging words.

Many experts in Afghanistan shared their wisdom, words, and ways. I trust that you know who you are—and how grateful I am to you. Staff of Women for Women International in 2002-2003: you inspired this research and taught me more than I can say.

Strong support sustained me, and kept me sane. Brothers Klawitter: you gave me a place to live while I wrote—and made it a home. And Wais: you were Afghanistan, to me.

Many in Papua New Guinea supported the metamorphosis from dissertation to book. Writing a book is easy as long as I can see the sea. Bona family, my PNG *wantoks*: thank you for adopting me. Patrick: we will always be "free from the inside." Erik and Topes, my salt and pepper: you held my hand

and cheered me on. I'd be stranded on a Pacific island with you anytime. And B: you stretched me, challenged me, made me laugh, and taught me to relax.

Finally, for the Afghan women I've had the privilege to work with: yours is the most exciting, exhilarating (and exhausting!) adventure I have been on. Thank you for teaching me the value of humility, for sharing your ways, and for inspiring me with your spirit. *B'aman Khoda*. I wish you peace.

Preface

This book marks the culmination of a twelve-year engagement with Afghanistan. My interest in this rich and fascinating country began in 1997 through my work on Afghan women's human rights in Washington, D.C. I sustained that interest across many other countries and organizations until the opportunity to move arose. I relocated to Afghanistan in 2002 to establish the Afghanistan office of an international non-governmental organization. In 2003, I joined the London School of Economics and Political Science as a Ph.D. candidate in order to refine my thoughts, hone my analyses, and delve more deeply into my observations. I continued to work in Afghanistan in various capacities — both as academic and activist. My professional engagement with the country ended in September 2006. I then moved to Sierra Leone — but continued my writing on Afghanistan. I defended my dissertation and received my Ph.D. in 2008, while I was living and working in Papua New Guinea. This writing has traveled the world with me, but with the publication of this book it can finally return home, to Afghanistan.

The question of women's role in Afghanistan has been an ongoing part of political discourse, linked to modernity and progress on the one hand and preservation of tradition on the other. Women, politics, and the state have always been intimately connected in Afghanistan, and conflicts have been fueled by attempts to challenge or change women's status. And yet Afghan women's experiences are more complex than mere pawns in political struggles.

At the level of rhetoric, Afghanistan can be viewed as one of the largest gender-focused aid interventions. At the level of action, however, the situation is less clear. Afghan women and men recognize that they face a great challenge in articulating their own definitions of progress in the face of strong international agendas. Many women argue that their cause has been manipulated for political reasons, and external pressures to fast-track gender equality would foment a backlash. The necessary foundations to secure human rights — economic, political, military — have been notably meager. And Afghan voices have been lost in the process.

Women in Afghanistan are used as the barometer for aid agencies to measure social change. But has there been an opportunity for Afghan women and men to find their place in the new gender order? Are they able to determine the direction and pace of social change according to their own priorities and agendas? Has the concept of gender become synonymous with imported and imposed ideals for women?

This discussion set out to investigate renegotiations of the gender order from policy to project outcomes, drawing primarily on the perceptions and experiences of Afghan women and men but also of those engaged with women in the aid industry. The study was inspired by a need to illuminate the perspectives and experiences of Afghan women and men during the social and political transition in the aftermath of conflict. In addition, this work set out to understand the discrepancies between policies and realities as perceived by the policies' supposed beneficiaries. Despite significant progress — and policy rhetoric — there remains a void in understandings of Afghan experiences.

My research was inspired by my experience running an international

Eidgaah mosque at sunset, Kabul.

NGO in which I was able to engage with Afghan women program participants and staff (both women and men) over a period of one year. I had been gifted with an insight to Afghanistan, and I benefited from observation, discussion, and debate, as women freely shared their concerns, experiences, and perspectives with me. I was in a rare and privileged position, with an obligation to nurse it delicately and share it wisely. I became very conscious of my responsibility to share the understandings that I had acquired. I saw the essence of Afghan recovery as an amalgam of these women's stories, and began to share them for that purpose. My work was inspired by these women. It is through their lived experiences that progress (or lack thereof) can be measured.

Methods Used

This study is conducted first through an examination of policy texts and media discourses, then through an investigation of program practice, drawing on the perspectives of policy-makers and policy implementers. The findings are then weighed against perspectives and experiences of women and men in Afghanistan. The year 2009 — eight years into the reconstruction of Afghanistan — is an opportune time to begin a discussion of the effects of gender-focused aid for both women and men in the country and to examine the implementation of policies in light of promised transformation of the gender order. Indeed, Afghanistan is facing a unique set of development challenges: poverty, insecurity, gender inequality. It is in this context that the following discussion takes place.

As both an academic and a practitioner, I have elected to retain the anonymity of individuals and organizations because of codes of confidentiality. Furthermore, it is not constructive to personalize issues and could obstruct from a more useful discussion on improving delivery of gender-focused aid.

Segments of this investigation build on previously published analyses that have appeared in a variety of articles and reports. All of these are cited where relevant. Further, these findings have been shared in several international conferences where I have been invited to speak and have benefited from critical feedback. The present conclusions are drawn from a fresh analysis of findings in the light of research material collected and reviewed during my period of doctoral research.

This investigation was both a political and an institutional ethnography in that it sought to describe and explain the lives of select Afghans affected by an aid intervention in a particular political period in the country's transition. The data is therefore strongly rooted in the context of Afghanistan's turbulent social and political situation with a view to examining the aid apparatus as an institution in its own right.

Qualitative methods have been used because, at this early stage in Afghanistan's development, the country lacks reliable data. Further, qualitative methods are appropriate because the focus is not to judge the outcome of aid interventions but to illuminate different actors' understandings and perceptions of gender-focused aid. In addition, I sought to pay particular attention to unanticipated effects — either direct or indirect. Use of various qualitative methods therefore took into account the possibility of such effects — and how these might impact the success of the aid intervention, based on the perceptions and experiences of those directly implicated. Qualitative research has the capacity to reveal both intended and unintended effects in aid interventions. Quantitative data collection techniques could abstract women from the relationships they participate in. My interest was in obtaining the perspectives of women *and men* in Afghanistan and examining them in the social settings in which they exist.

Positionality and Challenges

I recognize that my own identity as a researcher cannot be abstracted from the research process. Firstly I situate myself as a developing world feminist with solid experience in the developed world. I recognize that my feminist consciousness was born out of my own origins and experience, but that it took shape in the developed world. Although I am an outsider to the lives of women and men in Afghanistan, I have spent sufficient time working closely on the inside. In my experience, I established strong contacts with people affiliated with a variety of organizations in the country and therefore was better able to access information relevant to my research.

I was in a unique position to investigate Afghan women because I was able to gain their trust through my work. I had demonstrated my commitment to them, and also delivered for them in my previous work. For this effort, I was rewarded with an honesty and loyalty that many outsiders would not see. In addition, my skin color provided access to their private realms. I was frequently mistaken for an Afghan, and therefore in a position of privilege to hear the real story. My special access was not revoked when I corrected the mistake because I was assumed to be from the region and therefore familiar to them, and familiar with Afghanistan. During my four years in Afghanistan,

I was frequently placed in the role of cultural interpreter for outsiders — be they part of the aid apparatus or the media or other — who were too far removed from Afghanistan and its realities to understand the context. Because my origins are Arab, it was assumed that I was Muslim. As a result, the women assumed that I was also better equipped to explain to others the centrality of Islam to the lives of Afghans. I was therefore in a privileged position as both insider-outsider and interpreter of insiders in a language understood by those on the outside.

Translation and language were challenges that I overcame by employing two Afghan research assistants — male and female — who were fluent in Dari, Pashto, and English to accompany me. These research assistants were former members of my staff and were therefore very familiar with aid issues, accustomed to working with me, and highly credible and capable. These assistants served as my interpreters during interviews and my cultural and contextual interpreters after interviews. They also assisted in translating and transcribing the data. Following the research, my two assistants were married — united by a shared commitment and understanding.

Structure of the Book

Chapter 1 begins with an understanding of Afghan women's history to illustrate the political nature of all things "women." This is followed by a brief discussion of social indicators and aid dynamics. This chapter deconstructs the gender order in Afghanistan socially and historically, presenting a view to how gender-focused aid might be formulated. This is followed by a discussion of how the aid apparatus sought to transform the gender order, based on the view that aid interventions cannot transform, *per se*, but can support or hinder women's potential in achieving transformation through policies and programs. Finally, this chapter reveals a disconnect between policy and practice through the framework of technical and political interventions.

Chapter 2 highlights the "liberation" discourse with a view to understanding how this may have affected policy texts of aid institutions. This chapter uses the image of the *chaddari* as one way to understand media and policy discourses. It also brings in profiles of Afghan women to begin to understand their diverse experiences. A discussion of institutional support in the aftermath through the formulation of policy contributes to a better understanding of what was committed in terms of gender-focused aid and serves as a starting point to examine gender rhetoric. This information is then weighed against Afghan perspectives on the images that likely led to the formation of aid interventions.

Chapter 3 illuminates the journey from policy formulation to interpretation to implementation through the voices of policy-makers, policy implementers, NGO leaders, and Afghanistan specialists. Their experiences and perceptions are organized around emergent themes that are then checked against those of Afghan women and men. This chapter also brings to light the media messages that were discussed in Chapter 2 and places them in the context of policy interpretation and implementation.

Chapter 4 provides an example to illustrate gender policy in practice — the advancing of the gender agenda through Afghanistan's 2005 parliamentary elections. In so doing, a parallel can be made between the quest to bring democracy and gender equality as standard parts of the aid package. This is done through an inside view to the process as well as through the voices of Afghan women and men, and Afghan and non–Afghan activists and experts.

Chapter 5 presents data collected from interviews with Afghan women and men on identity markers, definitions of gender roles and relations, and evolution of gender roles in different periods throughout Afghan history. It begins with an understanding of how Afghans define and negotiate their various identities and what this means for the formulation, interpretation and implementation of aid interventions.

The next chapter presents an in-depth discussion of the major themes from interviews with Afghan women and men. These perspectives and experiences are then compared with group discussions to better understand the prominent themes that have emerged: the importance of honor, the existence of agency, and the need to rethink aid. These themes all highlight the significance of engaging men. Chapter 6 concludes by raising the possibility that violence against women could be an unintended effect.

Chapter 7 begins with comparisons and implications at the family and community levels using profiles of couples. In this chapter we begin to understand the importance of working with men and the possible consequences of sidelining them. This chapter also provides an analysis of women and men's views under the three themes raised in Chapter 6.

Chapter 8 focuses on violence as an unintended effect. This in-depth view starts with a discussion of violence in conflict and the aftermath and presents a comparison with other countries and cases. The chapter discusses perceptions of violence and concludes with a brief overview of documented cases. This chapter resumes the discussion from Chapter 1 on gender roles in the aftermath of conflict and what implications this might have for aid interventions.

Chapter 9 highlights the voices of Afghan women and men and their views of what the future holds. It then puts these voices in the context of a deteriorating situation in Afghanistan to better understand how this particular interface has played out for Afghans. This final chapter addresses the implications of a new occupation of Afghanistan and helps us to better understand how freedom is won.

1

An Agenda for Social Change

An Afghan man once told me: "The world thought they could bring freedom to Afghan women, but freedom is only won from the inside."

This discussion on gender-focused international aid[1] in the aftermath of conflict in Afghanistan[2] seeks to better understand how the promise of freedom has fallen short for Afghans. This is the story of an aid intervention — how it is represented at the highest levels to how it is understood at the lowest levels. This aid intervention is one historical moment in an ongoing institutional process, revealing that such interventions are political processes — with political outcomes. This story is told through the voices of policy-makers, practitioners, and participants[3] living in Afghanistan during the transitional period of the Bonn Process, December 2001–September 2005.

The investigation begins with a contextualized understanding of women in Afghanistan to better understand their role in social transformations throughout Afghan history. The first argument is that this history is in some measure incompatible with the discourse[4] on Afghan women that was created by aid institutions[5] to justify aid interventions.[6] It is argued that this discourse denied Afghan women's agency, abstracting them from their historical and social contexts. Aid sought to "empower" and "liberate" Afghan women, yet implementation of interventions did not reflect such goals. I put these and other key words in quotations to emphasize their use as part of the discourse. While I might not subscribe to this language — or its underlying belief system — I use this initially to illustrate the point. Illuminating the discourses that animated gender-focused international aid in the aftermath of conflict in Afghanistan might present one way to understand what effects these discourses have had on the gender order. This is the primary argument of my work.

There is also a secondary argument, namely that said aid interventions have actually made life more difficult for women, and that such difficulties might have been avoided if a more nuanced and sensitive approach had been taken. A causal relationship between aid interventions and the hardship experienced by women might be difficult to establish; however, there are elements of my analysis that support what is commonly known as the "backlash" phe-

9

nomenon. This is evidenced through the voices of Afghan women and men documented here.

It is through these Afghan voices that this work makes its main contribution. This investigation also adds to the gender policy discourse, particularly through discussions with Afghan women and men on gender issues, social change, and aid effectiveness. In addition, this discussion tests Western[7] development constructs in an Afghan setting. I have employed gender analysis in order to illuminate the roles and needs of both women and men in Afghanistan's conflict aftermath to understand what changes in the aftermath have meant to Afghans. Gender analysis is only one part of the story. This is about aid policy — about what is said as much as what is not said. This is firstly the story of an intervention, examining some of the practical implications of theory to better understand what effects aid policies have in practice. This discussion of the effects of aid could present lessons for policy and programming. There are tensions and conflicting views on what the outcome of development should be — and whose vision of development it is. As a result, this is also a story of the contradicting social realities that emerge when countries are presented with expertise-with-abstraction.

The term development can be employed in diverse ways for strategic purposes. To this end, I have opted to use aid instead of development as it avoids potential pitfalls in definitions and — perhaps ideally — carries less baggage in its application. A distinction should be made between development contributing to a modern society and development contributing to a better quality of life.[8] Because these two are often conflated in aid interventions, it becomes possible to offer a technical response contributing to a modern society as an answer to improved quality of life. In so doing, a project for rubble removal in the Ministry of Women's Affairs becomes a part of an aid institution's contribution to women.

A study of an aid intervention as a political process entails engaging with James Ferguson's work on "anti-politics" from his study of development policies in practice in Lesotho. Ferguson examined the aid apparatus[9] as a social institution[10] in its own right, with a view to deconstructing development discourse to understand its effects. In this vein, I extend the concept of antipolitics by examining it through a gender lens in Afghanistan. This case study exploring gender-focused international aid is not simply a critique but rather an effort to understand what this particular approach to aid meant to those who were implicated in its social reality.

The engagement of the aid apparatus in Afghanistan did not begin based on an analysis of real needs or a carefully planned process, but was a knee-jerk reaction following the events of 11 September 2001. Interest in Afghanistan was naively enthusiastic, but direction was lacking. As a result, aid interventions were supply-driven based on aid biases. This in turn fueled the belief that aid funding existed solely to fuel the presence of the aid community itself.[11]

There are many phases on a policy's journey from paper to practice. Firstly, a policy is formulated based on a perceived need. Certain images of the policy "subject" — whether accurate or not — are employed for this purpose. Once on paper, a policy's intent becomes apparent — but not to all. A policy can therefore be interpreted in various ways — with wildly differing outcomes depending on who does the interpreting and what strategic purpose it serves. Finally, a policy needs to be implemented through an intervention. There are many opportunities for disconnects in this journey, and it is often impossible to isolate a sole factor in this progression. The best we can do, therefore, is to tell the story as we have experienced it — from our own perspective — and hope to reveal some of the effects along the way.

In Afghanistan, the story looked like this:

(1) Policy formulation extracted women from their social, historical, and political realities, employing a discourse on Afghan women to justify a particular kind of aid intervention. Interventions for Afghan women were designed based on the discourse of a one-dimensional *chaddari*-clad[12] figure in need of assistance — with transformation of the gender order as the anticipated outcome.

(2) Policy intent sought to transform women's position, and policy interpretation attempted to fast-track social change, thereby denying the agency of those who were to be "transformed."

(3) Policy implementation tried to meet political issues with technical interventions and therefore failed to achieve transformation — an inherently political process.

(4) Depoliticizing gender-focused aid interventions can produce significant, unintended political effects.

This is an oversimplification of a complex historical moment. Most important is what the changes in Afghanistan's aftermath have meant *to Afghans*. Aid cannot be technical or neutral. It is political by its very nature. Aid is further politicized when gender issues are at the forefront of the agenda. Nowhere is this more relevant than in Afghanistan. Attempts at gender-focused international aid depoliticized a highly political discussion — and brought political effects in doing so. We can philosophize endlessly about the disconnects of the development business, but through this work I hope to let

Women wait in line to register for participation in an aid program for women, Logar.

the voices of Afghans tell us how freedom could have been won — for women and men both.

Understanding Women in Afghan History

The women's movement marks time in Afghanistan and tells the story of social change in a context where *evolutionary* change is repeatedly abandoned for *revolutionary* change.[13] An understanding of Afghan women's history therefore could begin in the 1880s, when Afghan rulers of the period launched one of the earliest attempts at emancipation and social reform in the Muslim world. However, these rulers also proclaimed men as the guardians of women, marking the beginning of a non-linear pattern of social change. Amidst various contradictory laws concerning women, the protection of women was employed as a call for Afghans to expel the British: "Should these foreigners overrun the country, the men of Afghanistan would lose hold over their wives, for, according to [British] laws women enjoy liberty and under them no husband has any control over his wife."[14]

During the 1920s, women's emancipation began to play a prominent role in the nationalist ideology of modernization.[15] Popular perceptions of King Amanullah's immorality and excessive Western influence fueled a strong resistance, and religious conservatives and the rural population met his attempts at reform with violent opposition.[16] This is significant in that the rural population has historically presented the greatest challenge to social reforms. This dynamic plays out again in present-day Afghanistan and is increasingly magnified by the rural population that is now displaced in Kabul city.

At this time, violence against women increased, perpetuated by those who considered women's families shamed by calls to abandon veiling and adopt Western attire. It is estimated that 400 women were murdered during this period as a result.[17] *Mullahs*, Muslim religious leaders, circulated a rumor that unveiled women's children would be stolen by the Communists and made into soap. *Mullahs*, feeling threatened at the challenge to their religious authority, further instilled fear by claiming that natural disasters would befall Afghanistan because of the women's sins. When an earthquake did occur in 1927, it was blamed on women who had shamed their families and communities by removing their *chaddaris*. Women eventually succumbed to pressure and those who had removed their *chaddaris* donned them once again to appease religious authorities and regain their respect in the communities.[18]

A young girl looks out over the village, waiting for a truck delivering blankets, Paghman.

Emancipation continued to be enforced and subsequently challenged. Despite incremental changes, responses to women's rights vacillated between enforced modernity and conservative backlash. And yet, attempts at modernity throughout history have always been imposed from above, without local foundations and popular support — and with little impact on the lives of the majority. Reforms have repeatedly flooded Afghanistan faster than the country can absorb them, should it choose to do so. Such modernity has also been selective: so-called modern contributions such as technology and advanced weapons are accepted, while movements towards women's public participation in Afghan society are not.

Afghan women were officially enfranchised in the 1964 Constitution and later were given equal rights in the 1977 Constitution.[19] The Saur (April) Revolution of 1978 introduced an aggressive program for social change, enforcing such modernizations as women's right to work, serve in the army, and choose their spouses. Mandatory literacy programs for women and the abolition of bride price were viewed as direct attacks on Afghan culture and honor, instigating yet another wave of violence. Afghans felt a total disdain for their values, so much so that an Afghan woman said that the Russians deliberately "came [to Afghanistan] to play with the dignity of women."[20]

Thus, Afghan women once again found themselves at the center of a conflict between Western concepts of modernization and Afghan codes of culture.[21] To most Afghans at that time, the government was perceived to be interfering with Islamic values and disregarding social traditions. It was further encouraging women to engage in public activities which were deemed "unladylike, ... undignified and detrimental to family honour."[22] The Soviet invasion prompted contradictory changes in lives of Afghan women — emancipation and greater opportunities for some (a minority, largely urban), and death and destruction for others. The Leftist group in power during Soviet occupation promised full equality for women but did not deliver on it. Women might have been more visible in Kabul during that time, but they had no real decision-making or power-sharing roles.[23] Soviet decrees were viewed as an unwelcome ideological occupation:

> The alien ideological rhetoric with which these programs were imbued, the haste with which they were formulated, and the zealotry with which the local officials attempted to implement them led to a massive resistance among large segments of Afghan society.[24]

The same could be said for present-day Afghanistan, and perhaps the many other periods in Afghan history where social change has been imported and imposed through foreign intervention. Thus efforts to emancipate women are not new — and have never been well received.

Social change and attempts to improve women's status have repeatedly brought strong resistance because of affronts to honor. Women's honor is the cornerstone on which the politics of women's rights rests. These fluctuations in women's rights — enforced by the state's attempt to exercise centralized control — have actually led to violent, fundamentalist backlashes.[25] As one example, opposition to Soviet reforms for women — and concern for the symbolic value of women's honor — fueled the fundamentalist movement that took hold in refugee camps. This in turn served as the grounds for the *Mujaheddin* opposition to expel the Soviets and regain control both of women and Afghanistan. The *Mujaheddin* (literally holy warriors) — U.S.-sponsored freedom fighters — continued to threaten women's honor by using their bodies as rewards for their wartime victories.[26]

In the 1920s, Afghanistan was a secular country working to extend women's rights, yet by the 1990s the country was a captive of religious fanaticism, tribal patriarchy, and underdevelopment.[27] Indeed, the combination of colonialism, economic dependence, and rapid social change is a recipe for Muslim fundamentalism to flourish. This phenomenon is exacerbated by the international pressure that is exerted at the intersection of Islam, the state, and gender politics. As a result, the place of women becomes "one of the few areas of relative autonomy left to societies whose ties of political and economic dependence severely restrict their choices in every other sphere."[28] Afghanistan repeatedly demonstrates the strong and yet volatile link between women's honor and external interventions.

The Taliban ironically drew world attention to the situation in Afghanistan. Prior to the fall of Kabul in September 1996, Afghanistan was hardly a part of the international community's agenda.[29] During the Taliban period, Afghan women were portrayed as victims of violence and oppression by the international media. Yet the situation of women in Afghanistan is not simply a product of Taliban policies, and the *chaddari* is not a Taliban invention. Nonetheless, the international shock at the Taliban's treatment of women took place in a historical vacuum, with little attention paid to pre–Taliban abuses and *chaddari* uses.[30] Belated discovery of the discrimination of Afghan women (discrimination that passed largely without comment during previous regimes) is a reflection both of the political agenda and of wider ignorance of the realities of Afghan society.[31]

Much has been written on women's abuses during this period. For these purposes, it is sufficient to say that women suffered under many regimes in Afghanistan, but women's sphere of influence under the Taliban was virtually annihilated.[32] The Taliban were able to manipulate the deeply embedded system linking women to honor, issuing policies that "wrapped entrenched customary practices and patriarchal attitudes in the mantle of Islam."[33] It is worthwhile to note that men also suffered under the Taliban, although this was hardly noted by the media. In fact, Taliban authority extended beyond women to non–Taliban men. The simplistic assumption was that the expulsion of the Taliban would bring women's liberation. Taliban out, women in. This facile logic exposed the so-called liberators' ignorance of Afghan history.

Women's rights were the call to battle around which the world appeared to assemble. The Bush Administration's vociferous concern for Afghan women's rights as justification for military intervention was undercut by their support to the lawless factions that have repeatedly perpetrated violence against women.[34] As such, the military campaign was launched with little regard for longer-term social consequences. Afghanistan's politicized aid history has left the country a graveyard for failed fast-paced efforts by outsiders.[35] Do we know if this attempt is any different?

Prescribing Aid Solutions

Few aid institutions existed in Afghanistan prior to 2002. This was due in large part to the difficulties of operating during the Taliban period and previous regimes. In the post–Taliban period, women's liberation and empowerment appeared to be the order of the day. Aid institutions poured into Afghanistan with women's issues at the top of their agendas. With this enthusiasm, programs failed to integrate a contextualized understanding of Afghan women — and in fact forgot to consult Afghan women at all.

The aid process in Afghanistan is said to have been "prescriptive and supply-driven, rather than indigenous and responding to Afghan needs."[36] Aid institutions in Kabul employed a generous supply of "conflict experts" whose experience did not coalesce with Afghan realities. This contributed to a failure to incorporate a contextualized analysis in interventions. International staff generally knew very little about Afghanistan when they arrived, and by the time they achieved a modicum of understanding, they were already in Iraq.[37] Indeed, in conflict and the aftermath, the same people are rotated and the same partnerships are formed in a pattern of free-floating expertise that lacks context.[38] As a result, existing disparities between local and international perspectives in Afghanistan were exacerbated by differing priorities regarding women's rights.

The concept of rights first became a part of the aid discourse in Afghanistan with the release of the *Strategic Framework for Afghanistan* (SFA) in 1998. Rights rhetoric was enthusiastically applied to the "women issue." Afghans viewed the concept of rights as something to be handled within the community and social environment, not by individuals. Afghan identities are grounded in communal structures and continuously redefined by economic, social, and political currents. However, the SFA presented — and therefore negotiated — rights in a largely Western (read: individual) framework. It was thus perceived by Afghans as a language that defined the aid apparatus' own agenda and ambitions in Afghanistan.[39]

Within the discussion of rights, the language of liberation was born. This high-profile focus on women came with controversy — and without context. Veterans of other crises, inspired by the liberation agenda, flooded Afghanistan in the early days of the intervention.[40] Many possessed little knowledge of the country, its context, or how to bring their plans to fruition. Afghans might have been initially pleased with this enthusiasm — and the funding it promised — but disillusionment was not far off. Afghan women were particularly uncomfortable with the rhetoric, their publicized plight, and their absence from campaigns waged on their behalf.[41]

Afghan disillusionment grew in the progression of a number of "events" offered to publicly reaffirm the aid apparatus' commitment to Afghanistan. The process of reconstruction was guided by the *Bonn Agreement*, a political timetable determined by international donors in Bonn, Germany, in December 2001 to set in train a three-stage journey towards democracy: electing a transitional authority, adopting a new constitution, and electing a representative government. The *Bonn Agreement* also established the Ministry of Women's Affairs (MoWA) — the weakest link in Afghanistan's national machinery — much touted but largely marginalized and under-funded.

The Constitution — adopted in January 2004 by the Afghan Constitutional *Loya Jirga*, or Grand Assembly — secured women's rights and ensured equality before the law, yet human rights and women's rights organizations quickly noted fissures in the document where women's rights vanished.[42] Women comprised 20 percent of the delegates to the Constitutional *Loya Jirga*. These women secured the passing of several articles safeguarding equality. Article 7 requires Afghanistan to observe the *Universal Declaration of Human Rights* and all covenants to which Afghanistan is a party. This includes the *Convention on the Elimination of All Forms of Discrimination Against Women* (CEDAW), which Afghanistan signed in March 2003 — without reservation. Despite ratification, the Afghan government has yet to submit its first annual report, which was due in March 2004 as well as the second report in 2008. Article 22 of the Constitution guarantees the legal equality of men and women. While it might be touted that women were present and active in the *Loya Jirga*, this should not overshadow the fact that these women expressed concern for their safety on the streets and at home, in addition to the harassment they experienced at the event itself. Despite progress on paper, these rights have yet to translate into practice.

In line with the Bonn Process, Hamid Karzai was elected President in October 2004. The final step in this process was the parliamentary election of September 2005. The *Bonn Agreement* is the document reflecting the "good intentions" of the aid apparatus and its role in fostering gender equality.[43] Following Bonn, donors met in Tokyo in 2002, in Berlin in 2004, and in London in 2006. In Tokyo in early 2002, conference participants renewed their commitment to the Bonn Process. According to the "'Co-chairs' Summary of Conclusions":

> The Conference emphasized the centrality of restoring the rights and addressing the needs of women, who have been the prime victims of conflict and oppression. Women's rights and gender issues should be fully reflected in the reconstruction process.[44]

The *National Development Framework* (NDF), emerging from the Tokyo Conference, claimed that gender was to be a cross-cutting theme.[45] In the paragraph to which gender was relegated, the report states that it does not want "gender equality to be treated as a ghetto," elaborating that programs must pay special attention to women and men, not merely including women as an afterthought. The report further states that "because our women are often invisible that does not mean they are always excluded." Finally, the NDF advocates a "societal dialogue to enhance the opportunities of women and improve cooperation between men and women on the basis of our culture, the experience of other Islamic countries, and the global norms of human rights." This particular line is problematic because of its assumption of a uniform culture. Further, the experiences of Islamic countries are diverse and open to vast and contradictory interpretations regarding women's rights. Finally, potential for disagreement exists in the concept of global norms of human rights.[46]

The following conference, in Berlin in March 2004, produced yet another tome. *Securing Afghanistan's Future* (SAF) renewed its commitment to gender issues, and strengthened the discourse to include more aggressive — and elusive — language[47]:

> The gender element is critical, given we are moving from gender apartheid to gender integration, addressing the capabilities of women in the culturally appropriate way requires special attention. However, as shown by the *Loya Jirga*, when women take on these roles they are accepted,[48] the key is not to discuss the role of women in Afghanistan, but to create facts on the ground regarding integration and women's roles.

In January 2006, 60 donors met in London to renew their commitment to Afghanistan and determine the next course of action. Although these donors committed military and reconstruction support for the country over the next five years, it is not clear how much has actually reached Afghanistan. It is not surprising, therefore, that Afghans remain skeptical. Given their history of abandonment following the expulsion of the Soviets in 1989, Afghans are once again fearful that they will not benefit from sustained international attention in the long term.

The Afghanistan Compact— the document emerging from the London Conference — is the successor to the *Bonn Agreement*, providing the framework for the aid apparatus to continue its assistance to Afghanistan. It is believed to be the last chance the aid apparatus might have to create sustainable structures. This window continues to narrow as donor fatigue, new emergencies, and low momentum set in. And yet, donors met in Paris in 2008 for yet another *International Conference in Support of Afghanistan*. This declaration offers one line in support of implementation of the National Action Plan for the Women of Afghanistan, the Ministry of Women's Affairs' guiding document adopted in May 2008.

In terms of what has been done, the aid apparatus has fallen short as many have argued that reconstruction in Afghanistan was attempted "on the cheap."[49] There are many arguments of misallocating funding, of commitments not disbursed, of money not reaching the country. It is difficult to trace funds allocated to — and accessed by — the Afghan people. But it is safe to say that funding received was in no measure compatible with the level of rhetoric, particularly considering the enthusiasm for the liberation agenda.

Aid to Afghan women perhaps has been meager because the bulk of funding has been swallowed for the War on Terror. Since late 2001, the aid apparatus has operated with a narrow definition of security, meaning the dominance of armed forces. As a result, interventions to win "hearts and minds" were not employed as a precondition for the realization of peace and human rights but actually sought to placate a potentially hostile population.[50] In addressing insecurity as a purely military matter, instead of adopting a broader view of security to encompass human security, women's concerns are relegated to "softer issues." This unfortunate omission was also brought to light in the 2007 Global Peace Index that failed to rank the most prevalent form of violence — violence against women — as an obstacle to peace.[51]

Afghan hearts and minds were certainly not swayed by the paltry aid they received compared to other conflicts. Significant amounts of aid in the first years of post-conflict interventions have brought relative success in other countries. Immediately following their respective conflicts, Bosnia received

$679 per capita, followed by Kosovo at $526 and East Timor at $233. According to studies, Afghanistan received a meager $57 per capita in 2006.[52] Other studies say that Afghans have received an even more dismal $42 per capita since 2002.[53] Regardless of the discrepancy in per capita figures, Afghanistan's lack of resources has resulted in a sacrifice of long-term priorities to achieve short-term gains. "This malnourishment at the formative stage has left Afghanistan today as a shell of a state facing daunting development challenges and an accelerating insurgency."[54]

Further studies suggest that Afghanistan was short-changed in its allocation of security forces. Compared to other conflicts since 1993, Afghanistan ranks lowest in terms of peacekeeper support per capita, with 5380 Afghans per peacekeeper in 2003, compared with Kosovo at one peacekeeper for 48 people.[55] To further illustrate this malnourishment, a 2005 security study asked Americans to rank the importance of 30 international concerns: Afghanistan ranked last.[56] The situation was aptly brought to light in a personal communication from an Afghanistan specialist on the condition of the country in 2006:

> It is not good — I guess I expected that. What are we all doing with this money and effort? So much goodwill, so many words, but we seem singularly incapable of actually putting ideas and words into practice. We have lost the plot — we observe, commentate, wax lyrical, recommend — then what? Check again, write another report, tie ourselves into bureaucratic knots to make people accountable but sometimes this results in a kind of paralysis. We can't move forward without a radical rethink — or rather redo. As I am writing to you I am feeling so strongly about our failures. I of course include myself in this — but recognition is necessary before you can tackle anything.

In late 2001, Afghan women's human rights and well-being were at the top of the aid apparatus agenda. We therefore need to recognize that good intentions, strong words, and high expectations have largely not been met. Progress has been slow, and, according to a 2007 World Bank report, "in some areas important progress during the first two-three years was followed by slowdown, drift, or backsliding — adversely affecting future prospects."[57] Women have suffered disproportionately from these adverse effects. Afghan women continue to be among the worst off in the world in virtually all aspects of life — health, education, poverty, literacy, civil and political rights, protection against violence, and political participation.

The Afghanistan Independent Human Rights Commission (AIHRC) report lists obstacles that women are facing in present-day Afghanistan: tradition, lack of available services, economic constraints, inability to take initiative and manage their own affairs, family obstacles, domestic violence, patriarchy, and illiteracy. Afghanistan ranks far below its neighbors with respect to literacy, especially for adult females. Female education is impeded by a lack of available schools, security concerns, poverty, and discrimination and gender inequality in customary practices.

In the health sector, Afghan women have a life expectancy that is at least 20 years shorter than most other women in the world. Afghanistan's Maternal Mortality Ratio, estimated at 1,600 to 1,900 maternal deaths per 100,000 live births, is one of the highest in the world.[58] Each Afghan woman will have approximately 6.6 children during her childbearing years. This is nearly one-third higher than even the least developed countries' average of 5.02 children per woman.[59] One million new Afghans are added to the population every year — onto an increasingly weakening economic and social infrastructure.

Despite recent progress in women's political participation, women are still a minority in public life and are often marginalized in policy-making and decision-making. There is a general lack of awareness of women's rights and certain vestiges of inequality remain in some laws of the country.

Afghanistan and Afghan women fall at the bottom of global poverty indices — with a Human Development Index value of 0.346 and a Gender Development Index value of 0.300, ranking Afghanistan as fifth and third lowest in standard of living and gender disparity in standard of living, respectively, in the world.[60] The average per capita income is less than $200, and only 13.5 percent of families have access to a sustainable source of income.[61]

Livelihoods are deteriorating. A context of prolonged war, continued conflict, and periodic drought has increased poverty and vulnerability, particularly in urban areas. Poverty has brought increased corruption, posing yet another risk to an already precarious and steadily deteriorating security situation. Displacement and urbanization have brought a transition from a largely agricultural economy to one where livelihoods are precarious and daily survival is tantamount. As a result, women continue to enter a variety of fields in order to support their families, the most dangerous of which is opium production.[62] Women are engaged in livestock and agricultural work and micro-enterprises, yet they lack access to capital, information, technology and markets.

In urban areas, Afghans have very little access to basic services and social infrastructure.[63] Resources are limited and those in control are unable and unwilling to meet people's basic needs. As a result, most of Afghanistan's urban population has no choice but to enter into informal employment. Increased vulnerabilities due to irregular incomes force women to supplement the income — at times through exploitative and hazardous work. The increased poverty has forced more women into sex work. The number of widows and female-headed households continues to increase. Their situation is far more serious because households with male labor are still better off than those without.

Afghan women continue to experience violence and threats of violence at home and in public spaces. Domestic violence and self-immolation are also increasing, although emerging statistics remain unreliable. Both women and men expected more from the reconstruction process, and yet today it appears that hopes of peace, security, and development have been thwarted.

> With the U.S.–led invasion came poverty, rural-to-urban migration, uprooting, crime, drug addiction, unemployment, alien culture: all these factors are leading to the breakdown of [Afghan] social relations as their basic safety net.[64]

Deconstructing Gender and Aid

For the purposes of this study, I have elected to use the term "aftermath" to define the period following a conflict.[65] The more familiar term "post-conflict" connotes an end to violence and a linear progression toward peace. In fact, post-conflict situations are circuitous and often entail relapses into violence. For countries that have undergone long periods of warfare, the boundaries between conflict and so-called post-conflict situations are sometimes indistinct. Afghan history demonstrates that relapses into conflict are not unusual. The country has yet to achieve peace, rendering the term "post-conflict" useless. Present increases of violence — and violence against women — are a manifestation of this dynamic.

Conflict can be defined as a complex socio-political struggle over processes of transformation. And therefore, the policies that guide interventions in conflict contexts are also political processes. Humanitarian aid has always been a political process. Attempts at denying the political nature of such aid only strips interventions of their political reality — making their application a mere technical exercise that has little relevance to local realities. Such was the case in Afghanistan.

In conflict contexts, meeting practical needs becomes a particular imperative as aid interventions focus on immediate humanitarian concerns. Research on aid interventions in emergency contexts reveals that interventions can often inadvertently increase the vulnerabilities of the communities they aim to serve through misguided policies that neglect to take longer-term political interests into account.[66] Such interventions can facilitate violence by failing to recognize the political nature of so-called political emergencies. Humanitarian assistance thus increasingly becomes a process both politicized and colored by political considerations.[67]

It is assumed in the so-called relief-to-development continuum that conflict — similar to development — is a linear process.[68] However, the progression toward peace is long-term, multi-dimensional, dynamic, and unique to each context.[69] In Afghanistan's aftermath, programs transitioned from immediate relief to longer-term development interventions, yet political implications were not addressed in this intervention-evolution. The aid apparatus viewed the rising levels of violence, instability, and inequality in Afghanistan as part of a standard post-conflict package — not as possible effects. As one result, aid became conflated with security, and aid-as-security became the primary means of international assistance. Despite this, the track record of aid in reducing social risks and promoting stability remains unproven. Afghanistan represents a case in point. There remained an imbalance between short-term, visible interventions and long-term strategic interventions that change the ways power relationships are expressed as part of a *process* of transition.

Aid is political — and even more so when we add gender to the mix. In aid parlance, the term "gender" is employed to demonstrate an agency's understanding of and commitment to women's empowerment and equality. However, static and technical understandings of the term strip gender of its political implications, resulting in isolationist and reductionist interpretations. In other words, gender becomes a politically neutralized euphemism for women. When gender is conflated with women, the language of aid becomes centered around women's objectives. While "gender" is a political term, "women" lends itself more readily to technical solutions.

To illustrate this tension, I use the term "gender order" to represent the way in which society is organized around women's and men's roles, needs, and interests in various contexts. This term reintroduces the underlying power and politics that animate gender. The gender order does not exist in a vacuum. It is socially and historically constructed, and influenced by other identity markers. The gender order is a political process that changes and evolves — although it might appear resistant to change. It is a dynamic concept — varying not only between men and women, but between different types of women.

An examination of the gender order in the aftermath of conflict is particularly relevant as Afghan society is undergoing a process of transformation, one result of which is the fluctuation of gender identities. There is a burgeoning literature on women's roles in conflict and the aftermath, but no consensus exists on whether these new roles are, firstly, advantageous to women and, further, sustainable in the long term. Conflict can stimulate a shift in gender roles while simultaneously provoking a retreat to conservative notions of masculinity and femininity.[70] While these changes in gender identities are largely indigenous, they can be supported or hindered by external influence, in this case aid interventions. Afghanistan presents an interesting case study in this regard.

An understanding of the Afghan historical trajectory — particularly regarding gender politics — can illuminate patterns and problems that might pose obstacles in present attempts to restructure the gender order. Researchers and experts have warned against taking shortcuts to understandings of Afghan history and society as this is the entry point to an informed and contextualized gender analysis.[71] More profound analyses of and engagement with Afghan society could prevent women from being addressed in a social vacuum, allowing space for the creation of programs that complement women's realities.

The gender order is not historically static, but changes over time and has a relationship with other systems of oppression. The term does not reflect a particular gender hierarchy, yet the reality in most countries is one of patriarchy.[72] Patriarchy alone is an insufficient argument and could serve to obfuscate the agency of both women and men. Contrary to common understandings of patriarchy in Muslim contexts, patriarchy in Afghanistan is more tribal than Islamic. Tribal practices often overshadow Islam — particularly its more enlightened messages on gender issues.[73] Therefore there is a need for a nuanced understanding of power and patriarchy that shows their interconnections — and their fluctuations based on current political projects. Contexts of rapid social change, where patriarchal controls are being eroded by socio-economic transformation, create a "favorable climate for the emergence of a conservative backlash against the emancipation of women."[74] Thus patriarchy — like the gender order — is a political process but is also influenced by political processes.

Afghanistan is similar to other patriarchal societies in that its gender order is shaped by socio-cultural factors largely based on women's role as keepers of the family honor.[75] Attempts to separate women from family and community are met with strong resistance. It is neither possible nor appropriate to refer only to Afghan women since their lives are viewed in the context of interrelationships. Aid programs targeting and isolating women (read: excluding men) find little foundation in Afghan society.

In Afghanistan, gender has been conflated with women, and the language of aid programming has been oriented around women's objectives, without a broader understanding of gender. This is not unusual. In the context of conflict and the aftermath, there often is little clarity on what "doing gender" really means — and what the political implications might be. An examination of the gender order also places men as a subject of analysis as they too have a role to play in gender order transformations. Men have agency in gender politics; they can advocate or oppose women's struggles. Examining the role of men, particularly in traditionally patriarchal societies such as Afghanistan, helps us to better understand women's agency in its social context. In so doing, we recognize the challenges that men face — and men's need to search for new identities and redefine masculinities. Building on these arguments, understanding men's perceptions provides insights to their own interpretations of reality and to their perceptions of how social change is received — or resisted. This is the crux of a gender perspective.

It is useful to trace Afghanistan's path alongside political sociologist Sylvia Walby's understanding of the progressions of gender and how they influence aid interventions.[76] She sees four phases of engagement with women and gender issues. The first phase entails the near-total neglect of gender, or the mention of women as an aside or footnote. This is followed by a second phase that exposes the flaws and fallacies from the previous neglect. The third phase adds women as a special case to compensate for previous neglect.

Nuristani men greet the arrival of a helicopter of foreign visitors, Nuristan.

Afghanistan sits here in its approach. Walby elaborates that this approach presents women's activity as exceptional and restricts gender analysis to women only. This third phase is limited in its view of women's activity as a deviation from the norm. In Afghanistan, this can be represented by the media's obsession with the few gender heroines as an antidote to the downtrodden *chaddari*-clad woman — whether they adequately represent Afghan women or not. Furthermore, this approach omits men as actors in gender politics "as if the existing studies take men as gender neutral and only women as gendered subjects." Walby places her emphasis on patriarchal practices, but the contributions of male advocates and supporters — not just opponents — are crucial to advancing gender politics. Finally, the fourth phase represents the full theoretical integration of a gender analysis. This cannot occur until there is a body of empirical work that relates to both sexes. To this end, I examine the gender order based on the perceptions of both men and women as key players, with a view to pushing analyses of Afghanistan into the fourth phase.

Transforming the Gender Order

Aid is often conflated with radical social change.[77] For aid agencies, their proclaimed target for women in Afghanistan was indeed such change. Rhetoric of women's liberation, empowerment, and other terms were used frequently to justify intervention — an intervention that was fueled by the propagated discourse on Afghan women. This is further magnified in contexts of conflict and the aftermath where gender identities are in flux, offering space for women to access new resources and claim new roles. As Afghanistan moves beyond an immediate post-war situation, aid interventions become increasingly conflictual and contested processes, as people negotiate priorities and resource distribution in an effort to secure their livelihoods.[78] In the aftermath, gender-focused international aid can play a role in helping women achieve greater security. I do not doubt the sincerity in seeking to provide for women's (political, social, and economic) security, but interventions were hampered by inadequate understandings of the intersection of poverty, gender, power, and security.

To this end, one intention of intervention in Afghanistan for women was to transform the gender order. In theory, transformation is achieved by a strategic impact on the gender order, a fundamental structural change in gender relations that brings women closer to equitable relationships with men.[79] Transformation is a long-term process, working at a deep structural level to address gender inequalities. Transformation is also more than an outcome; it is a non-linear process to be put in place entailing consciousness-raising and women's agency. Indeed, the most important transformations are not simply introduced by aid interventions but are being negotiated through a complex process that involves all those with something at stake.[80] In theory, transformation is not a difficult concept to grasp. Implementing programs that raise the probability of transformation, however, is not as apparent. Aid interventions themselves do not transform, per se, but they support or hinder women's potential in achieving transformation through their policies and programs. For these purposes, I do not seek to measure transformation or to judge its success. Transformation in this case is relevant in that it was used as a discourse that was not matched in practice.

A discourse on transformation can produce certain ideas — whether applied or not — that generate their own effects. An analysis of intervention should therefore include an examination of battles over the interpretation of images and meanings that take place at the interface between outsiders (aid institutions) and local groups.[81] In the case of women in Afghanistan, language was used as a political practice to present a specific picture and to achieve particular ends. There is little existing scholarship on Afghan women's agency at the interface between aid interventions and women's needs and interests. An examination of transformation in practice should therefore begin with an examination of aid institutions' statements of intent.

The *Afghan Women Empowerment Act of 2006* presents a good starting point for a discussion of discourses animating gender interventions in Afghanistan.[82] This act provides evidence of the above discussion, namely that certain terms can carry a moral imperative to act and an assumption that the action must come from the top, in this case the U.S. government.

The Empowerment Act began in January 2004 as the *Afghan Women Security and Freedom Act* championed by U.S. Senator Barbara Boxer. This Act authorized $300 million per year through 2007 and earmarked funds for the Ministry of Women's Affairs, the Afghanistan Independent Human Rights Commission, and Afghan women's NGOs. Two years later, Barbara Boxer attempted to revive the dormant act. She argued that President Karzai himself "admitted that we are falling short on the issue of Afghan women." She continued: "As we work to foster democracy in Afghanistan, we must be vigilant in ensuring that women take their rightful place in Afghan society." [83] This bill never became law.

The Act is problematic because it begins with a denial of Afghan women's agency and assumes a moral imperative to act. It further insists that funding shall focus on the adherence "to international standards for women's rights and human rights" and includes a commitment "to disseminate information throughout Afghanistan on the rights of women and on international standards for human rights." Senator Boxer's message was sent to me through a small distribution list with the following preface from an Afghan woman leader: "I hope on the Afghan side this humanitarian money is spent wisely and efficiently in the right spots for the right reason."

It is not unusual for empowerment discourses — not unlike the act — to reveal an assumption that empowerment is a top-down effort. The underlying assumption is that the present is restrictive and that women are oppressed — unable to empower themselves. This approach, combined with contradictions in the discourse, could inevitably lead to difficulties in implementation. Indeed, implementing empowerment is often less clear, despite its triumph at the level of discourse. There is no agreement on the meaning of the term or how it is to be brought to fruition — through acts of government or aid interventions. Despite its centrality to the concept of power, the term is frequently used in a way that strips it of political meaning.[84] Indeed, "empowerment" has achieved buzzword status, making it increasingly more slippery to put into practice. And yet, such buzzwords frame solutions, giving aid policies a sense of purpose and suggesting a world that can be neatly repaired through technical solutions.[85] In Afghanistan, technical interventions were applied to address political and structural issues, further masking social problems. Technical interventions in isolation allow little room for Afghan feminists advocating for structural change in their own contexts.

The discourses surrounding aid interventions — and the buzzwords that animate them — are not neutral. These buzzwords assume meaning as they are employed in policies which then influence how the aid apparatus understands what it is doing — and why it has a moral imperative to do it. The agenda for transformation brings such a responsibility, and provides the legitimacy that the apparatus needs in order to intervene. The empowerment discourse mysteriously becomes stripped of politics and power — its core values — and assumes a depoliticized aid identity that no one can disagree with. The term is then negotiated and operationalized in different ways in different settings. In so doing, it is further stripped of any understanding of, or engagement with, the local contexts in which it is applied.

The empowerment discourse can be seen as emanating from the rights-based development agenda where empowerment is defined as an awareness that one is a subject of rights with a capacity to act on the world and change it to benefit individuals, collectives, and society.[86] However, elements of this discourse are contested on the grounds that they are seen as a Western imposition and an act of moral imperialism, further representing an individualistic worldview that counters the collective identities of patriarchal societies.[87]

The perception that "rights" is a Western import holds much weight in Afghanistan, based largely on the means by which the rights message has been delivered. Many theorists have argued this point, particularly in the Afghan context with the link between liberation of women and the War on Terror. There is an inherent contradiction between the rhetoric of women's rights and the reality of stealth bombers.[88]

The rights agenda is not easily put into practice, and runs the risk of failure when translated into action. The rights discourse needs to undergo adaptation and translation in context as a first step to ensuring that local priorities are represented. This does not compromise its underlying principle of equality. On the contrary, it offers a more solid foundation for sustainability, grounded in local contexts.

In Afghanistan, there is no hegemonic aid discourse, per se, but some perspectives have become more powerful than others, leaving little room for alternative (perhaps indigenous) discourses on women.[89] The discourse on women in Afghanistan suggested that aid interventions would transform Afghan women from their position of subjugation to empowerment and liberation. Implicit in this message is the idea that women are *prevented* from achieving aid because of socio-cultural constraints, as if it were simply a matter of changing attitudes and values.[90] Such a perspective dislocates women, reinforces victimization, denies agency, and leaves women no role in their own empowerment. It is problematic to assume that Afghan women need to be liberated, developed, and empowered. Further, in Islamic contexts, international pressure exerts influence on gender priorities and policies,[91] making it difficult for women to demonstrate agency in a context of pre-determined international opinion about the status of women in Islam. The West's view of the Muslim woman as needing to be "saved" is Orientalism.[92] There is a conflicting worldview in the notion that Afghan women are *bourka*'ed damsels in distress awaiting salvation from knights in shining tanks.

Feminisms exist. And many women can exercise agency to "save" themselves. Local interpretations of feminisms are not alien importations. These evolve like all social movements — in response to issues women face in their own contexts. Indigenous feminist movements evolve when there is a desire to challenge circumstances to create better alternatives. Afghan women have struggled and negotiated the various fluctuations in their social status throughout history, using long-established mechanisms to achieve gains on their own terms. An Afghan feminism — perhaps not labeled as such — has a long history in Afghanistan. Afghan feminism seeks firstly to distance itself from a Western feminist model. Although the underlying principles are the same, a link to Western feminism could appear to be a cooptation by the aid-occupation, thereby undermining Afghan women's long struggle. Further-more, Afghan feminists challenge dual oppressions: imperialism and patri-archy. In such cases, the feminist struggle is often superseded by the national struggle. Afghan women have always been exercising agency — despite the aid apparatus' inability to recognize it as such.

Depoliticizing Political Interventions

The aid business is animated by an array of acronyms. Words lose their political power — and potency — when amputated. The gender discourse trav-eled an acronym evolution: the phrase "gender and development" (GAD) evolved from a focus on its acronym predecessor, WID ("women in develop-ment").[93] While WID can be credited with bringing women to the fore, it also

> continued to create a colonized poor and marginalized woman who needed to be managed and educated; whose capacity for work and local decision making needed building; and who needed to be controlled reproductively and sexually through a series of development interventions designed for "women's empowerment."[94]

The WID/GAD distinction presents an interesting point of entry into the dis-cussion on technical and political interventions. WID creates an artificial dichotomy based on sex — without an understanding of the power and poli-tics that comes into play. I will argue that aid interventions for women in Afghanistan have progressed much along the same lines as the evolution of WID and GAD — only backwards. Afghanistan began with a GAD–centered discourse, but resulted in WID–style implementation. A WID–style imple-mentation is more conducive to technical solutions and a standardized aid package — the ideal scenario for an aid intervention.

It is helpful to make a distinction between technical and political inter-ventions to examine implementation of gender policies in light of intent. Political issues include women's strategic interests, addressing structural issues and transforming the gender order to bring it closer to equality. Politics is about the distribution of power — resources and influence — and understand-ing who gets what, when, and how.[95] A key political question they are not equipped to answer is the *why* of it all. Technical interventions, on the other hand, are apolitical. They dangerously ignore the political nature of gender issues and shy away from confronting imbalances of power. Technical inter-ests can be the basis for political transformation. However, this is difficult to measure as it requires women themselves to transform technical interventions into political gains. The aid apparatus is equipped to provide technical solutions, although such inputs are less likely to achieve transformation. Whether the intent is technical or political, aid interventions are always received as a political tool — with a political message.

Political and technical gender interventions need to work in tandem in order to instigate longer-term strategic change in gender relations. There are possible consequences in prioritizing one over the other. An understanding of the distinction between technical and political interventions helps to unpack the tension between policies which seek to distribute resources in ways that preserve and reinforce inequalities and those seeking to challenge inequalities.[96]

In Afghanistan and other aftermath contexts, aid interventions focused initially on practical needs. The discrepancy in Afghanistan is between the rhetoric (political) and the implementation (technical). Aid interventions are not equipped to address political concerns, nor are they necessarily driven by policy intent — transforming the gender order. The gendered effects of aid policy and practice cannot be divorced from the operations of aid institutions. There is an increased risk that aid interventions will have unanticipated effects when policy rhetoric does not match actual implementation. Gender-focused aid policy in Afghanistan employed a discourse of transformation, using terminology associated with political and structural issues with the goal of encouraging social change and redressing gender inequalities. However, implementation of those policies focused on meeting practical needs through technical interventions.

This measure may not be applicable to Afghan realities in its current form; however, it presented a useful starting point for analysis and an opportunity to engage with a concept that originates from a Western gender and development agenda and to test its relevance in another context. This distinction is more apparent in theory than in practice, yet it serves as a starting point to measure actual implementation in light of intent. This political process should be seen within a larger context of social change, one in which aid agencies are both products of, and actors in, particular political processes. This framework allows space for strategic examination of existing aid interventions with regard to the goal of addressing social and gender inequalities, revealing the ways in which women's interests and needs were formulated and subsequently implemented by aid institutions. In so doing, it is possible to examine what aid institutions *say* and measure it against what they *do*. However, it is more important to understand how Afghan women — and different groups of Afghan women — define transformation and what it is they hope to see transformed.

2

Discourses on Chaddari *Politics*[1]

Women's rights issues have become depoliticized and have been hijacked.... In this context, everybody and everything responsible for gender equality in Afghanistan equates to nobody and nothing being responsible for putting women's interests and experiences of injustice on the political agenda.[2]

The point of departure for an examination of discourses of transformation and gender in Afghanistan is through media and policy discourses — understanding the trends, themes, and similarities that characterize aid and gender documents of international and national institutions. This is checked against the perspectives of the policy-makers and policy implementers charged with bringing those texts to fruition in order to understand the political subtexts that underpin articulations of technical and political issues.[3] This analysis is followed by the experiences and perceptions of Afghan women and men. It is through these perceptions that the entire aid intervention in Afghanistan should be understood. Therefore, this story prioritizes Afghan women and men's experiences and interpretations of their own realities in the context of the aid apparatus in Afghanistan's aftermath.

The concept of a domain can be used to understand how areas of social life are organized by reference to a central core of values.[4] Domains reveal a social order. Differing domains clash at the point of interface — where conflicts of value and social interest are likely to occur. Afghanistan's interface is one that has played out repeatedly in history, that between a foreign occupier and Afghans in Afghanistan.

We can distinguish between two types of approach used in aid interventions to initiate social change: the improvement approach and the transformation approach. The transformation approach attempts to establish new forms of social organization, making a radical break with existing systems. This is similar to my distinction between technical and political issues. In addressing political concerns, or a transformative approach:

There is no one-to-one relationship between policy commitment and the actual consequences of policy. This is most strikingly the case with the attempts at implementing a transformation approach, which generally spawns a large number of apparently unintended consequences.[5]

32

Chaddaris dry on a line in front of a house, Kabul.

Interfaces occur more readily when outside agencies intervene to implement aid interventions.

"Liberation" from "Gender Apartheid"

The media is one such interface as it plays a strong part in galvanizing public opinion around selected causes, regardless of actual interpretations of events. Indeed, in Afghanistan, the media portrayed Afghan women as eager to embrace liberation. This rhetoric permeated public perception, leading to a moral imperative to act, and thereby also influencing the design of aid interventions for Afghan women. When I interviewed a senior gender advisor for an international institution, she explained that the discourses and images employed by aid institutions and the media are "typical" and should not come as a surprise. She elaborated: "This is orientalism and this is racism.... The media has to have shorthand ways because it has a short time to convince anybody of anything.... I think it's also the need to have symbols that are very easily translatable." As a result, images of women in *chaddaris* become the dominant image.

The situation of Afghan women was at that time an effective tactic to manipulate public opinion in the Western world. However, it might appear to Afghans that the sudden feigned devotion to women looked more like political instrumentalization than concern and compassion. Activists noted that Afghan women had been neglected for years, only to be discussed on exotic list serves and forlorn internet petitions,[6] the most notorious of which, from a student at Brandeis University in the United States, was the first introduction that many American feminists and activists had to the situation of Afghan women.[7] I received the petition 17 times from different sources in a period of two months in 1999. Excerpts from the petition follow:

> The Taliban's War on Women:
> The government of Afghanistan is waging a war upon women. [List of Taliban offenses].... It is at the point where the term "human rights violations" have become an understatement. Everyone has a right to a tolerable human existence, even if they are women in a Muslim country in a part of the world that Americans do not understand. If we can threaten military force in Kosovo in the name of human rights for the sake of ethnic Albanians, Americans can certainly express peaceful outrage at the oppression, murder and injustice committed against women by the Taliban.
> STATEMENT: In signing this, we agree that the current treatment of women in Afghanistan is completely UNACCEPTABLE and deserves support and action by the people of the United States and the U.S. Government and that the current situation overseas will not be tolerated. Women's Rights is not a small issue anywhere and it is UNACCEPTABLE for women in 1998 to be treated as sub-human and so much as property. Equality and human decency is a RIGHT not a freedom, whether one lives in Afghanistan or the United States.

Few voices expressed concern about the images and stereotypes in this petition and the additional risk this might place on Afghan women. Regardless, the petition had already served its purpose as a political tool.

Following the peaks of public interest generated by the petition and, years later, Afghan women's subsequent liberation, the media's interest in Afghanistan — and the *cause-celebre* of Afghan women — became limited to press-worthy events. Analyses of the change in media focus through different periods of time indicated that press attention on Afghan women abated from late 2001 until discussions of the Afghan Constitution and the Afghan Women's Bill of Rights were proposed in October 2003.[8] This attention was short-lived. Afghan women again hardly appeared in the media until the following year for the presidential election of October 2004. There was silence yet again for another year, until the parliamentary election of September 2005. And, predictably, without the anticipation of major events where women's participation can be showcased, the media will pay even less attention to Afghan women in the foreseeable future. A senior gender officer for an international institution reinforced this point, arguing that the aid apparatus has the responsibility to correct images that appear in the media that give the impression "that Afghan women are now emancipated and 'de-*bourka*'ed' through international intervention [and therefore] can be forgotten — again."

Indeed, the media can be credited with bringing attention — and therefore funding — to Afghanistan in the first place. For many, this is the only exposure they might have to the country. According to the senior gender officer of an aid institution:

> The less there is a focus on women's crisis, the less direct funding there is for women specifically. Without the horrors of the Taliban presence, less attention is paid to the progress being made by women and the support needed for that to continue. It is more or less business as usual.

A further question to be explored is what the implications might be for those who do *not* receive media and donor attention and how they seek out their own ways — positive or negative — to rectify these externally imposed imbalances.

The sudden, excessive attention paid to Afghan women centered around a particular garment. The *chaddari,* described by a journalist as a "body-bag for the living," became the international symbol of the Taliban's oppression of women and the galvanizing point for many American feminist groups.[9] This is an unfortunate choice as it is not *our* opinion of the *chaddari* that matters, nor *our* campaign against it that will succeed. Nonetheless, international feminists debated their roles in supporting women in Afghanistan, and the familiar camps of universal human rights and feminism-as-imperialism emerged. Despite this attention, an Afghan specialist argued that:

> Unprecedented international interest, misinformation, and hysteria have surrounded the situation of women and girls since the Taliban set foot in Kabul. In recent years Afghan women have been used by countless media, political, and humanitarian entities, as well as publicity hungry women's rights' groups, to pursue their own objectives.[10]

The "Gender Apartheid" campaign was launched by feminists with the "body bag" in mind.[11] While high-profile campaigning on behalf of Afghan women might serve well in terms of consciousness-raising, it created difficulties for aid operations on the ground.[12] Such campaigns waged by American feminist activists limit discursive openness by centering their agendas around certain moral convictions, therefore stifling debate. These agendas then become the foundation for the group's moral perspectives.[13] Afghan activists expressed concern with the campaign and the possibility that it could alienate the very women it was trying to help. These Afghan voices were relatively silent in comparison, despite their concern that their opinions were largely absent from campaigns waged on their behalf.[14]

The "Gender Apartheid" campaign was deemed successful with the 2001 "liberation" of Afghanistan — and therefore of Afghan women — from the Taliban. Many years after the campaign, images of Afghan women as oppressed creatures beneath *chaddaris* still permeated popular perception, although the media's silence led spectators to believe that Afghan women had been liberated and there was no further need to discuss them. One author expressed the views of many:

> The veil was probably the clearest example of the perverse nature of media coverage.... The fall of the Taliban has led to the virtual disappearance from the media agenda of the issue of the veil, and indeed of Afghan women in general.[15]

Indeed, the cause of Afghan women had been taken up and largely forgotten, while Afghan women continued to struggle under external pressure to defend their agency and their cultural integrity. Meanwhile, Afghan women had "good reason to suppose that if their lives were to become the subject of feminist discussion, their own perspectives might be discounted."[16] It is wise to be critical of this sudden interest in the perceived victimization of women in non–Western cultures and the perceived moral obligation that accompanies it. Indeed, there is arrogance in the notion that the aid apparatus knows better than the women involved about their needs and interests.

In March 2005, I tested popular perceptions to better understand the extent to which these images still held sway, and to assess the influence of media on these perceptions.[17] The discussion started with general descriptions of Afghanistan after the Taliban — not very positive. Images of Afghan women were mixed. Most included the *chaddari*[18] and veil, noting that Afghan women are "oppressed but wanting change." It was interesting to note the contradiction in each answer as many conveyed the sense that things are bad, *but* could be good. For instance: "Hidden but struggling to better the life of their people."

The respondents largely felt that the media contributed to whatever negative images they might have had about "helpless women who don't have rights or privileges." The media "perpetuated negative image of repressed women, veiled unhappy victims." They felt that there is currently very little focus on Afghan women, particularly since world attention has shifted to Iraq and other issues. Another said: "We see images of women under the *bourka* but we hear [former U.S. President] George Bush tell us that women's rights have been restored." The media presented a biased and sensationalized view, victimizing Afghan women further. Afghan women are presented "as either victims, or as victims-turned-success-stories."

Can We See "Beneath the *Bourka*" Yet?

The *chaddari* is not a new object of Western obsession. In 1985, Nancy Hatch Dupree wrote that women in Afghanistan during that time "dismiss the stereotyped image depicted by most Western media which insist on picturing Afghan women forever enveloped in billowing veils."[19] In November 1997, the Special Advisor on Gender Issues and the Advancement of Women wrote the following in her report following an inter-agency gender mission to Afghanistan:

> External observers and interlocutors often mistake symptoms and causes: the bourka, for example is not considered a major problem for most Afghan women with whom the Mission spoke, but is treated as such by many assistance workers in the country, agency personnel at headquarters and sometimes, opinion-makers outside the country.[20]

The *chaddari* should be viewed in its socio-political and historical context. A nuanced understanding will reveal that the *chaddari* can also be seen as a symbol of resistance. Its earliest uses by the Pashtun elite provided freedom of mobility and anonymity. During the Taliban era, the *chaddari* was used strategically to transport messages, weapons, cameras, and banned publications in anonymity.[21] Indeed, imagining the *chaddari* as a tool of freedom is beyond the understanding of the aid apparatus, who saw only a one-dimensional vehicle of oppression.

"More responsible action in the use of images is needed,"[22] particularly regarding the use of the *chaddari* as a tool to advance Western campaigns for Afghan women. The pervasive image of the *chaddari* was reduced to a symbol of Afghan women's oppression. As a result, many of those interviewed viewed representations of—and focus on—this garment as part of a larger confusion regarding the intersection between Afghan women, culture, and religion. In fact, the obsession with the *chaddari* obscured other gendered consequences of the Taliban's decrees for men. The Western construction of this garment fosters an artificial construct of Afghan men against Afghan women.[23] A gender specialist elaborated:

> Too much focus can push women into a position of defending their culture and it can become a symbol of resistance to "tyrannical Western influences" against "good Afghan women." It also simplifies the complex situation of gendered identities and roles within Afghan culture. By this I don't mean to suggest that women do not have less access to power or control of resources in Afghan cultures but that it's too simplistic to suggest that once women remove their *bourkas* they are free and everything has been made right.

The head of an aid institution working with women expressed it this way:

> The world's image of Afghan women was that they were horribly oppressed and abused — the worst image of women anywhere in the world. This has continually fuelled programs attempting to help Afghan women. That *bourka* is the ultimate symbol of the backwardness of Afghanistan. Westerners gasp at its sight. There is nothing more reproachable in terms of the absence of women's rights. Even though the quantity of coverage [of Afghan women] has obviously reduced, the quality hasn't. It's still catchy to talk about how oppressed and wretched they are.

A woman dances to celebrate her graduation from a vocational training program, Kabul.

However, this garment can be credited with bringing much (read: largely Western) attention to Afghanistan. It continues to play a prominent role for the aid apparatus, particularly the Western media, producing myriad documentaries, articles, and photographs claiming to offer a glimpse "behind/ under/beneath the *bourka*."[24] This unconstructive image of Afghan women serves only to feed stereotypes and deny Afghan women's agency. In the words of another head of an aid institution:

> We live through symbols, through assumptions. Because it is too difficult to understand. The assumption is that a woman who is more Western in terms of dress is empowered. That will take you to a conclusion that all European women are empowered, which is not correct. It will also take you to a conclusion that there is gender equality if there is no *bourka*.

It is not unusual for any act of veiling to be misconstrued as a denial of women's agency. Afghanistan is not unique in this case. Many have documented a history of Western obsession with the veil. Despite this obsession, Afghan women repeatedly fail to conform to stereotypical images. The most facile of constructs is the use of the *chaddari* as a barometer to measure social change—or lack thereof.

In my own capacity as an NGO director, I was approached by many journalists about the *chaddari*, to explain why it remains in post-liberation Afghanistan. One American journalist told me that, during a five-day visit in early 2002, he estimated that ninety-five percent of Afghan women were wearing it. He returned for seven days in November 2002 and told me that now perhaps ninety percent of Afghan women still wore the *chaddari*. As a result, he said, he felt that I had "failed" to do my "job" in "liberating" Afghan women. To him, the *chaddari* was the problem, and the aid apparatus the solution—the means by which liberation would occur. Therefore, the persistence of the *chaddari* on Afghanistan's streets indicated a failure of the aid apparatus. His words remained with me during my four years in Afghanistan.

That journalist might note with dismay that the *chaddari* persists. And yet, as Afghan men and women will clearly articulate, the presence or absence of this garment does little to indicate liberation. It is more important, however, to distinguish between the transformation of customs—such as veiling and the prevalence of Western clothing—and institutional change in the form of laws and women's sense of their rights and roles. In fact, one might assume that men have been transformed based on the prevalence of Afghan men in Western dress. The change in men's clothing style does not constitute a Western influence, or an indication of liberation. Indeed, it is assumed that culture is static when it comes to women, and that the sex of the actors is a determining factor in labeling a change Western or not.[25]

Choices and Voices

Both Afghan women and men interviewed noted that the *chaddari* served as the image under which all others were determined. As part of a reflexive journal, I wrote the following excerpt in my capacity as NGO director to document my first impressions in September 2002:

> My sense is that Afghan women long for choice. The choice to wear a veil, or a *bourka*, or nothing at all. The issue extends well beyond the actual fabric of the *bourka*. It is more important to address the psychological *bourka*, and its progeny — the fear *bourka* and the poverty *bourka*. Social evolution is a slow process, and our task in this is to offer women the tools with which they can achieve self-sufficiency, a choice, and a voice.

And yet, today both the choice and the voice are notably absent. And the *chaddari* remains the preferred garment. Afghan women repeatedly expressed exasperation with this facile construct, saying that the world thinks "Afghan women are only *bourkas*." As a result of this image, the world felt compelled to save them. An Afghan woman explained that the world thinks of them as "oppressed and weak." This is not accurate, she said, "but the world wants to see us this way." An Afghan man elaborated strongly that the aid apparatus wants Afghan men and women to have:

> Freedom like the Western world. Western women wear clothes, not *bourka*. So Afghan women should wear that, too; otherwise they have no rights. This is a completely incorrect image. We don't approve of it. Afghan men and women are Muslims and have their own culture and they do what is in their culture.

A senior gender advisor for an international institution told the following story to illustrate this:

> I remember talking to the public relations person in [the NGO] because I had argued as a policy that we would not show images of women in *bourkas*. They can be in the background but this is not the dominant image. And she said to me "But how else will we know that they're Afghan?" And I said "But look at those pictures of women from Bosnia, from Iraq. You can't tell that that Bosnian woman is not from Iraq and that she's not from Kosovo and that she's not from Afghanistan because they all look pretty much the same."

Below are two stories of Afghan women at seemingly opposite ends of the spectrum.[26] Both of these women spoke at great length about their lives and offered detailed profiles. They present an interesting comparison: one woman is career-driven, successful, and employed in a traditionally male field in a high-ranking position. She does not represent the norm. The other is uneducated and relies on charity and aid interventions for her livelihood.

The former has chosen to remain without a husband. The latter woman is burdened by a husband who cannot support her and feels she has suffered more because she lacks male protection. One feels like a victim, the other like a survivor. These women share some perspectives, however. They both believe that Afghan women can stand on their own and can act on their own behalf to better their lives. They both believe that an Afghanistan with foreign influence has only served to retard progress for women. They believe that the right pace of social change is one that is instigated by Afghans — men and women — and that only this way will Afghanistan achieve liberation, finding freedom on its own terms.

Mariyam: Waiting for Change

Mariyam was 35 years old. She was a mother of two small children. She couldn't read and hoped that one day she would have enough "free space in [her] head to think of such things." For now she must find a way to support her children because her husband could not. Her family lived in one small room and shared a cooking space with the family in the adjacent room. "This is how our lives have become, in this time of *peace*" [emphasis hers], she said. Her husband was unemployed. He tried to find work as a day laborer but was not able to bring home a steady income. "He is angry," Mariyam explained, "and so he has turned on me, and turned to drugs. What can I do but tolerate this? I am a woman, after all."

Mariyam told the story of how her life had changed:

> My husband was kinder to me during the Taliban time. We were both scared. I felt safer then. We both had no opportunity for work or leaving the house. Life was very difficult but we struggled together. We were equal in our suffering.

Today, she said:

> Afghan men are not given chances. But this is not our fault. Afghan women have always been patient, strong, brave, silent. We do what we must do to support our families and feed our children. If I don't go out and take advantage of this [waves hand around organization office], how will we live? He cannot. He wanted to before, but now he is an addict and he is useless to us. But he is my husband and I have no choice.

Mariyam felt that relations between men and women were deteriorating, not just in her household, but in those she saw around her.

> Women are still struggling to make better their relations with men. It is not easy because there is still violence against them. It is a man's job to take care of the family and children financially. In most families that I have seen, rela-

tions have gotten worse because of poor economy. It is a bad thing, this change.

Mariyam explained that part of the tension between her and her husband was primarily because she had become the man in the family. Further, she was going out of the house. And, even more serious, she was "involved with foreigners." It was not just her husband, she explained. "Men don't like their women out of the house, especially with foreigners." She elaborated:

I wish that women would work in local and governmental organizations and schools, not in foreign NGOs. It will cause them problems with the men if they work with foreigners. But I am here because this is where I get money. If there were opportunities for men to work, and for [Afghan] men and women to work together, things will change. But I do not know what opportunities men have. I see many of them without opportunities. Organizations are promising rights that women cannot achieve and cannot understand. On paper, women have been given rights and freedom. But in my mind, women expected more rights because that was what was promised to them.

Mariyam was not unlike other Afghan women she knew in that she was able to make astute observations about the work of the aid apparatus and the impact its presence and programs have had. She explained:

Women are the center of interest for everyone. I never imagined I would see a day where foreign people don't stop talking about Afghan women. Every day in this organization some people come, some journalists come, and they want us to tell them that our lives are better. They want us to tell them that we are not wearing *chaddari*, that we are happy. They think we are stupid. And when they go away, we laugh because we have nothing else we can do. The world is watching, and this is what they want to see.

Mariyam had the following to say about the international obsession with the *chaddari*:

The foreigners say, "remove your *bourka, bourka kharab* [*bourka* is bad]," but I say Afghanistan *kharab*. Afghan men *kharab*. Until we change this — and we will never change it — my *chaddari* protects me. I put it on and "where is Mariyam?" No one knows. And Mariyam comes and Mariyam goes. And Mariyam stays safe. What choice do I have?

Still, Mariyam was able to end on a positive note. "I hope for a bright future," she said. "What else can we do but hope?"

General Nazari: Making Change

General Nazari was the Deputy of the Human Rights Department in the Ministry of the Interior (MoI). She also represented the Afghan Independent

Human Rights Commission in the MoI. She was tasked with training and assigning women police officers to handle women's security issues. General Nazari also worked to sensitize men in the MoI to women's human rights and security.

General Nazari's story was a rare one. She had served with the Afghan police for 31 years. In 2002, she became a general. Her father was in the military, and, although he was a liberal man, he did not want his daughter to follow suit. General Nazari recalled her father taking a trip to Turkey and returning with new ideas about women. He began to advocate for women's education, and he expressed opposition to his wife wearing a *chaddari*. At age five, while watching a military parade with her father, General Nazari had decided on her course in life.

General Nazari was serving as a police officer at the beginning of the Soviet invasion. She sent her husband abroad to protect him, while she remained in Afghanistan with their three small children. He returned many years later, but she had decided that she did not want a husband. She continued to invest in her career and served as a role model for women. She expressed concern with the current direction of her country, and asked why organizations were not working with men. She explained: "It is not only women who need help. In Afghanistan you may think that women don't know anything and men do. But this is not the case. Both need help."

When asked about women's security issues and the prevalence of violence against women, she strongly stated that violence against women has increased recently because men are having difficulties dealing with changes in women's rights and status. She elaborated:

> In all the world, violence against women is increasing, not just in Afghanistan. But we are Muslim people and we need to study gender issues and women's rights in the context of Islam and society in Afghanistan.

General Nazari explained that the large international presence has prevented women in Afghanistan from defining their rights for themselves. Furthermore, it has created resentment with men who feel that their own issues are not addressed. Even in the context of violence, she explained, violence against men and violence against women by other women are unacknowledged problems and are never discussed. She elaborated that the international community only talks about women's rights in relationship to men. General Nazari put it this way: "Women and women! That's what the men say. This makes difficulties and problems in families because all men hear from the outside is 'women and women.' They no longer know where they fit."

On the concept of gender, General Nazari explained:

"Gender" has not had a chance to define itself in Afghanistan. It is unknown here and does not translate. People think gender is brought from other countries and doesn't belong to Afghanistan. But when we say equality of men and women, then the people say "Yes. This is in Islam. Yes. This is in the Constitution." But "gender," this is foreign to us still. In this society, it is difficult for people to accept changes so quickly.

Despite these diverse lives, the liberation discourse was instrumental in creating a particular image of Afghan women. This image served to create a picture of an oppressed Afghan woman beneath a *chaddari*, in turn contributing to the design of programs and aid interventions. Such an image denies agency and did not resonate with Afghan women and men. There are discontinuities in analyses and assessments of the condition of Afghan women and how best to empower them. This presents a good starting point for a discussion of policy formulation from the perspectives of those actively involved. Given the tenacious nature of the perceptions surrounding Afghanistan and Afghan women, one might question the extent to which these images have informed aid interventions.

Examining Policy Texts

It is essential to question how far national and international instruments have been influenced by pervasive images of Afghan women. In this vein, a brief investigation into policy formulation begins here with a textual analysis of aid and gender policy papers of large aid institutions operating in Afghanistan. Five aid institutions were selected based on their roles as core members of a high-level body charged with supporting the Ministry of Women's Affairs and providing strategic direction on all things gender in Afghanistan. This high-level body works to ensure that gender is mainstreamed across the various thematic areas of focus as outlined in Afghanistan's aid interventions. Such a group is not new. When it was established, it was comprised of nearly equal numbers of foreign and Afghan women. "The foreigners did all the talking. Only when you asked one of the Afghan women a direct question would she come forth with her observations."[27] Today, the group likely comprises far fewer Afghan women. And their voices are still silenced.

In the policy texts of these aid institutions, I examined the documents with a view to the presence of gender issues — and the quality of that presence. My approach was informed by a number of studies where aid policy documents have been analyzed for their gender content or to discern their approach to women and gender. I was further concerned with the extent to which gender has been "mainstreamed" in the document. Despite rhetoric, very often gender is *not* a cross-cutting issue but has in fact been isolated in the document. It merits questioning when a claim to mainstream gender issues is substantiated by an isolated paragraph on gender.

Such an approach could also result in an emphasis on the media-driven image of women as victims as opposed to a focus on women's agency. Further, this approach facilitates the creation of technical solutions to a political problem, clearly designating space for the aid intervention as the only alternative for women. Given these conditions, it becomes difficult for the aid intervention to assess progress made for women. This is usually done in terms of quantity — money spent, women trained, and so on — in lieu of actual improvements made in women's lives.

A further contradiction entails the mention of men in so-called gender documents. In these cases, men are included in the document only as obstacles to women's development, or when making negative comparisons to women.[28] This is also reflected in popular perceptions of Afghan women and is problematic as it negates men's roles in women's development — and negates the importance of their own development. As a result, interventions assume that gender relations and power are a zero-sum game, and that interventions for women should offer no alternatives for men.[29] In addition, simplistic formulations and facile analyses label man as exploiter and woman as exploited. Imagery of *chaddari*-clad women also supports these deductions.

Most texts make lofty claims to instigate social change, yet they provide few practical applications to bring this to fruition. A textual analysis therefore should include an understanding of the presence of terms like empowerment and gender in order to illuminate the extent of this intervention priority shift on paper. This is the approach adopted here.

One report makes vague references to women, such as "women and men of Afghanistan," and makes negative comparisons of women's suffering as compared to men. There is little indication of women's agency and in fact emphasis is placed on women's poor condition. No mention is made of solutions to address this condition. The report further refers vaguely and unconstructively to "gender issues" and a "gender-sensitive approach," while failing to define what the term might mean in Afghanistan. Therefore, while "gender issues" are present, they appear to lack a robust definition. In addition, use of the term is concentrated in the paragraph on "human rights and gender issues" and not throughout the document.

Another report fails to provide definitions or operational guidelines on how to address the various "gender issues" it raises. Other references to gender include "gender training modules," "the gender perspective," "gender task force," "gender-sensitive amendments to law," and others. All of these are used in the abstract, without a clear understanding of how this is to be put into operation. The only indication given in these documents to operational-ize concepts is to incorporate technical solutions: add women, or isolate them as an "object" of aid interventions. These reports also give little indication of women's agency in Afghanistan, implying that the presence of the aid insti-tution is therefore justified as it is the only way to achieve gains for women. Media images and popular perceptions have influenced policy in this regard.

Yet another report juxtaposes the Taliban ("the problem") with the orga-nization's activities ("the solution"). This plays into popular perceptions of how to "solve" Afghan women's "problems." Each statement regarding Afghan women's poor condition is qualified by Taliban abuses. This constant justification for action, coupled with a moral imperative to act, is simplistic at best. It is also important to note the frequent employment of liberation rhetoric for such purposes. Additional documents from this organization advo-cate "fast responses" to what it calls "political problems." One might argue that Afghanistan needed precisely the opposite. It also assumes that aid inter-ventions are equipped to provide political solutions. The solutions proposed are hardly political but are in fact technical. Claims of improving women's roles in society are articulated but not substantiated. No mention is made of analyses defining what women might believe to constitute an "improve-ment"—or whether they sought this "improvement" in the first place. Fur-ther analyses have revealed that such projects are not founded on Afghan community needs and demands. Afghan women have articulated that they were not consulted and felt compelled to accept the projects that were designed to benefit them as a *fait accompli*.

Such efforts would have likely benefited from a contextualized under-standing of Afghanistan's social dynamics — particularly gender issues. This was notably absent from most public discussions on "the situation of Afghan women." Neglect of this understanding demonstrates the propensity to offer technical solutions to political problems and the tendency for elevated claims that could not be met through these technical solutions. Further, moving from program rhetoric to reality was extremely challenging and was met with much resistance.

Another organization did not finalize its gender strategies or release them to the public. Such documents frequently employ vague terminology that recognizes Afghanistan's "cultural context"—viewing it as a static element that presents a constraint to the women's "liberation" agenda. It was implicit that—while neither a workable definition of gender nor a plan to mainstream was provided—aid interventions are best suited to do the "mainstreaming"—whatever that entails. This gender policy was not specific to Afghanistan, but was — according to one official — built from gender policies in other countries and "tweaked for the Afghan context."

Other reports reflect similar trends. The uses of the term "gender" do not represent a contextualized understanding and lack any definition of the term. More often than not, the term is used in place of sex, such as "gender-disaggregated data." The report refers sporadically to women's "vulnerable" status and to their suffering under the Taliban. Beyond language referring to "gender imbalances" and the subsequent need for "special attention" to be paid to women, there is little reference as to how to rectify imbalances. Such documents leave no alternative beyond that of an aid intervention to provide balance and bring equality. Through such texts, it is made clear that only the aid apparatus can bring "liberation" to Afghan women, and that this "liberation" can only come in the form of technical solutions that constitute the standard package of interventions.

The ranking shown below was created in order to compare texts and analyze documents:

- **Low** entails use of the words "women" and "gender," but no or limited understanding of the meanings and how to bring them to fruition. This category also entails a lack of contextualized analysis for women and gender yet heavy use of gender-related rhetoric. The terms "women" and "gender" occur as tokens. Further, there is little or no mention of Afghan women's agency.

- **Medium** includes a brief discussion of the terms and a limited understanding of women and gender concerns. However, this category represents those documents that lack concrete strategies as to how to bring gender issues to fruition in program plans.

- **High** demonstrates a solid understanding of gender and women's issues. The terms are used in relevant contexts — in particular gender is used in the robust sense of the word, including definitions. This category suggests a direction for programs and concrete action to be taken. It also represents a contextualized understanding of gender in Afghanistan.

Based on the above discussion, it was clear that most organizations ranked low. None of the organizations achieved a high ranking. This analysis of texts from reputable institutions in Afghanistan is used to illustrate the similarities in the discourse and the pervasive extent of this particular discourse. This would likely also be the case if popular media reporting on Afghan women was to be graded along a similar scale.

In addition to their poor ranking, the texts share a few key commonalities. First, they offer no definitions for terms used, or an understanding of the application of these terms in Afghanistan. Practical applications are notably absent, making it challenging for gender to translate from paper to practice. Gender issues might be sprinkled strategically throughout the documents, but the value is lost and mention is largely tokenistic.

Next, they offer no recognition of Afghan agency but instead leave room to justify their own existence by problematizing "the women issue" so that the only solution is an aid intervention. The rhetoric uses gender terminology but reflects a women-in-development approach. In this case, women's empowerment is a means to achieve economic development.

A parallel can be made between textual references to gender and agency and Sylvia Walby's progression of engagement with gender issues, as mentioned in Chapter 1. I extend this approach to address men's issues in gender programming using a five-phased process. The first phase, near neglect, sees men only as perpetrators, and therefore women as victims. The second phase exposes the previous neglect, addressing men as obstacles to women's development. The third phase entails engagement with men only to advance women's interests. The fourth phase is that of exceptions: men who are advocates and supporters of women's issues. Finally, full integration of men — the fifth phase — entails working with men in their own right. Most of the texts sit in phase one. None of the texts have moved beyond phase two.

The documents all frame women's issues as social problems, stripping them of any political content. And yet the texts all promise transformation that they cannot deliver on. Proposed transformation is not met by real interventions. Political interests are not embedded in the texts and only receive lip service without practical applications. Some prefer to focus on technical solutions with outcomes that are quick and visible (to their constituents and countries). All of the documents treat mainstreaming as a technical project well suited for aid interventions.

This analysis of policy texts takes the discussion one step further in an effort to understand the constructed image of Afghan women that began with the media and popular perceptions. In this step, Afghan women's problems are framed as social, enabling aid institutions to create a situation to fit their standardized solutions.[30] In the case of Afghanistan, it was not difficult to find the image that necessitated an intervention. Calls for "liberation" were quickly met with technical packages of aid institutions. An academic discourse, on the other hand, might not have created the space for such packages. An examination of the academic discourses might have revealed Afghan women's historic ability to act on their own behalf. An academic discourse would expose an Afghan feminism and a socio-cultural context filled with demonstrations of agency. The lines between the academic and development discourses are blurred in practice, but the purpose is to reveal gaps in the development discourse that might have been found in the academic discourse. It might be worthwhile speculating on the following: If an academic discourse had prevailed in Afghanistan, would there have been room for a gender-focused aid intervention and public support for the liberation of Afghan women?

3

Gender and the Aid Apparatus[1]

> Some interventions can be very disruptive. Badly conceived and facile analyses based on the assumption that Afghan women are vulnerable individuals living in a vacuum may eventually isolate rather than reintegrate women.[2]

This chapter takes the discussion one step further to illuminate the journey from policy formulation to interpretation to implementation through the voices of 45 policy-makers, policy implementers, NGO leaders, and Afghanistan specialists. Within this community, gender is a buzzword in contemporary aid discourse that peppers aid reports, policies, and program plans. Among the Anglophone aid elite, "gender discourse was privileged and pure; the word women was *passe*.... Never mind that gender did not translate well into many languages."[3] In a discussion with a senior staff member of an aid institution, he said:

> We generously employ lots of buzzwords ... like gender, I don't even know what that means. But I'm told I have to mainstream it. Even our gender person, she sits in her own container on the compound. She's not even physically "mainstreamed."

Both the definition of gender and its implications remain under discussion in Afghanistan. And yet the term continues to be coupled with other ambiguous words — empowerment, equality, mainstreaming. "It has never been gender mainstreaming," an Afghan human rights activist explained. "It is gender segregation, just highlighting the differences between men and women. Dividing them, not bringing them together.... And that creates a reaction.... It's the first thing internationals talk about."

As a result, Afghans quickly learned that use of this term would guarantee them international support, regardless of their understanding of the concept itself and what it might take to bring it to fruition. The language animating the agenda of transformation has also been debilitating for some Afghans. According to one woman who runs an NGO for women, the rhetoric of empowerment leads the aid apparatus to believe that "we are here to save the poor victims, and [as a result, Afghan women] are so good at playing the victims." Indeed, Afghans understand what themes are marketable in

A woman waits for a rope to be tied around her waist before she swims in Band-i-Amir, a lake believed to have healing powers, Bamiyan.

the aid apparatus, and use the right words accordingly to achieve gains on their terms. The aid discourse is one that has been mastered very quickly by the communities. Women use the right words because they think that this is what foreigners want to hear, although the depth of the terms has not necessarily been absorbed. Men also use the language, as I observed in my work when, on many occasions, I was confronted with men who sought to start NGOs for "women's empowerment" and approached me for funding. Communities are sufficiently informed to know that the presence of aid institutions is transitory and that they may need to subscribe to the lingo now: including women — on paper — to attract aid. Regardless of their use of the rhetoric, Afghan groups know how to apply the terms and how far they can push the gender agenda in their own contexts. A woman head of an NGO felt strongly about the contagious nature of aid lingo and said that "Afghans are very good at saying whatever they think the donors want to hear — about 'empowerment,' 'right to work,' 'veiling issues' — and will ask for just those things."

An international gender advisor working with an Afghan women's organization illustrated the dynamic this way:

Many of the women I encountered wanted their position in society to be improved — through better health, better support — rather than changed. And I wondered whether they used the term gender because it was the term used most often by donors.

Despite being able to manipulate the lingo, Afghans nonetheless perceived these terms to be items "in the toolbox of those who were party to Afghanistan's wars."[4] In other words, the discourse took the form of an ideological occupation. As a result, Afghans became resistant to these discourses (not the concepts — an important distinction) because of their perceived ties to Western (largely American) individualism. The aggressive promotion of this agenda, and the means by which it is transmitted, therefore serve to generate further inequalities. Thus, it is possible to argue that — to Afghans — the quest for empowerment, for rights, for equality, for liberation is an aid-induced myth. Imposed liberation, however, will only leave a vacuum between ideologies and real people.

To further complicate matters, there is still no agreed-upon translation of gender in Dari and Pashto. To illustrate this point, all of my business cards for positions with gender in the title have been written as "gender" in Dari, as if it has become a Dari word. I use the example of my previous position as "Senior Gender Officer" as case in point. "Senior" and "Officer" were translated. "Gender" was not.

In Dari, the most commonly used word, *jinsiyat*, meaning sexuality, is still heavily disputed and is only used to fill a linguistic void. "What I see," an Afghan woman leader explained, "is that most people translate things from other languages and bring these things here. In Afghanistan, no one asked what gender means. This word, it is different everywhere. For us, it's important to know and to find out for ourselves what gender means in Afghanistan." The infiltration of English terms also gave Afghans the perception that their language and culture was under threat.[5]

In a meeting on gender issues in June 2006, Afghan women made the following points regarding the word gender: (1) The aid apparatus lacks a robust understanding of gender in the Afghan context, (2) There has not been an agreed-upon translation, and (3) The word has became loaded with the perception that it is part of a Western-driven agenda and is used when it is believed that it is "what foreigners want to hear." Later that month, an update on gender activities was circulated, ending with confirmation of plans "to settle the definition issue." It is interesting to note that this issue was, firstly, an afterthought, and secondly, still not resolved — four years into so-called gender efforts in Afghanistan.

Experiences based on the perspectives of policy-makers and policy implementers reveal that gender programs default to women's programs when translated into practice. Gender is not employed in the robust sense of the word. In aid interventions in the context of conflict and its aftermath, this is even more problematic as women as a category tend to be singled out in isolation from their wider social, cultural and family contexts. This point could not be overstated by those interviewed. An Afghan woman working for an aid institution articulated that "gender is a Western concept, or another word for women in Afghanistan." She continued to explain that aid interventions have not addressed the root causes of women's subordination and have therefore failed to affect gender inequality in any significant way. She said that "most mainstreaming approaches to women's development have not been based on analyses of the overall reality of women's lives."

A woman from the region who works with women expressed the views of many:

> I am sorry, but I am not sure I understand the difference between "gender" programs and women's programs! I am tired of this whole "gender" topic anyway. Seems to be an incestuous topic amongst a group of foreigners, having little to do with the realities on the ground there. I think Afghanistan is not the place to experiment with a Westernized construct of women's liberation.
>
> Aid agencies ... are just a bunch of propagandists that have mastered the art of talking for their funders, not for the people they are supposedly here to assist. It's such an embedded system, it is impossible to even step back and see how miserably flawed it is. The repercussions are that people are left with an overly backwards view of countries in the region. The aid agencies have gone too far in creating these clichés and now we are stuck with them forever it seems.

A head of an international NGO was trying to demystify the concept of gender to a colleague. She relayed the conversation to me:

> I was trying to tell her that what she understands gender to be is wrong. That is not gender, it's promotion of women. If you give it the title "promotion of women" then it's fine with me. I can definitely share in the need for that. But then don't call it gender. Of course it makes men angry. So at least try to be honest about it.

An Afghan woman working on gender issues with an aid institution put it this way:

> [Gender] is considered as a weapon against men — which is totally against the concept of "gender issues" in the first place. Gender programs should be designed in order to reduce existing problems between men and women. Side effects should be prevented. The way gender issues are undertaken in Afghanistan now will not work. Because gender issues are introduced as

women's issues, the whole gender thing is considered to be against the cultural and religious values of the country.... To stop and change the present concept of gender issues in Afghanistan, gender programs need to be transferred to both women and men equally. For successful implementation of gender programs in any country — Afghanistan or not — a few basic things should be considered: religious values, cultural values, social structure of society, level of education, and techniques for implementation. Obviously, a successful gender strategy in the United States cannot be successfully implemented in Afghanistan, and similarly a successful gender strategy in Afghanistan can't be successful in Iraq. And, most importantly, empowerment of both men and women cannot happen by outsiders. Men and women should be able to empower themselves to make choices and decisions. To reach this stage our society needs proper and successful gender programs within the framework of our religion and culture.

Many Afghan women activists believe that "talking gender and doing women" actually undermines efforts towards equality: "It has created a big problem in Afghan society. Men were already sensitive to women's issues. And now the international community is trying to talk about women. These things will again make men sensitive." The programmatic separation of men and women likely reflects a Western-oriented individualistic approach, and yet the rights discourse should dictate that, in the words of one Afghan woman, the same rights should apply for men and women as human beings: "Do not try to separate them. People are trying to separate them." A dangerous outcome of this separation is that it fuels men's perception that gender is a negative word. To them, gender has become synonymous with women's power *over* men. An Afghan man working with an NGO explained: "Most of the people, they think that gender is making women in power and decreasing the power of men. Women over men." A gender advisor working for an international NGO explained that the idea of "gender" as an abstract concept fails to manifest itself as equality. In fact, she explained that it was creating an imbalance between men and women:

> In Kabul, the reverse situation already takes place where women get supported in such range that men are falling behind also in the job market, women earn much more and get easier jobs than men. Is this what we wanted to do with empowerment of women? And is this the way to include men in this gender awareness process?

An Afghan woman implementing women's programs with an international NGO had this to say:

> Gender programs are mostly failures. Gender training is never held for those men who need it. We are talking about big changes and transformation of women, and women's organizations are giving hundreds of little trainings for

> women but they are not taking serious action in making changes they talk about. Millions [of dollars] are being spent on conferences and seminars and this has made no difference in women's lives. There is still violence. Gender programs should have worked with men rather than women!

In the absence of thorough gender analyses, programs were unable to adequately integrate men — or women. Extracting Afghan women as a target group sans context rendered both women and men's voices silent. It is important to note that gender interests are not met simply by adding both sexes to aid interventions. The addition of male and female bodies does not necessarily represent gender issues.

Opportunity Lost?

> Gender relations in Afghanistan are complementary. This juxtaposition — men versus women — reflects individual rights and a Western capitalist context. This isn't applicable to Afghanistan because traditionally there is coexistence.

These words of an Afghan-American gender researcher and activist were shared by many. An Afghan-American gender specialist felt strongly about the importance of integrating men in gender work, as she stated in a speech given at the World Bank in Washington, D.C.:

> We need a full gender perspective because without men and boys, gender work is not possible.... Be careful not to provoke a backlash. There are examples of this in Afghan history. Instead let the message slowly come from Afghan women themselves, not the international aid community.... We can't empower women without empowering men, otherwise there will be a backlash again and it will provoke increased domestic violence. The more disempowered men feel, the more resistant they will be to change.

This counsel was shared in 2002. Today, her words proved to be prophetic, as many believe that a backlash is indeed underway. Attempts at engineering a social transformation will have serious repercussions for women as long as women's agency is denied in the process. In conversations with Afghan women, many felt that there was room to work in partnership with men, to make gains in the contexts of the family and community. Indeed, policy-makers and policy implementers agreed, yet no one was aware of such efforts. In fact, many women working with aid institutions felt that an opportunity to engage with potential male supporters and advocates had been lost. In the few cases where men were involved, many interviewees expressed their initial surprise that men supported women in ways that they had not anticipated. They elaborated to say that they regretted not having reached out to men from the onset. However, many aid efforts to target men often pathologize or essentialize them as deviants or as perpetrators of violence in the context of conflict.

Many advocated supporting men — in their own right and as allies to women — to make gains for women. In this vein, it is therefore essential to understand masculinities within a study of the gender order — and the impact of aid interventions on masculinities.[6] When men are studied, it is primarily the experiences of men in northern industrialized countries — the rest are rendered "exotically ethnographic." Research on masculinities could offer an understanding of both men and women and perhaps provide alternative visions of male identity in order to reduce negative effects.[7] Gender equality is not possible without men's involvement and support. This should be done with a view to reaching the fifth phase of engagement with men, as illustrated in Chapter 2.

It is a particular imperative, therefore, to understand the role of men as participants in aid interventions, and the possible negative effects for women when men do not participate. While women's issues made gender visible as a category of analysis, there is a lack of understanding on the impact of such interventions on men. Neglect of men has political effects and renders the quest for gender equality futile. So-called gender frameworks are applied to focus on women and exclude men. Coupled with a perceived male exclusion, this can result in a backlash against gains made in favor of women.[8]

In preliminary understandings of Afghan masculinities, it has become apparent that men view gender equality as a zero-sum game, fearing that they will lose some of their advantage as a result. Conflict contexts reinforce a hegemonic masculinity. In the aftermath, men work to retain this masculinity, driven by a fear that their traditional roles have eroded. Studies of men in countries in transition demonstrate that men carry the burden of the role of provider — and loss of this role can be emasculating.[9] This is compounded by the effects of poverty, displacement, and economic and social change experienced in the aftermath. As a consequence, men may seek affirmation of their masculinities in other ways, such as domestic violence. Interventions for women must therefore offer men alternative sources of domestic and political power and credibility.[10]

For these purposes, it is relevant to understand that aid interventions do not operate in a gender vacuum, and that men are an essential part of gender efforts. Studies from other countries reveal that men have largely been absent from gender equality efforts. A study conducted in several African countries noted that those organizations that engaged men and women together succeeded in reducing not only male resentment over a focus on women, but also reduced domestic violence.[11] Respondents to the research frequently reinforced these ideas and expressed a desire to engage men in gender processes, and also to employ men as agents of change to work with other men. Many interviewed felt that they would rather reinforce, and not undermine, men's traditional roles. An international feminist activist explained: "Just like we are encouraging the government not to ignore one-half of its population — women — we need to start encouraging aid organizations not to ignore one-half of their beneficiaries — men."

An Afghan gender specialist had the following to say in an email to me as part of a discussion on work with men:

> The way that women's roles are drawn in Afghan society adversely effect every aspect of women's lives.... Men's roles in Afghanistan are also rigidly defined, leading men to bear the brunt of economic responsibility. It is also evident that Afghan men are increasingly frustrated and perceive the international community to be exclusively focused on women's rights without addressing the ways that the men have suffered from the decades of war.... The majority of vocational training programs and foreign education opportunities are geared towards women. In the long run, it will be important to create programming that addresses men's needs as well as women. In virtually every post-conflict country, the presence of large numbers of unemployed and unskilled men and boys poses a risk to stability.... More will have to be done to ensure that Afghan men find constructive means of engagement and employment in society ... [in order to prevent] the alienation of men and subsequent backlashes to women's advancement.

A gender advisor explained it this way:

> Of the programs I have seen, most have had a women-only perspective — often with lip-service to male inclusion. I don't believe that strategy works best here. Emphasis should be on the inclusion and acceptance of women as community members first and foremost before focus is given to women's ability for self-determination and the often intangible notion of "women's rights." ... Personally, I myself tend to focus on women when thinking of gender and have a hard time really including men into the picture, which leads me to think that the problem might be in the application of the word "gender" being that it is applied to practically any and all woman-focused projects or discussions.

In the words of an Afghan woman NGO leader: "The best way to make gains is to convince men to give freedom to women.... Get their collaboration and cooperation, [and] any program will be successful." And another gender advisor lamented: "Stop excluding men that are qualified and can help women if we help them!"

An online discussion between an Afghan woman implementer in an aid

A girl stands in the doorway of the office of a local women's group, Logar.

institution and me illustrates the point further. I am "LA" and the Afghan woman is "SR" in this discussion.

> LA: What have your observations been about the trainings for women?
>
> SR: I noticed that the men are angrier because women are in training and they are not.
>
> · LA: What do you think the men think about the women focus?
>
> SR: Same as the women think. They see it as less effected, especially the gender awareness for women.
>
> LA: Do you think they would prefer to stay home and have the men work/train instead?
>
> SR: No, they prefer equal opportunity for both, because now the opportunities are mostly bound to women.
>
> LA: Would the MEN prefer to work/train while the women stay home?
>
> SR: I think yes. There are rumors about NGOs being not fair to men.
>
> LA: Why the rumors?
>
> SR: I know a woman whose husband is jobless, he will be trying to find job. He didn't like at first that his women go out at all, but later he had to let his wife join the training.
>
> LA: Because it was the only source of money?
>
> SR: Yes, and from our culture and people's point of view it's considered a shame for husband to sit and eat the money of the wife.
>
> SR: Though the lady did not point at this issue at all because she was afraid. But I heard it from her colleague, that she is not being treated well because her husband is being more aggressive since he is not working.
>
> LA: Are there more women like her?
>
> SR: Yes. I think women will also not say the truth like that woman, because maybe [they are] afraid to lose the present opportunity of working.
>
> LA: What is the solution?
>
> SR: If there would be equal opportunity, that will be better.

Thus, Afghan women would likely have argued in favor of the fifth phase of engagement with men — but they were never asked.

Afghan Women's Agency and the Myth of Liberation[12]

In the transition from formulation to interpretation, women's agency was sidelined while the myth of liberation gained momentum. Such myths serve a strategic purpose but often fail to reflect women's realities. There is a tension between the speed at which aid agencies are expected to operate and the time it takes to understand the dynamics of a particular situation. More often than not, understandings are trumped by quick fixes. As a result, many of those I interviewed admitted to misunderstandings of Afghan women, and a failure to understand how best to assist them. They also felt overwhelmed by stereotypes — many of which they often subscribed to. The head of an international organization working with women explained that, even after these last few years of active engagement, "donors and Western implementers still do not understand the 'mind set' of the women of Afghanistan." She continued to explain that the aid apparatus was unable to view Afghanistan — and Afghan women and men — through a lens other than their own.

The liberation agenda denies agency, resting on the premise that (1) Afghan women need to be saved; (2) Afghan women can't save themselves; and (3) Afghan women need to be saved *from* Afghan men. Such perceptions might just do more damage than good. Attempts at engineering a social transformation will continue to have serious repercussions for Afghan women as long as their agency is denied in the process. In a 2004 article entitle "Bourka Politics," I wrote the following:

> The media and international agencies only present opposite sides of the spectrum: the few heroines who have attracted the media's fickle eye, and the oppressed masses who remain victims. Even this limited picture of Afghan reality fails to capture media attention today. Isolating Afghan women — from the bourka-clad to the lipstick-wearer — is not the best way to make changes and achieve gains. Focus on Afghan women is lessening, leaving the masses with a false perception that Afghan women have been "liberated" and our task now lies elsewhere. In Iraq, perhaps.[13]

Despite Western perceptions, Afghan women have always been historical and political actors struggling against patriarchy. Their cause is emancipation — not only of themselves, but of men as well. Aversions to Islam, particularly pervasive in the U.S. feminist movement, undercut efforts to empower women. The implication is that after "liberation," Afghan women will toss aside their *chaddaris*— along with their Islamic and Afghan identities — and become secular.[14] Afghan women have struggled and negotiated the various fluctuations in their social status throughout history, doing so within the context of Islam.

Many Afghan women are still struggling to find the space within which they can rectify this image and demonstrate their ability to act in their own interest. The head of an aid institution explained that "there is a seemingly uncontrollable urge to overlay the experience of 'the Afghan woman' with the

Americans' worldview and to create programs that thrust that woman into the American design of what is good and beneficial for them." The head of an aid institution explained it this way:

> Supporting women was not about understanding social dynamics. It wasn't about understanding the culture. It wasn't about the causes of poverty. It was very superficial. Many of the development agencies were appalled with what is happening with women. But then we never did look at it from a gender perspective. It was women under bourka. It was never about men in shalwar kameez.[15]

The above quote raises an often overlooked but extremely valid point. Discussions of agency in Afghanistan are not exclusively about women. Discussions on policy formulation revealed that men's agency was also denied in the discourses promoted by the aid apparatus. Afghan women themselves reinforced this view, further articulating that the juxtaposition of "civilized American men to barbaric Afghan men" was based on the view that Afghan women were mistreated by their own men. As a result, "American men assume the role of the global protector of women, and by extension, civilization."[16]

Global protection of women manifested itself as an agenda to enforce social change, something that is not without historical precedent, particularly when coupled with the perception that it is externally enforced. Those interviewed generally agreed that the aid apparatus would do better to proceed cautiously and build on local momentum to ensure a solid foundation and sustainability. "The international community has to do its homework first before going into a country," an Afghan woman activist explained. "Do homework, and then bring in the project." The importance of contextualizing interventions cannot be overstated. A socially and historically informed analysis could guide aid institutions in how to proceed — and how *not* to proceed — in order to achieve gains for women and men in Afghanistan. This includes taking into account the idea that gender is defined differently in each conflict and in each context, and therefore basing gender-focused efforts on gender analyses of contexts. "Doing homework" entails not only learning about the communities that aid institutions will work in, but also giving time for the communities to become acquainted with the institutions themselves and to build trust. "If they don't know where you are from or what you are doing and you set up your office with your flag and you tell them what to do, you see what happens," an Afghan woman leader cautioned.

"Afghan people do not accept things by power or pressure on them," an Afghan woman leader explained. "If our aim is to change Afghanistan's situation, to change the things that people don't like, we have different ways to reach this goal. We should gain the support of the Afghan communities." It was generally agreed that, in order to be sustainable, the process of social change must come from within. Under such circumstances, it is difficult to remain humble and neither overstate the roles nor impose the particular worldview that animates the aid apparatus. Interventions must assess local demand and support for an agenda of transformation. Without such support, externally driven change cannot be effective or sustainable. The haste of the aftermath period and the hype surrounding Afghan women prevented many institutions from taking account of Afghan women's perspectives. Many argued that it was not the message but the *method* and the *means* that were problematic. An Afghan man with an aid institution emphasized the importance of a moderate approach: "Through force [the Afghan people] won't accept anything. They will fight and they will resist. But if you approach well, people will listen." A gender specialist continued: "I think we do Afghans a disservice if we assume they do not want change. What matters is how things are negotiated and presented. You can do a lot if you understand the cultural ways of negotiation."

In addition to the aid apparatus *modus operandi*, their mere presence — as a diverse community of international women and men — has a social impact. The influx of non–Afghans from different countries brings customs and traditions that might appear to be threatening or challenging to Afghan ways. Further, the perception is that the influx of *kharijis*, foreigners, tends to travel hand in hand with alcohol, parties, and pornography. An international gender advisor put it this way: "We are witnessing the interaction of cultures.... Maybe it increases fear in men, thinking 'Is that what it means to be empowered?' and it raises questions in women like 'Do I want to be like that?'"

Afghan men are at the same time increasingly influenced — and increasingly threatened — by this new environment. And Afghan women may suffer decreased mobility — either imposed or preferred — as a result. It is difficult — and in fact counterproductive — to lay blame on any sole factor, but many Afghan women have expressed concern that this new (urban) dynamic has led to increased harassment on the street. "On one level such sexual aggression is almost the inevitable product of the Taliban years ... on another level it is clearly a statement of what many Afghans think about the takeover of their capital by foreigners."[17]

Gender Anti-Politics

There is a vacuum between the stated policies on paper — gender/liberation/empowerment — and an implementation that translated these ambitious agendas into a WID–style intervention, where loaded terms are at once depoliticized, replaced by practical and technical solutions. Indeed, highly charged and politicized issues will not automatically find resolution based on stated goals on paper. Further, such processes are not conducive to quick-fix solutions. An Afghan policy implementer working with many women's groups explained that international priorities — on paper — guide aid interventions in Afghanistan and these bear little relevance to Afghan needs and priorities. She expressed the views of many:

> The means of aid in Afghanistan, in particular under this fashionable word "gender," is totally focused on international policies and priorities. And these are more to show off to each other in the aid community than to help Afghans. Though most of the fuss has been made about women, even less has been given to them. And even less than that is focused on their needs. So those of us who have to do the work are left trying to sift through the talk and seeking out ways to use the little left in hand as efficiently as possible.

An Afghan woman NGO leader continued:

> The influx of foreign aid workers [results in] decision making being done by foreigners who know less about the ways and customs and effective solutions than local residents. Local residents, particularly women, should lead the way. Aid agencies should provide the money and simply document progress to make sure the money is being spent on what it was supposed to be spent on.

An international gender advisor explained the importance of working with all members of the community and sharing opportunities:

> Raising a community out of survival mode and into economic stability will be of significant benefit to all members and will thus create a more conducive environment to address gender roles and relations. And more often than not, the community and family will address the subject without external interference!

A former Minister of Women's Affairs had the following to say:

> The mistakes maybe have been not proper usage of resources. Not proper planning and targeting. Maybe they didn't have enough time to think about the investment that they were doing. Because it was an urgent situation, and emergencies are like that. But now we are not any more in emergency. In terms of women's status, it is the worst in the world. So in that sense, that is still an emergency. It is like Tsunami for women in Afghanistan. But still we need to take the time to think more about what we are doing and where and why we are doing it.

A reflexive exercise — a questioning of "why we are doing it" — could have been useful in illuminating the extent to which technical solutions were imposed by aid interventions to address political concerns. Policy failed to translate into practice upon implementation because the policy was largely political while the implementation of it was technical. The distinction between political and technical interventions is relevant in implementation because women are not often treated as if they know what they need, with the result being that aid institutions tend to then make decisions on women's behalf based on what they are equipped to provide. It is therefore wise to question the extent to which aid interventions have penetrated the surface and challenged real power issues in Afghanistan, particularly as most interventions were not designed based on Afghan women's political interests, nor with Afghan women at all.

It has been argued that the true strategy in Afghanistan was that of military objectives under the guise of women's rights. In the words of an Afghan woman NGO leader: "The U.S. government's loud and public promise that they will never again allow Afghan women to be forgotten has done damage. They still funded military operations much more than women's programs." Indeed, the link between the rights agenda and military objectives was not clear. In Afghanistan, the U.S. policy is informally described as "sex, drugs, and rock 'n' roll" to represent gender, poppy, and terrorism. This three-pronged policy has led to a conflation of objectives on the ground, and a sense among Afghans that the liberation of women was merely a byproduct of military action.[18] A report from a U.S. general in Afghanistan clearly exemplifies this confusion, stating that the protection of human rights is a military objective.[19] If it is argued that women's human rights have been violated, by extension Afghan men are therefore the perceived targets of the "military objective." It is therefore not a stretch to understand how Afghan men might feel personally under attack.

These experiences of policy implementation resonate well with James Ferguson's observations from his research in Lesotho.[20] Ferguson did not set out to present a critique of policy. Instead, he hoped to reveal outcomes — whether intended or not — in light of planning. He viewed aid interventions as inherently political and linked to the distribution of power in terms of resources and influence. Ferguson argued that the aid apparatus viewed its own interventions as apolitical. His "anti-politics machine" illustrates the way aid interventions are stripped of their political content, no matter how politically charged they may be. The case of Afghanistan fits neatly within Ferguson's anti-politics framework. One Afghanistan specialist explained:

> In spite of the predisposition of the international aid system to treat peace and development as apolitical products created from a set of discrete technical tasks, actual peace and development can follow radically different path-

ways and arrive at very different destinations, each of which will generate alternate sets of winners and losers.[21]

To assume that technical solutions can address Afghanistan's gender concerns is to ignore the most highly politicized situation of all. This type of linear transitional thinking was not well suited for Afghanistan's complex socio-political environment and served to ignore Afghanistan's overlapping social realities.[22] The aid apparatus revealed its inability to understand the extent of the political project it was undertaking: it failed to realize that its attempt to change women's roles and engineer social transformation through technical interventions would initiate a political response. With the unprecedented attention placed on the situation of Afghan women, it is important to understand how that attention has manifested itself and what effects this attention might have. It might be too soon to judge if aid interventions have helped Afghan women foster long-term transformation, and it is beyond the scope of my work to pass judgment on perceived success and failure. It is possible, however, to understand the foundation of the initiative to determine what it actually intends to do. In this vein, the distinction between technical and political interventions is relevant.

And yet, the two interventions are indivisible as together they are more likely to achieve transformation. Despite the strategic language that was used, including the rhetoric for empowerment, ambitious interventions were destined for failure because the aid institutions charged with social change through their assistance to Afghans lacked the capacity and the political backing to deliver on such targets. They therefore failed Afghanistan far more than if they had gone for less ambitious targets and achieved them.[23] The few gains that have been made for Afghan women in recent years have served to increase the presence, but not the power, of women.

Women and Chickens

The propensity of aid institutions to promote "'feel good,' gimmicky programs with very little analysis" have added little value to women's lives — making them present, but no more powerful.[24] To capitalize on the large amount of aid in Afghanistan during early phase of aftermath, interventions opted for quick-fix solutions — the road of least resistance. This reinforced women's traditional roles and did little to inspire transformation.

> It should be obvious from looking at the last twenty years in Afghanistan that six months' funding for a handicraft or chicken-rearing project purporting to transform gender relations is utterly useless.[25]

Income generation projects provide a good example of this "road of least resistance," reinforcing traditional skills for women and focusing on low-paid, gender-stereotyped occupations. These initiatives and their corresponding trainings are too short, too small-scale, and too little profit-oriented. "Anytime you need to do something for women," a head of an international organization explained, "it was all about handicrafts and tailoring.... In a way it reinforced the social construction of women's roles ... as if there is no other thing that women can do." The market in Kabul is saturated with women tailors who are unable to find employment. "You cannot just have classes and pour in millions of dollars and then have the women go back home. There is no follow-up," an Afghan woman leader stated. Income generation efforts did not take the time to ask women if they actually want to work — or if they were doing it because there is nothing available for men. "You have women who want to be employed," a head of an international organization explained, "and you have women who say they want their husbands to work instead. It is not always that women are being prevented from such things. It depends." Economic necessity was stronger than the need to preserve honor. Women paid

A woman sells her handmade blankets on the street, Kabul.

a high price for the "opportunity" to work, striking a delicate balance between challenging stereotypes and establishing new gender norms while maintaining behavior that would retain their honor within the family and community.[26]

Numbers are used to measure the success of income-generation projects for Afghan women. These indicators drive funding, and projects that achieve their numbers are touted as a success. Aid interventions carry the whim of agencies who reset their priorities based on funding available. Implementers work to please their donors, not the women they are helping. While feedback on the success of income-generation projects is mixed, Afghan men expressed their dislike for the initiatives, particularly in their promises for dramatic changes for women. This presents a further illustration of strategic rhetoric and technical implementation. One man expressed the views of many, saying that "Afghan women should not be the clothes-washers of foreigners."[27] An Afghan woman echoed this: "After this much work has been done and promised to women, all women are doing is washing clothing in the offices and that is it."

How, then, can one understand what constitutes empowerment in this context? The Human Development Report cites measures of empowerment from a human development perspective, but these can be extended to a focus on gender.[28] The following variables can be used to analyze intervention priorities in Afghanistan from a gender and empowerment perspective. A key factor is the extent to which there has been participation in the elaboration of strategies and implementation of programs. Clear indicators to the contrary include lack of consultation with communities, rushed design of programs in order to meet deadlines and access conference-related funding, and preparation of documents in English by foreign advisors.[29] There is a battle between the "quick-fix" mentality and the time required to make non-cosmetic changes.

Since women's rights — and attempts to change them — are highly politicized, this battle plays out in unanticipated ways, with disempowering consequences for women.[30] It is only through anecdotal evidence or qualitative measures that we can begin to understand the effects on Afghan women and men. To reinforce this, a gender officer for an international organization said: "The general impression I get is that there is a lack of indicators and a lack of quantitative and qualitative tools for measuring change/progress. If you know of any, tell me!" She also expressed strong doubts that interventions had consulted women or felt that they were accountable to women. As a result, the aid apparatus might not feel responsible for what has happened since they intervened.

Aid interventions are limited in their ability to foster empowerment for women. One effect is the perceived disempowerment of men, often resulting in increased domestic violence. It would be wise to question whether promoting women's empowerment at the expense of men is beneficial to all in the long-term.[31] We need to take this line of questioning one step further to find ways that promote women's empowerment without undermining men.

An Afghan woman NGO leader urged that Afghan women comply with the country's social and cultural values because "any rapid changes could result in a revolutionary reaction." The senior gender officer of an aid institution elaborated:

> There has not been an overnight revolution, a shift from oppression to liberation. Change does not happen that fast. Also, women are savvy enough to know that the last times there were dramatic and sudden shifts toward a Western model the resultant backlash undid any gains made. There is no need for a revolution, rather for a gradual *evolution* towards more gender equality.

The following themes can be gleaned from this analysis of the journey from policy formulation to interpretation to implementation: interventions possess neither a clear understanding of the definition of gender nor the understanding of how to bring its programs to fruition. The de facto definition of "gender interventions" is "women's programs." The agency of both women and men has been denied through attempts to import an agenda of social change coupled with the lack of contextualized analysis that accompanied program design. In practice, aid rhetoric fails to match implementation reality because technical solutions are offered to solve political problems. This reflects a disconnect between policy and practice, and a further disconnect between an understanding of technical and political issues. The argument is not a simple one. To argue that interventions focusing on technical over political issues destabilized men's honor is almost counter-intuitive. Interventions presented their goal as strategic, and in principle this should have been met with high resistance. But when these interventions manifested themselves in technical ways, it undermined men's sense of manhood and ate at their honor. One might question how, if political interests had been met alongside technical interventions, Afghan women and men would have reacted. In this vein, meeting men's practical needs through technical interventions could have resulted in strategic gains for women by allowing them the space within which they can define and address their own interests.

4

Transplanting Democracy

The aid apparatus seems to be basing its success on the political project of fast-forwarding history to remake Afghanistan as a democratic and gender-sensitive state.[1] Afghan women policy-makers, policy implementers, and NGO leaders have expressed concern about this agenda. "Bringing democracy" is a challenge, according to the head of an aid institution:

> We might "bring" democracy. You can bring experts and you can organize the elections. And you might have mechanisms for the institution, for the building of democracy. But institutionalizing it is going to take 100 years. We know that from other countries' experiences.

As previously mentioned, the Afghanistan of recent years has witnessed the aid apparatus repeatedly import terms that correspond to the latest aid trends, with little regard for their relevance in Afghanistan. Democracy, civil society, empowerment, and gender are but a few that are used liberally in Afghanistan. While the concepts exist in Afghanistan, the terms appear to be the recent additions to a succession of ideological frameworks as models for change — implying transformations that provide a pretext for conflict rather than a focus for unity.[2] This helps to explain why Afghans are reluctant to embrace what appears to be Western-imported and imposed ideals. It is important to reiterate that these concepts do have roots in Afghanistan. Indigenous forms of Afghan democracy and gender equality do exist — if we look.

It is wrong to assume that democracy and gender equality are Western products. In fact, there is "nothing exclusively 'Western' about valuing liberty or defending public reasoning."[3] Yet labeling these ideas as Western can bring resentment and build resistance. A speech by a political science professor at Kabul University articulated that creating an environment of respect for democracy and women's rights is not through the help of foreign countries, but is a social progression in line with the national and historical values of the country.[4] In this sense, the push for democracy is not unlike the pressures for gender equality — in seeming opposition to such values. The terms are used liberally, but without meaning and context.

A young boy with an AK-47 looks out over the city, Kabul.

Democracy based on a Western individualism rather than traditional Afghan Islamic communalism, gender-blind social interaction, and the elevation of the individual above society, do not appear to be part of the emerging ... Afghan worldview.[5]

As a result, women's organizations criticize "the way in which many men frequently bandy the word democracy in a meaningless manner, without implementing these democratic principles within their own families."[6] The outcome is that terms like democracy — and gender — have been saddled with negative baggage, making men increasingly resentful and outcomes for women increasingly deleterious. An Afghan woman policy implementer put it this way:

Kharijis cannot try and change Afghan culture. If they do, it will bring more problems for women. It has brought more violence upon women. Women will ask for changes when they are ready. If a foreigner comes, she cannot help me. I do not think NGOs for women are such a big help. If an organization comes to help men and brings them work and training, it will be better for them — and better for women. But we must wait a long time for men to change. Every man is old in his head ... [but] give them training and jobs, and then afterwards start talking to them about women.

"Many men are the victims of too much gender training," the head of an international NGO elaborated. "And now they just make fun of it. It's the same development we have seen in Western societies. If you push too hard, you make it into something which is politically correct but not accepted and understood by the people."

An Afghan NGO leader expressed the sentiments of many:

In Afghan history, we have imported policies from other places. This is why it doesn't work. If we want democracy, we have to go step by step, starting from the beginning, and not running. If we run, we will fall down. We should walk slowly and look around us in order to be successful. Again today, just like before, Afghans are running, running after democracy, running after gender. And when we fall down no one will be able to rescue us. Not even the international community.

As this example of the parliamentary elections will show, it is not the underlying principles of democracy or women's political participation that is in question, but the way the terms are used as part of a Western agenda, leaving Afghans to adopt them publicly but resent them privately.

Prior to the 2004 presidential election, I wrote the following for an article on Afghan women[7]:

Presidential elections in Afghanistan are scheduled for October 9. In the past few months, a major campaign has been launched to bring women to the polls. This entails a poster campaign, but little else, [a gender advisor] explains. "Women should be called in a meeting forum at a local mosque or school so that they can learn about their rights. From what I know nothing of this sort was ever done...." As a result, many women will not vote since they may view it as a "'man's duty.'" In a country with little history of or faith in central government, exercising civic duty is not a priority. In discussions of women's role in politics, one [Afghan] woman told me, "What good is politics? Look at where it has brought Afghanistan."

Current security risks in Afghanistan have made voter registration a difficult task. Violence has increased in recent months, and agencies are concerned about sending staff to rural areas. The recent deaths of female election workers has slowed the registration process. Further, the process is a lengthy one as most women will need to be approached individually and within their own homes, [a senior UN official] explains.

Although many women have registered, true representation is a challenge. It is unlikely that women will vote differently from the men in their household, and men will vote to keep themselves secure. [A gender expert] explains that "most rural areas have commanders whose word is law, and no one would be likely to vote against the commander's preferred candidate for fear of persecution. In other words, both women and men will do what they are told."

As the final step in the Bonn Process, the "free and fair" parliamentary elections of 18 September 2005 were an ambitious and controversial undertaking. The Afghan Constitution of January 2004 established that 25 percent of the seats in *Wolesi Jirga* (House of the People) and Provincial Council were to be reserved for women. This is a very progressive quota that only a handful of countries in the world have in place to ensure women's representation. Such a quota would place Afghanistan as 20th in the world in terms of women's representation in a parliamentary body. The quota itself is hailed as a victory achieved through pressure by Afghan women's groups and the aid apparatus, including such countries as the U.S. where women hold only 14 percent of congressional seats.[8]

However, while this may seem impressive at first, many of those interviewed expressed skepticism. They were concerned that women were once again being used as window dressing and that this progressive quota served to appease international donors at the expense of laying a foundation for genuine participation. In countries in transition, it is not unusual to see social and economic rights decrease while formal political rights are put in place. Quotas have been used both for the Emergency and Constitutional *Loya Jirgas* to ensure women's participation in the political process. Many interviewees felt this to have been a good start, but it also appeared to be tokenistic. "Right now our women are all over the place, being used for politics, used like dolls," an Afghan woman head of an NGO lamented. "Every event they are in front of the TV, the camera. They are being used just to show that women were there." Interviewees felt that, at worst, quotas and external pressure for a male/female balance could run the risk of generating a community backlash. Indeed, women were harassed during the Emergency *Loya Jirga*, the Constitutional *Loya Jirga*, and the presidential election. This clearly did not set a good precedent for women's political participation. Experience in other countries reveals that affirmative action measures are perceived to be an external imposition. It is this perception — more than men's fear of lost power — that fuels resistance.[9]

The parliamentary elections were initially expected to coincide with the October 2004 presidential election. The unstable security situation prompted a delay, and the elections were then scheduled for April 2005. In the months prior to the April election date, there were concerns that the elections would be delayed further. The pervasive sense, according to myriad discussions with organizations, was that the country was ill prepared for elections. While one arm of the UN apparatus was plowing forth with elections, another arm was counseling caution. The UNDP Human Development Report warned against conducting elections too soon after conflict and before peacetime politics had a chance to take root. The report stated clearly that "ill-timed, hurried, badly designed or poorly run elections can actually undermine the process of democratization."

Moreover, the completion of this last step of the Bonn Process was met with fears and rumors that the aid apparatus would begin plotting an Afghanistan exit strategy. Researchers and political analysts in Afghanistan cautioned that the country would need many years of continuous international support. Plans for a premature exit of the aid apparatus could destabilize — and most likely collapse — the country's tenuous foundation. Elections, with their deadline-driven nature, bring the impression that the work is done when the election has been held. As such, they are the "holy grail of western transition formulas, providing moral cover for exit."[10]

The parliamentary elections were finally held on 18 September 2005, despite security issues, threats, and warnings. These elections signified the end of a period of transition and represented a chance not to repeat the breakdowns of state and society that characterize Afghanistan's recent past. In the months leading up to the elections, female candidate participation was widely visible, particularly in Kabul city. Campaign posters peppered city walls, and anecdotes of women's participation abounded. For instance, in the northeast of the country, one pregnant female candidate traveled by foot for eight days in order to present her candidacy to the *Wolesi Jirga*. And so the stories went, liberally employed as evidence of the Afghan people's commitment to democracy. Afghan women's groups have argued that women's participation in political life in Afghanistan appears to be a favorite subject of aid institutions and the media, but Afghan women themselves have barely broached the topic.

It could be argued that proof of women's commitment to political processes comes from the numbers of their participation. However, the figures emerging from elections — particularly the parliamentary elections — have been highly contested. This is due in part to suspicions of fraud, ballot stuffing, and unclear procedures in polling stations. The aid apparatus might boast the participation of women in elections, but inequalities remain because women continue to have symbolic assignments in the cabinet and other key positions. Very few women have been given the opportunity to access higher positions and use their leadership skills.

Interviews with gender policy-makers and policy implementers revealed concerns that the limitations to women's political participation have not yet been addressed. These include lack of security, warlords, and a sense that politics is men's domain. In addition, it has been argued that the physical presence of female bodies occupying parliamentary seats would not automatically give them leverage or authority. Most of those interviewed agreed that injecting women into all aspects of the democratic process will not automatically address women's interests. Indeed, numbers do not necessarily translate into equitable participation and might not lead to an understanding of issues of power when measuring participation. Leaders of Afghan women's NGOs felt strongly that women's participation should be for a purpose, not to appease international donors or to satisfy aid institutions. An Afghan woman captured the views of many:

> Why should I vote? ... This election is for you not for us. You will have it and then you will go, leaving us with a system that has no roots in our country. You can grow new systems, yes, but it takes time; they need to put down roots. And the Pashtun women in the countryside, they will be herded like cattle to the voting stations. They will be just voting fodder. What meaning does this have?[11]

An Insider's View

As an insider to the parliamentary elections process, I often found myself asking similar questions. In 2005, I worked in some measure on things "women and gender" for Afghanistan's parliamentary elections. In assuming the position, I was told by a senior gender advisor of an aid institution that I was just a "warm body" filling a politically motivated post that the aid apparatus felt should exist because "this is Afghanistan, and everyone wants to know about women here. The issue of gender is so contentious and everyone expects that someone will have to do it." Indeed there was an obvious pressure to have someone "do gender," whatever doing gender really means.

I took this as an opportunity to apply my experience in Afghanistan and familiarity with the context. I hired a man on my staff, and began a campaign working with men to help them better understand the role of women in the political process. This entailed meetings with *mullahs* and the heads of Afghan political parties (all men). The challenges that women were facing became clear to me when I was told by a particularly bushy-bearded political party leader that he would under no circumstances endorse women's political participation because: "Women have no wisdom, Women are 'sick' for seven days of every month. They cannot think. They cannot judge. Their judgment is impaired. They cannot make decisions for the country."

This was not a unique sentiment. And this sentiment was not at all unique to men. An Afghan woman staff member told me she did not "believe in elections" when I asked her why she did not vote. She had taken the job for financial reasons and felt that the pressure for women to vote was nothing more than an opportunity for journalists to photograph lines of *chaddaris* as evidence of "democracy in action." These sentiments were pervasive. It was believed that the pressure to "get the numbers" outweighed the quality of civic education and participation. A massive campaign was underway to reach the most remote villages, but the result was shallow. In one village, the elder greeted a training team asking: "Are you coming here to tell us the results from the last election?" In the end, the elections were characterized by a relatively poor voter turnout and a discrepancy in figures that took months to resolve. In an international press briefing at the close of election day, a colleague turned to me in surprise and said: "I didn't know the elections were such a 'success'!"

In a discussion with international journalists on gender issues in the elections, I was told that we — the aid apparatus — were too smug in our boasting of 25 percent of seats for women. In reality, women outnumber men in the population, and therefore the representation in parliament should reflect this, I was told. This came from one male journalist in a room of 15 European and American journalists — 13 of whom were male. It was at that point that I realized that Afghanistan was being subjected to unrealistic goals and standards that did not even apply in the so-called developed world. A nonrepresentative group was demanding women's representation. Not too long afterwards, an article appeared asking:

America has had democracy for 200 years, and during that time no woman
has been nominated to the presidency, nor are there large numbers of women
in the cabinet ... so why are they imposing on others what they don't have or
don't want?[12]

This lesson was again brought home to me one Friday as I listened to
the sermon coming from the mosque down the street. "Do not vote, I tell
you!" the imam wailed. "These foreigners are trying to strip away your Muslim identity by imposing their 'democracy'!"

In the end, "doing gender" proved to be difficult to coordinate with an
elections timetable that is deadline- and deliverable-driven. There was little
recognition among the aid apparatus that gender is a process that requires a
long-term investment — not unlike civic education. These entail political
consciousness-raising and cannot be brought about through technical solutions
and numbers in polling stations. The one-time presence of women at the polls
did nothing more than appease the aid apparatus. The presence of the aid apparatus (read: funding) could have put pressure on Afghanistan to set a high quota
for women in parliament through its Constitution. Many women that I spoke
to in my research and professional capacity felt that the aid apparatus unknow-
ingly put women at risk by aggressively promoting their public presence.

Women expressed much concern — and fear — when faced with the question of presenting their candidacy. Two women I spoke with had considered
running for office but were discouraged by their husbands. Another woman
decided not to nominate herself when her husband and brothers learned she
would have to be photographed for the ballot. They told her having her photograph taken and displayed publicly would bring shame upon the family.
One female candidate told her story:

> I was going to different villages and places when I was doing my campaign.
> When I was talking to women, it turned more into a "woman gathering" and
> women started talking to me about their problems. I found out that there is
> a huge difference between women activists and intellectuals and educated
> women — and women in those villages and remote areas. There is a need for
> us to find solutions and ways to help these rural women. There is a huge dif-
> ference between village and cities. I noticed that my speech for women was
> too difficult. They didn't know what I was talking about. They didn't know
> what was voting and who to vote for. When I noticed that they had difficul-
> ties presenting themselves and understanding, I decided to stop my cam-
> paign to them and instead spend time talking to them to understand their
> issues. The result was that in election day, they were going like cattle in a
> group with a shepherd, leading them to the election and putting them in the
> centers. They were told what to do. They didn't have any independence or
> the room to use their right to vote in the way they wanted. What does elec-
> tion mean for these women?

Voter turnout was much lower than expected because of a campaign marked by intimidation — particularly against women candidates and voters. The Afghan Independent Human Rights Commission (AIHRC) produced three reports in conjunction with the UN Assistance Mission to Afghanistan (UNAMA) to track progress on the parliamentary elections and raise concerns. These reports, known as the *Joint Verification of Political Rights*, frequently mentioned women and gender issues as primary concerns.[13] The first report, for the period 19 April to 3 June, noted that "there is a broad perception that intimidation and limitations on political rights are pervasive or will increase." "Female candidates ... have also voiced concerns about their security. In some areas women only registered in the last days of the nomination process to avoid security threats." The report also explained that Afghan society is ambivalent about women's participation in political life, stating that women "internalize these norms and fear bringing dishonor to their families if they expose themselves to public critique by standing as candidates." The pervasive sense in the report was that the country was just not ready for such aggressive change.

The second report (4 June–16 August) did not report improvements.[14] During this period, acts of intimidation against female candidates forced some of them to withdraw. Female candidates continue to feel threatened and have been intimidated and attacked. There were also numerous threats and attacks against women election workers. Further, many mosques have been publicly condemning women's participation, calling it un–Islamic and anti–*Sharia*.[15] The situation continued to deteriorate. The final report, for the period of 17 August to 13 September, reported that four male candidates were killed and that "women candidates have been the target of a number of acts of discrimination, intimidation and violent attacks."[16] Religious leaders also continued to dissuade people from voting for female candidates and from permitting their wives to participate in the election.

Human Rights Watch was also actively monitoring cases of intimidation of female candidates, stating that security in Afghanistan had deteriorated in conjunction with the elections, particularly in the form of high-profile cases of social and political violence against women.[17] Women were increasingly targeted, the report elaborated, and they feared that pushing social norms would incur greater retaliation. The report continued:

> Women candidates exposing themselves to public review risk retaliation for disrupting social norms. Violence and intimidation against these women is highly symbolic and sends a chilling message to other Afghan women considering expanded roles in public life.

Another article stated that Afghan men believed that women have become candidates at the "command of Laura Bush"—otherwise it would never be allowed, as it is perceived to be un–Islamic.[18] It was not only Afghan men who believed that the parliamentary elections were a decree from the Bush family. A more provocative American article stated:

> Females, once considered worth less than scum by Muslim males, are now coming into their own in Afghanistan, thanks to an ongoing democratic planting. There is no other answer but to recognize that it is because of the Bush administration and U.S. assistance in that Muslim country that much progress is being made on numerous levels.[19]

I Don't Vote for Women

According to research conducted by the Women and Children Legal Research Foundation in Afghanistan, 58 percent of 600 people (525 women, 75 men) surveyed believe that women should not be involved in politics.[20] In a further survey of 130 women, 85 women did not feel that women should be politically active. These findings can be confirmed by research to gather perspectives of Afghans. Prompted by a concern that Afghan voices were not heard in the days leading up to the elections, I decided to send my staff out to collect voices from the street. A random sample of Afghan men and women was selected and 20 on-site interviews (10 women, 10 men) were conducted prior to the elections. Of the ten women, five said they were not in favor of women running for office. Six of ten men said they do not believe that a woman should have a role in the public domain, particularly not in political life—a realm traditionally reserved for men. One woman who was interviewed had the following to say:

> I don't vote for women, because I don't want a woman to act as a leader or have the authority or power, because women are not capable of playing this role. They will lose themselves easily. It is important for women to vote, but they should support men candidates more than women. People in Afghanistan don't want women to take on prominent roles among the people.... There are many obstacles for women. And maybe they cannot be removed.

Another woman also shared this view:

> I'll never vote for a woman. And it has reason, because in Afghanistan women can't do anything without men's permission, so they are not independent and always want to be with men and look to men to support women.

When asked if she thinks it is important for women to vote, the woman explained that these kinds of things are nice to have on paper. "For policy, it is good," she stated. She elaborated that women voting serves to appease the aid apparatus and fulfills its agenda. "For real work, it is not perfect," she continued. She explained that in reality these things do not work as one would expect. She felt that women are powerless in the home, and therefore they would be powerless in a public office. She explained it this way:

> · Women candidates can't do anything without their husband's permission and can't even make small decisions on their own. And also security is not perfect for women candidates. For example, in some provinces women can't distribute their posters and they are not allowed to go to rural areas and cannot be far from their homes.

She concluded by asking: "What is the point of women in office with all these restrictions? Afghanistan is not ready."

A man who was interviewed on the street of Kabul expressed concern that women would not be able to serve the people any better than men:

> In my opinion I won't vote for a woman, because I don't trust that she will work more than a man does. Also if we have good men who are very educated and more capable than women, why shouldn't I vote for a man?

He recommended that women should vote, and had the following to say: "My advice for women is to vote for men candidates, because as I mentioned men are more powerful than women and they are capable of doing every type of work."

The man felt that the biggest obstacles to women's participation are their lack of credibility, security issues, and cultural obstacles. He elaborated:

> There are different issues [between men and women's participation]. As an example if a man stands before people in a public area and starts his campaign everyone will stand and listen to him. But women can't stand in front of a crowd except in some areas because of lack of security and inappropriateness. First their families don't allow them, and if their families let them work the society is not familiar with that type of situation. It is better for women not to try hard because they must keep themselves quiet otherwise they may receive punishment or harassment.

When asked if he believed that women should be represented in parliament, he had the following to say: "It is good if we have some female representation in parliament and if not it is okay also. We have our men and they do whatever needs to be done for both men and women."

One man believed that women in Afghanistan are facing fewer obstacles than men — in terms of participation in political, social, and economic life. He felt that men should be the focus of attention as well as the primary political actors. One man said he would not vote for a woman because she would be biased towards women and would thereby rob him of the rights he enjoys now. The sentiment of political power as a zero-sum game was heard frequently on the street. Another man said he would rather cut off his own hand than vote for a woman. He did not feel the need to elaborate any further on his sentiments.

In a discussion with a former Minister of Women's Affairs on women's participation in the parliamentary elections, she emphasized the importance of support from husbands and families of female candidates. "Without support of their husbands or families, they cannot do this." She illustrated her point using her own example during her campaign:

> My husband often accompanied me to provinces. I did not have guards so he acted as my security too. Sometimes, if I was at a gathering and I was tired after speaking so much, he would speak for me. He said, "She is my wife; she has a lot of experience; she is capable." This is the best endorsement — because he knows me well. Husbands and fathers should be supportive. They should help by going out to speak to male voters.
>
> Ours is a male-dominated society; they have the political power at the level of making decisions — whether in parliament or as head of the family. The best way to tackle the issues is to convince men to give freedom to women and daughters. Local *Mullahs* are very influential. If we can secure the cooperation of the religious community, it will have a positive effect on opportunities for women.
>
> It is very important to target men. The programs should contain very primary messages and should encourage men and influentials to come forward and cooperate. It should be done with the target audience in mind — and should speak their language.

These views are reinforced by myriad press articles with quotes from Afghans — candidates and voters — expressing discomfort with the democracy agenda. For instance, in a local paper, a male candidate for the *Wolesi Jirga* claimed that women who hold political office will "eat the rights of men." Another article reported a political party leader as saying: "We will never accept the Western interpretation of democracy in our Islamic republic which they are trying to implement in Afghanistan."[21] Another candidate said: "The rights the West talks about are not the rights we accept. A woman's rights as given in the Koran are enough."[22] Yet another article reported that candidates are "not happy" with the quota for women, saying that Afghans were "overdoing things under the pressure of the international community."[23]

In the Afghan press, from the weekly publication *Rozgaran*, an article entitled "Imposed Parliament" appeared, stating that: "The Afghan government, the Western world, and the electoral commission had no other objective but to have a parliament for the country no matter of what standards."[24]

Indeed, Afghans were not impressed with their new parliament, or with the elections process. In 1980, Louis Dupree wrote the following prophetic words: "Take dry constitution, combine with fluid elections and stir, and voila, 'instant democracy'—without the agony of generations of development."[25]

Instant Democracy

While the strong performance of female candidates is touted — many won seats in their own right and not based on the quota — these are the minority. It is generally believed that most of the women would not have reached the parliament without the support of the quota. In a discussion with the head of an international foundation supporting parliamentarians, he explained that the members of parliament face death threats if they return to their constituencies. Even during parliament recess, the parliamentarians fear returning to their provinces of origin because of security. The climate following the election in 2005 was not conducive for an effective parliament, he explained:

> The parliament hasn't made one decision yet. They have nothing to show their constituencies. They have no idea of their own job because it hasn't officially started yet. How can they convince their constituents that democracy works when they have nothing to show for it? No roads, no schools, nothing.

He continued to say that it is moot to discuss so-called higher issues when basic concerns such as security have not been met. As far as the aid apparatus is concerned, the parliament is an old issue. He explained that the parliament received much attention leading up to the elections, but now there is a general sense that "the job is done." As for the international media, if they speak to parliamentarians, "it's only to good looking women — or warlords." Indeed, the "warlord problem" has yet to be resolved. Many have noted the parliament's domination by "warlords, criminals, and discredited politicians responsible for much of Afghanistan's woes since the Soviet invasion in 1979."[26] It is these very warlords who continue to harass female parliamentarians and question their presence in what they believe to be male political space. The presence of these women was meant to signify the starting point of women's political participation, not the end. It is worth speculating whether these women exist merely as "symbolic gestures meant to appease the international community."[27]

A few weeks after the elections, gender advisors from various agencies participated in a post-elections debrief on women's participation. On the quota, participants felt that the aid apparatus had promoted this aggressive program with little regard to the risks that women would face as a result. In the words of one participant: "There is a security issue we need to consider here. And implications such as violence against women. We might need to rethink this." One participant asked:

> Is [the organization] gender-sensitive? Is it the role of elections to do "gender"? What will happen when the international staff leave and no one is there to push the "gender agenda"? Gender receives much attention, it is politically important. But for the next election this attention might fade and then there needs to be more push to get gender on the table. It needs more than a "gender section." It needs a section with authority. Not just calling itself gender because that's what everyone expects.

In an online communication about the future of the Afghan government and its obligation to uphold a "[Western]-engineered Afghan democracy," one Afghan man had the following to say about the presence of the aid apparatus and its dictates in Afghanistan: "There is one thing unique about Afghans: we do not appreciate when we are told what to do. Millions of Afghan have died declaring we rather die proud and free than to live a life of bondage."[28]

The Dangers of an Education

To conclude, it is worthwhile comparing the effort to transplant democracy with one that is touted as successful. Education is likely the sector that received the most kudos in Afghanistan's aftermath. It was widely believed that great progress was made, but the below suggests that, not unlike democracy, any perceived successes would be premature.

> This is to warn all the teachers and those employees who work with Companies to stop working with them. We have warned you earlier and this time we give you a three days ultimatum to stop working. If you do not stop, you are to blame yourself.[29]
> Taliban *Shabnam*, or Night Letters, from Zabul

This brief example of the deleterious impact of insecurity on the education sector provides a strong diagnostic indicator of the costs of insecurity more generally.[30] Historically, schools in Afghanistan have been at the frontline of hostilities that are directed at the central government and at perceived foreign interference. In the Human Rights Watch report *Attacks on Education in Afghanistan*, research was conducted on violence and threats against the education sector. One hundred ten attacks against schools, teachers, and students have taken place between 1 January and 21 June 2006.[31] Many of these involved girls' schools. One NGO worker had the following to say:

Street girls in the city who spend the day on Chicken Street hoping for donations from foreigners, Kabul.

> We always have to be careful when we do women's activities ... [so that] women are not targeted.... Something that can take a month may take us four to five months because we have to be so careful. This makes us look bad to someone in Washington.... But it is the insurgency that hampers us from moving faster.[32]

Fear of violence has a profound effect on women both because they are targeted for violence and because of the stigma they face if they are victims. Groups opposed to girls' education have used threats of violence as a deterrent, keeping an increasing number of girls out of school every year. Indeed, it is not unlike the force to keep women out of public office. The forces against girls' education are stronger than the communities' will to resist them. A member of a women's group in Kandahar explained it this way: "Culture is an issue, [but] security is more important because even those people who want to break tradition are not able to."[33]

Shabnam, or Night Letters, are threatening letters left in public places or on the doors of individual homes at night. This tactic was frequently employed during the parliamentary elections to intimidate female candidates.

Shabnam frequently make the case that those Afghans who are "associating with infidels" are thereby "betraying Islam and Afghan culture" and will be punished:

> Muslim Brothers: Understand that the person who helps launch an attack with infidels is no longer a member of the Muslim community. Therefore, punishment of those who cooperate with infidels is the same as the [punishment of] infidels themselves. You should not cooperate in any way — neither with words, nor with money nor with your efforts. Watch out not to exchange your honor and courage for power and dollar.[34]
> Taliban *Shabnam* from Helmand

It is therefore wise to rethink how we measure progress — for education, for democracy, and for "development" more broadly — and what the effects of our efforts might be. The only true measure of progress, therefore, is through the voices of the Afghan people, for whom the progress was intended in the first place.

5

Afghaniyat *and the Gender Order*[1]

Gender relations represent the most stark example of the difficulties of working in a context of rapid political change and slower social change, where international voices have the potential to supersede local priorities.[2] Feminist movements are endogenous and generated in women's own interests, but the conflict occurs when the voices of the international political project — in this case the reconstruction of Afghanistan and the quest for gender equality — drowns out local voices.[3] To this end, this chapter starts with local voices to provide an understanding of how Afghan men and women define their own identities and priorities.

The gender order merits examination in the Afghan context in order to illuminate the relations between women and men within social processes — in this case, within the context of aid interventions. The gender order is a culturally, socially, and historically embedded concept that can change and evolve, as Afghan history has demonstrated. It is therefore imperative that the gender order is contextualized using Afghan voices to determine how men and women construct their relationships to one another and how these relationships might be changing in the aftermath. It is essential to recognize that these concepts vary between and within Afghan men and women. While there might be similarities, there is no uniform situation of Afghan women. Further, if women are singled out as a homogenous group with shared interests, gender issues — at the intersection of power and context — are sidelined. In an examination of diverse identities, we begin to understand how Afghans define themselves and how different aspects of their identities might be more salient at different times. Characterizing women and men exclusively on the basis of genitalia, therefore, might not present a robust view of their dynamic realities.

Identity in Afghanistan is a fluid concept and has experienced shifts over time and in different phases of conflict and peace. An understanding of Afghan identity in the aftermath is an important starting point to determine the ways in which Afghans define themselves and how these identity markers are reinforced or sidelined by external influences. With the focus on reconstruction, nation building and developing a civil society, the renewed struggle for identity merits investigation. The term *Afghaniyat* represents the sense of Afghan

Men in Istalif, a town famous for pottery, Parwan.

national identity that fluctuates in different periods of Afghan history. *Afghaniyat* is not based on the individual but is deeply embedded in the collective units of the tribe, clan, and family. "These reinforce accepted norms of behavior and function as economic, political and cultural units that act on behalf of those who comprise them."[4] It is this collective nature of *Afghaniyat* that determines Afghans' sense of self and place in the world and how they deal with alien ideologies.[5]

Similarly, women's identity is also part of the collective. Despite this knowledge, and the myriad efforts to mainstream gender, women are continuously singled out as a category in isolation from their wider social, cultural, and family contexts.[6] For a more thorough understanding, researchers on Afghanistan have suggested that it is worthwhile to examine the development of policies pertaining to women's roles in Afghanistan since the beginning of the 20th century. Nancy Hatch Dupree argued strongly that the family, as a social institution, warrants investigation.[7] Such investigations will reveal that Afghan women traditionally play the role of wife and mother, and the conduit through which Islam is passed from one generation to the next. Therefore it was unwise to ignore diversities and contradictions in identity and focus on gender (read: women).

Similar to other patriarchal societies, gender roles in Afghanistan are shaped by socio-cultural factors largely based on women's role as keepers of the family honor. "Women don't exist in isolation," a married Afghan man explained. Attempts to separate women from family and community are met with strong resistance. However, many programs have focused on women by excluding men, thereby perpetuating an environment that is unable to find roots in Afghan society. Contextualizing sex reveals that it is superseded by other social categories and identity markers. Aid will only be successful if it recognizes these interrelationships. In interviews with Afghan women and men, most of them did not identify themselves as women/men over other identity markers (such as nation, religion, class, lineage, tribe, clan, and ethnic group).[8] A head of an international NGO explained the importance of contextualizing identity this way:

> We work within the family context and do not talk "gender." I was advised early on by associates to "talk gender" to the donors but "do family." You express the issue of gender so well — change in gender roles vs. change in gender relations.[9] It cannot be emphasized enough.

An understanding of identity markers is essential for policy-makers and policy implementers firstly because it explains how aid can reinforce divisions or cohesion, particularly in context of conflict and the aftermath. Aid interventions that have not taken identity markers into account could not only reinforce divisions, but also foster new divisions. Aid institutions in Afghanistan demonstrated their feeble understanding of the Afghan "order" through the manner in which they sought to distribute aid. Lacking this knowledge, aid institutions sought to isolate segments of the population for aid, following which the community undertakes its own redistribution according to the social lines that make sense to them. The problem arises when aid exclusively targets one social segment and the community is not given the opportunity to redistribute.[10] The notion that aid interventions might be divisive is not unusual. Aid can be divisive in the context of conflict and the aftermath when it is distributed according to crude divisions in society instead of based on opportunities for peace. In this vein, it becomes important to recognize where the particular fissures are in the society and where connections can be made. Such choices can determine whether the effects of such efforts are positive or negative.[11] These choices also carry implicit ethical messages. In the context of Afghanistan's highly gendered intervention, one might wonder what perceptions the men might have of the focus on women. These strategic and seemingly apolitical decisions end up sending political messages and destabilizing deeply rooted social structures.

It was generally agreed that it is the responsibility of the aid apparatus and its policy-makers and policy implementers to understand that women in Afghanistan do not see themselves as individuals as much as part of the community and family. It is possible, therefore, to make gains for Afghan women by designing interventions that reflect an understanding of the context and that builds on these inter-relationships. On the importance of a contextualized understanding, a former Minister of Women's Affairs had the following to say:

> We are from the community. We know our community. We are better at finding the right approaches. We know the problems. We can recognize and identify them better. We know how to transfer the information in the right language, using the right words. We have this advantage. We will work better together than the international community would alone. Reaching the last woman in the farthest place of the country is only possible if international agencies come together in partnership with us.

Work on gender equality should be grounded in the local contexts and should understand the processes of socialization and historical resistance. Change imposed from the outside is strongly resisted, as experience in Afghanistan has shown. Working within the local cultures and traditions helps ground interventions in contexts that are understood. Reports and myriad examples explain that men specifically may be less resistant to changes when the changes are grounded in their own traditions. Therefore, without assuming *a priori* that sex is the most salient category, the analysis of this data begins with the possibility that sex might not be a category of particular relevance in the Afghan context and that it might in fact extract women and men from their contexts. Therefore, it is important to first determine the social categories around which interests are articulated.

An Identity in Crisis

Gender identities are embedded in other social categories: family, community, village, tribe. Underlying this is the foundation of Islam, the strongest unifying force in Afghanistan. Even these seemingly fixed categories have fluctuated over time and as a result of various political projects and powers. Conflict also instigates these changes in identity affiliations — as well as how conservative a given group might be.[12] Due to ethnic conflicts and ongoing tensions, it is often assumed *a priori* that ethnicity is the most salient aspect of *Afghaniyat*. Contrary to these assumptions, the various ethnic groups have evolved into a fairly common culture, psychology and ethos.[13] The fluidity of ethnic identity is a social and political construct, changing according to the pressure put upon it.[14]

Individuals balance many identities simultaneously, and any pressure to partition them under a sole identity label is futile. Choice of identity depends on context and is susceptible to external influences. These external influences could even go so far as to fabricate conscious difference where none previ-

A man stands on an old tank overlooking the city, Kabul.

ously existed. Forced singular affiliations of identity could be divisive, instigating social tension and violence.[15] In the context of Afghanistan's historical and political changes, Afghan analyses of their own identity were likely
to be affected by the attention of the aid apparatus and its "object" of focus.

Aid interventions in Afghanistan adopted a singular view of identity — in
this case, sex — and in fact made those in question more conscious of their sex,
particularly in that one was prioritized over the other. The question that should
be asked is to what extent aid interventions allowed program participants the
freedom to prioritize their identities. As a part of this investigation, interviews
were conducted with 71 Afghan women, selected based on their participation
in aid interventions through local NGOs, and 50 Afghan men. Twenty-five of
the men interviewed were husbands or male agnates of the women participants — fathers and brothers. Such interviews allowed for a more detailed analysis at the household level and provided useful comparison between women and
men's perspectives. Twenty-five men were selected randomly.

The majority of the women interviewed (63 percent) originated from
rural areas, were married (55 percent), and had no education (59 percent).
They represented diverse ethnic groups and age groups. None of the men
interviewed were engaged in aid interventions. The majority of the men also
came from rural areas (66 percent) and were married (56 percent). However,
the majority of the men had seven or more years of education. This reflects

Afghan realities as boys' education is prioritized over that of girls. As with the women, their ages and ethnic groups varied.

Participants were asked to rank five different aspects of their identity in order of importance to them.[16] The options were as follows:

- National Identity
- Religious Identity
- Ethnic/Tribal Identity
- Sex
- Family Identity

This exercise challenged the assumption that sex was the most salient category for Afghan women. Indeed, religious identity ranked first for both women and men as the primary social category within which they were more closely affiliated. This was followed by Afghan identity, ethnicity, sex, and family.

Identity Ranking—Women

Identity Ranking— Women	Number of Votes (out of 71)	Percentage of Total for Women
1. Religion	34	48%
2. Afghan	16	23%
3. Ethnicity	15	20%
4. Sex	5	6%
5. Family	2	3%

Men ranked identity markers similar to women. Religion received the majority vote (60 percent). Afghan identity was tied with family affiliations. Sex received 6 percent of the vote, followed by ethnicity at 2 percent.

Identity Ranking—Men

Identity Ranking– Men	Number of Votes (out of 50)	Percentage of Total for Men
1. Religion	30	60%
2. Afghan/Family	8	16%
3. Sex	3	6%
4. Ethnicity	1	2%

The ranking of religious identity reflects the prominence Islam has in Afghanistan, and the consequences if Islam is sidelined or perceived to be so, as Afghan history aptly demonstrates.[17] The role of religion is therefore deserving of particular focus, given its prominence in the lives of Afghan women and men. Islam provides the parameters by which Afghans live — focusing specifically on relationships between the sexes. Both women and men explained that they define themselves by these parameters.

Many expressed that they are content within its boundaries, electing freely to abide by its tenets. "Islam is the primary point of guidance," one woman articulated. "Without it, there cannot be progress." Many men said that their religion is "everything" to them, and therefore those of a different religion are "outside of [Afghan] society's laws." Most women argued that their role in Islam is no different from that of a man, stating that it is the duty of both women and men to be good Muslims. "There is no difference between Allah's creatures," one woman explained. Afghan women in the focus groups felt strongly that Islam, more than any other religion, guarantees equal rights to men and women. "Women have the right to work, to study. Women have lots of rights," they said. "Women have rights in Islam. They can work outside of the house," one woman added. Women explained that they prefer to find ways to defend their rights within an Islamic context. They want to search for answers in the Koran, or through another practicing Muslim. And they want to know more about Islam and the rights that it affords them. One woman explained: "When a baby is born, the family says 'you are Muslim, you are Muslim' but the child is never taught why ... so they have a hard time differentiating between the culture and religion." In Afghanistan, this line is further blurred as tribal customs merge Islam with their own practices. Norms governing women in Afghanistan are often based on tribal codes that trump Islamic laws — particularly in the case of Islam's more enlightened messages on women. A woman explained the dynamic this way: "There are lots of rules for women in Islam, but people weren't educated enough and didn't have much information about their religion. So people preached some wrong words about Islam."

Most men expressed a strong need to safeguard Islam — particularly its measures regarding women — from foreign interference and influence. One younger man put it this way: "Religion is an important factor for Muslims. To defend it they will sacrifice everything." "Islam provides and respects any opportunities for women, but unfortunately a non-respectable culture has been mixed with Islam," one woman said.[18] Many *mullahs* are to blame, they say. "They want to change Islam and mix it with culture and custom." Respondents viewed the Taliban as a manifestation of foreign influence that has "soiled" the true nature of Islam. "They tried to act like Muslims and they tried to alter Islam and disrespect the culture of Afghanistan," one woman said. "During the Taliban regime, it was just the name of Islam, but not real Islam. They were like wild animals." "All of their ideas were wrong. They said that women should wear the *chaddari*. They said we must cover. All things were wrong." "Taliban regime was a dark regime," one woman said. "They forced people to do things that they wanted."

Discussions on the role of Islam in Afghanistan quickly became expressions of duty to safeguard the religion and concern that it could once again be threatened by outside interference — especially ideological occupations. Many felt that the aid apparatus sought to undermine Islam by their failure to work within a Muslim context. This was fueled by Afghan perceptions that foreigners view Islam as oppressive. Thus many Afghans saw engagement with aid institutions as a willful dismissal of Islam. Many women were quick to blame "invading cultures and customs," expressing a dislike for foreign intervention and a desire to regain Afghan autonomy. "Now that we are a little bit free," one woman explained, "I will not be a servant of human beings. I am only a servant of God."

Women and men who selected Afghan as their primary identification expressed pride in being Afghan and a strong sense of *Afghaniyat*. Both men and women in this category generally felt that an Afghan identity is what will bring cohesion to a fragmented society. They expressed a desire to re-invigorate the concept of Afghan and, as one older woman put it, to "try to be as one people." An illiterate woman of rural origins put it this way: "We are all Afghans first. The rest just divides us." This is a sentiment shared by many in this category. Another older woman said "being Afghan is what holds us together. It should be our strength."

Of those who selected Afghan, many connected their Afghan identity with their ability to drive non–Afghans away. An older man stated that the "importance of being Afghan is because Afghans never want to convert their Afghan identity." Another man reinforced this point by saying: "We don't want to lose our identity and sell ourselves." Many of the men in this category expressed a belief in the strength of Afghans as a force to act in unity against non–Afghans. A teenage male of rural origins said:

> Afghan also means national unity, brotherhood, balance. The first factor to fulfill all the mentioned aims is to be an Afghan. And our national interests are in being an Afghan. It is our responsibility to protect it.

A few of the women who selected Afghan also connected their role as women to their role as keepers of men's honor — and therefore national honor. One 23-year-old married woman with two years of education explained that being Afghan means that "the women shall be kept at home and no one shall see her. Her role is to do the work of the home and to act as men wish." Another woman from the countryside put it this way: "I put women last because men are the highest degree and women are the lowest. It is more important that we are all Afghans." One woman ranked her Afghan identity lowest, explaining that "Afghan is last because Afghanistan has done nothing good for women." She ranked ethnicity as her primary form of identification.

Very few women and men selected sex as their primary identity affiliation. For many, they noted that sexual identity has only recently become important, since "foreigners started talking about it." Indeed, while most recognized that sexual politics have destabilized Afghanistan at many interfaces in Afghan history, they felt that "being a woman is now important in Afghanistan, before it was not."

Only one woman — and one man — expressed a more positive and hopeful sentiment. A 31-year-old woman with no education said she "believe[s] in the strength of Afghan women." A man from rural Afghanistan with primary education held a liberal view, using words like "equality" and "rights." He explained that "in recent years, relations between husband and wife — and all men and women — have turned very bad. To remake these relations is an important factor."

In Afghanistan's aftermath, very few respondents chose to identify with their ethnic group as this was a divisive issue during the conflict. In fact, one older woman put it this way: "During the conflict, ethnicity became the most important thing for us." She explained that she still clings to these views and is not ready to look beyond ethnic lines. The other respondents — mostly women — guard these identity markers because, as one 21-year-old woman explained, "this is how we understand each other, as tribes and groups." Ethnic identity also included tribal affiliation as these are interconnected in Afghanistan. Another woman from rural Afghanistan reinforced this view, stating that "we are closest to our tribe because this is where we find the most similarities." A 39-year-old widow expressed her connection to ethnic identity in opposition to gender, stating that "I selected ethnicity because these are the things that identify us first, not gender roles and relations." I took interest in her use of the word gender as it was the only part of her response that was in English. This emphasizes a reoccurring theme in the text: that gender has become an imported buzzword for use by Afghans for non–Afghans — and a word for which no translation exists.

Many of those who identified with their ethnic group expressed a need to be in a familiar context with their own people. In the context of conflict and displacement, many Afghans have found themselves removed from their families, communities, and tribes and are now without the social safety net that these networks provide. The expression *nufus-dar* was employed in this regard. This term literally means "having people," having a sense of safety and belonging, for example, within a tribe or clan.[19] Despite the importance of *nufus-dar*, family affiliation was not a popular answer for women. The men who said they identified firstly with their role as a male member of a family explained it this way: "I am a member of a family first and have an obligation to protect them." Indeed, men who selected family as their primary affiliation likely did so because of their prominent socio-cultural role as head of the family and the sense of duty that this brings. Along with this duty comes the obligation to protect the family honor as it is intimately linked with the man's own honor — and therefore his credibility in the community.

A young man from Kabul felt that family identity connected him to his ancestors, explaining the prominent role of older generations in forming the young. He put it this way:

> Parents mean responsibility, developing knowledge, culture, humanity, religion. They explain to us what other divisions and identities like ethnic groups, man/woman, and Afghan mean. But parents could also pass on poverty, ignorance, and darkness to their children.

Identity Ranking—Women and Men

Identity Ranking— Women and Men	Percentage of Women of Total	Percentage of Men of Total	Percentage of Men and Women
Religion	28%	25%	53%
Afghan	19%	13%	20%
Ethnicity	17%	2%	13%
Sex	5%	5%	6%
Family	2%	13%	8%

It is significant that the majority of male and female respondents (53 percent) selected religion as their primary identity affiliation, while only 6 percent felt that they identified with their sex. It could be argued that aid interventions underestimated the importance of Islam on the lives of women and men in Afghanistan — and did not view it as a channel by which to make change. In fact, Muslim identity is more than a religious label. It also is an indicator of a person's reputation and a certification that s/he is credible and trustworthy. The expression *khub musselman ast*, literally meaning "he's a good Muslim," is employed for this purpose.[20]

It is also worthwhile noting that 17 percent of women and only 2 percent of men identified with their ethnic identity. Similar to gender identity, ethnic identity has been manipulated by leaders and foreign invaders and is both political subject and object. Gender and ethnic identities are subjects of political forces, but also political issues in their own right. Women might identify more strongly with ethnic identity because they have periodically undergone the political processes of identification that accompany their own identities.

Understandings of Gender

Generally, men felt more comfortable answering questions about women than the women were in answering questions about men. On both sides, however, many expressed a sense that they were not qualified to answer questions about the other sex. When asked questions about women, most men answered using "we" — on behalf of all men. They felt qualified as individuals to express views that they believed were held by all men as a collective. The women, on the other hand, answered questions as individuals. Both men and women emphasized a division of public (male) and private (female) roles common to other patriarchal societies.

The male research assistant who conducted interviews with the men noted the following:

> There were men who welcomed me and answered eagerly, while some men tried to avoid the questions. Answering questions about gender didn't make them happy. They hear too much about this, and they are tired of it. To them, gender means woman. And "woman" means more important than man to the internationals. I am an Afghan man so they told me openly about these things.

The female research assistant explained it this way:

> I had discussions with [the male research assistant] and learned many surprising things. During my interviews with women, impressions were different than with men. Most of the women were comfortable in answering questions and did not have trouble addressing issues. Some of them were happy to complain about men! A few of them didn't have answers to some of the questions because they had not thought of those things before. Generally, it was nice to compare ideas of a man and woman from a family. We learned that there are actually very few couples who are thinking the same.

The majority of the women interviewed initially had a difficult time answering questions about what it means to be a man in Afghanistan. They hesitated at first but were able to articulate quite clearly upon reflection. They compared being a man with being a "lord," possessing power, responsibility, and authority. Some of the women expressed a desire for greater equality and a dislike for men's disproportionate share of power, noting that "men have all the rights they want." One woman said that "men are better than women in all aspects, meaning they can do most of the things that women are not allowed to do." Another recognized that men "have a good position [and] will not give it up." A few women clearly articulated that inequality is not exclusive to Afghanistan. One married woman expressed it this way: "Not only in Afghanistan, but everywhere from the first day men have been more powerful, strong, and responsible." During the group discussions, women's opinions gradually became stronger, often fueled and encouraged by the other women. For example, a widow in her 40s with little education laughed and said: "A man has to be a caring father, a kind husband, and an active citizen. I do not know how many men fit this image." Men interviewed were far more animated in their responses about what it means to be a woman in Afghanistan. Men agreed that women are the responsibility of the male members of the household — husband, father, brother, and son — and that they must "obey the commands" issued to them by the men.

Many Afghan women felt that they have always exercised agency, despite foreign perceptions that they are oppressed. In fact, women expressed concern that they were beginning to see themselves through the eyes of the world — and not as the strong and resilient women they felt themselves to be. *Nang*— honor — represents the honor that women manifest through their behavior. Most of the women recognized that they carry the burden of the family, community, and national honor. As a result, they are expected to safeguard this honor, or women — and by extension their families and communities — will suffer the consequences.

Many women expressed discomfort in being the center of attention and the "object" of international pity. A single woman in Kabul pointed out that "being a woman is now important in Afghanistan, before it was not." Another woman articulated that "woman in Afghanistan is a very popular object today." Her use of the word object was deliberate and emphasized. She expressed a sentiment echoed by many, namely that Afghan women are objectified in the eyes of foreigners, particularly the media — and that Afghan women are an object of the discourse animating the aid apparatus.

Women expressed concern that men feel lost in the new Afghanistan, wanting to bring back old ways. Many also felt more comfortable with a reversion to traditional roles, with men in the public sphere. Men's *namoos*, or pride, is under threat, and women feel greater pressure as a result. Afghan women might represent honor, but Afghan men are under obligation to defend it, especially if it is under attack by foreigners.

Men generally felt very strongly about their role as provider and repeatedly defined themselves as such. Many men echoed the sentiment expressed by a 47-year-old married man that "a man is responsible to work outside the house and feed his children." A 19-year-old single man with nearly 12 years of education stated that "man means leader, power, principle. And his every order should be accepted by the woman." This presents a clear example of a sentiment that is shared across age, level of education, marital status, and other demographic indicators. A few men expressed fatigue with the responsibility of supporting the family, particularly in the context of the aftermath and the economic challenges it presents. One man put it this way: "Man means one who is wandering in search of food 24 hours a day."

Mamus throughout History

Mamus is defined as men's duty to protect and respect women. In this sense it links *nang* (honor) and *namoos* (pride) and can be used to explain gender roles and relations in Afghanistan throughout history. Both male and female interviewees generally agreed that the period before the 1979 Soviet occupation was good for both men and women. Most interviewees expressed that men and women were satisfied with their position. Women felt that progress was being made toward equality. Men generally felt that there was equality, and that no one was concerned with place and position. A 44-year-old married man added that "the eyes of people were shut — they had no idea about position of men and of women." Many men expressed that everyone was generally content — a period of "respect, friendship and love." One man articulated that "both men and women had a good position before the war. They were able to come out of their houses and work safely and live to their potential." Another agreed, elaborating that "women could work with men shoulder to shoulder and they could take advantage of their new freedoms." A 24-year-old married man with little education explained: "Men and women

Hazara men sit near the holes where the Buddha statues once were, Bamiyan.

coordinated with each other and they were solving their problems easily and helping each other in every way." Some interviewees were more critical. One man put it this way: "Women didn't know much about their rights and were satisfied with what men expected from them." A few women noted that this period was more contentious and that "women were beginning to fight for rights, but men were resisting changes." A married Kabuli woman complained: "Women were trying to be equal. People say that there was equality, but I think it was not there and it could not have remained without much resistance."

The period of conflict was easier for male and female interviewees to define. There was general agreement that roles and relations suffered and were superseded by the conflict and ensuing violence. However, responses were split on two issues. Some believed that men and women suffered equally, while others — mostly women — believed that the various conflicts affected women more than men. A young single man articulated that "positions were very bad because women and men were living in very deep sorrow because they were put in war unwillingly." One 53-year-old man put it this way: "During that time there was no difference to be a man or woman — both of them were punished the same." An illiterate 19-year-old woman agreed, saying that "things were very bad for women, and even for men." It was generally agreed that the period of conflict destroyed any progress that had been achieved in Afghanistan — particularly in gender relations. One man from rural Afghanistan explained it this way: "All people were unsheltered, displaced to different parts of the world, and their love changed to violence." Another man from Kabul reinforced this point, explaining that "during the war, relations between men and women were destroyed because of ignorance and poverty — and instead violence and tortures started."

A few respondents felt that women suffered more during the conflict. Women stated that "there was much cruelty on women," adding that war stopped all progress between men and women and "women's lives became a prison." Another woman held the view that "all groups took their anger out on women." A man in his 40s stated that "women suffered a lot more than men." Another man articulated that women's position deteriorated because "they were living in violence and struggling to survive, and men were oppressing women." An unmarried man in Kabul explained that during the period of conflict "women didn't have any relations with men, and women were not able to go out and work because they were afraid." One man recognized that women had to take on additional responsibilities, stating that "all women were in search of shelter and protection since male responsibilities came to them because of war." Only one man expressed a preference for women's behavior during the conflict, because "women were more safe under the *bourka*— not like today." It is interesting to note that during interviews, Afghans recognized that the word *bourka* was one that was used more frequently in the aid apparatus and amongst non–Afghans. They therefore used the term *bourka* when referring to foreign images of Afghans, but continued to use the more common term *chaddari* in their daily discussions with each other. This reveals the extent to which the preferred terms of the aid apparatus have become part of Afghan daily discourse.

Responses were mixed on the question of gender roles and relations in the aftermath. One woman complained: "Now we are in a situation that we were in before, fighting for rights and men not wanting to give them." Another said: "Only God knows how women will be." And yet another woman reinforced this point: "Today I am not sure which way things will go. Women are struggling for their rights, but that does not mean they will succeed." A 19-year-old man with no education put it this way: "Conditions of the country have a big effect on gender relations. I do not think changing roles and relations is a good thing. In Afghanistan today, destruction is easy, but building is difficult." Only one woman — a 25-year-old from Jalalabad — expressed a small sense of optimism amidst frustration: "Laws are now equal for men and women, but we have to realize these laws in our lives." One woman made an important parallel that was echoed in various conversations as a response to a broad range of of questions:

> Before the war men and women were under the government's control. During the war they were under the control of different regimes. Now again men and women are under control — this time it is the control of the international organizations.

This is a particularly worrisome sentiment as it compares the aid apparatus to an occupying force or a dictatorial regime that seeks to control the lives of Afghans. A few were quick to align the three "occupiers"— the Soviet Union, the Taliban, and the aid apparatus — in their similar quests to restructure gender roles and relations.

When asked about gender roles and relations during different periods of history, some interviewees presented a fuller picture. Both women and men expressed the sentiment that things were "better" before the war. They recognized that conflict presents changed circumstances and therefore gender roles and relations change — generally to the detriment of women. However, notable differences occur in their perceptions of gender roles and relations in the aftermath. Women generally believed that men sought to cling to power and were resisting change. A 17-year-old illiterate woman told the story this way:

> Women were free in the early days and men were learning to accept women as equals. During the war, both men and women fought for freedom, but war put men in charge again. And now we are told to believe that there is freedom, but men are still wanting to be in charge.

Some men also expressed optimism and saw that change can be positive, although these were in the minority. The narratives of two men below illustrate the ambiguity within which they feel they are operating regarding gender roles and relations today, as compared to different periods in history:

> (1) Before the war, everyone understood their role. Both men and women wanted — and sought — love between them. And they wanted those things which can create love. Before the war, very few women were in government. Although they were not in the public eye and did not have impact on men, they were content. They did not have violence. During the conflict, violence increased. Not just between men and women, but also homelessness, bad economy, other things. All of this caused corruption. Men and women lost their position. During the war, women had no impact. Violence against them increased. Men didn't have good relations with women. Everyone was lost in his work and grief. After the peace agreement, roles [of women and men] were expected to get better. Contact between men and women increased but we can't see dramatic changes in relations.
>
> (2) Before the war there was not any discussion of rights, but still women's position was getting better day by day. Their relations were good. Both were living with respect and love. Life was good. There was an understanding that men and women's position had to be different. During the war, men's position was good but women's was not, because war converted their ideas completely and their previous ideas were ruined. Their relations were not good because war again had its bad effects. Weak economy and displacement drove them to violence. Now we hope for a better future. We are looking forward to a day when — like before — man and woman will both have a significant place in the society within their traditional positions.

The majority of men interviewed were not happy with changes and felt that women are stepping out of their prescribed role — and are encouraged by aid interventions to do so. As a result, many men felt that they were losing their place, as this 18-year-old articulates:

> Before the war, man and woman had their rights. They were in a very peaceful atmosphere. They had no problem together. They had a very good relationship. Violence level between men and women was very low. Men had respect for women — and so the women to men. During war time, women lost their rights, and their roles in the society. Violence increased incredibly. Previous respect collapsed. [Women] lost their dignity. After peace was built, democracy has given rights to the women which are not part of Islamic rules. And now sometimes violence is coming again.

This sentiment is reinforced by a man from Kabul with nearly 12 years of education:

> Before the war, man had his place in the society and woman had her place. During war time, relations between man and woman were demolished. No one was paying attention to their place. After the war finished, man and woman received their position and their rights. There must be a difference between man and woman. Woman has her place and man has his.

Some men felt that the issue of power and rights is a zero-sum game, and that women cannot gain these things without men having to lose them. As a response to various questions, men expressed a sense of feeling lost, less important, and neglected because of women's newly granted power and rights. One man with 10 years of education put it this way: "First, there wasn't exactly such a thing as 'woman.' Then, both woman and man did not exist. There was war. Now there isn't such a thing as 'man.'"

Most men feel that changes in relations between men and women are not a good thing. They prefer that each understands and respects his/her role as Afghan culture and Islam have prescribed. Many of the men recognize that circumstances in Afghanistan have changed gender relations, and that fluctuations in women's roles have been largely a result of political processes. A 28-year-old unmarried man explained:

> Social customs of different regimes in different periods have negatively influenced the relationship between men and women. It will take time to ignore the ignorant customs that are imposed on society. And "relationship" also means women in the house, not only outside.

Another man explained that relations change when situations change, and that these changes would be good "if men also got advantages." An elderly man with a few years of education reinforced this point, explaining that changes in gender relations are "not a good thing, because most of the people do not like these changes." Another man expressed that change can be a good thing—"only if it is not against what Afghans want." A man with 12 years of education expressed concern, explaining that in the past "men had an active role, and they were the ones who supported their family. Now that women have a better place in society, I am not sure what will happen to men's roles." One 19-year-old man lamented:

> Extremely bad changes are happening in relations [between men and women]. All of these things are bad—this urging of UN for women's rights all the time. We haven't seen a female president in USA so far, but here we saw female candidates in the recent election. And still people are putting pressure on Afghanistan to make more changes.

Some men expressed willingness to advance toward equality and a recognition that women's roles are changing and expanding. These men were not in the majority. For example, one middle-aged married man explained:

> It is like a dramatic thing to say that rights of women and men are same. Everybody knows that this is not true. It is too early in Afghanistan to say that. Maybe it takes 20 or 30 years. People are learning now to practice democracy and things like that.

Women held a more cautious view. Some women, like this married woman with no education, felt that change must happen at a pace that works for both women and men. She explained that "it is a good thing that relations change, only if they change in a positive way for women. And the change must be slow or men will not be able to follow it." Most women agreed that change should happen slowly, should be led by Afghans, and should fit within the context of Islam. The following women shared this sentiment, amongst others:

- Relations are changing because the world is paying attention to Afghan women. But not all the changes are good. The good changes take a lot of time. In time, we can work with men as equals.
- Any changes that are too fast are bad. People will not accept them.
- If the men and women together decide on the changes, they will be good. If someone else from the outside makes the changes, no one will be happy with it.

A few women expressed the view that "relations are not changing in the way [they] want" and that "relations change because rules and regulations of government change." This reinforces previously stated sentiments about gender relations at the whim of various regimes and occupying forces.

One woman explained that gender relations have changed throughout Afghan history, but that this particular change is different because women are "protected objects." She shared her perspective:

> I think that relations between men and women change because in different periods, the lifestyles of people were different. During the war, men had learned to be the cruel lords and force women to do whatever they liked because the government was supporting them to do so. But now men can't do anything because everyone supports women instead.

I Hope It Will Get Better in the Future

A few common themes emerged repeatedly in conversations with both Afghan men and women. A few interviewees — all men — held the view that women are doing better in their quest for equality. One man explained: "Relations are good — or almost good. Women can work alongside men. Women can defend their rights, but they cannot take advantage of their liberty." He elaborated to say that some men might present obstacles in women's path. Others felt that full equality has been granted. One educated middle-aged man explained that "now women's position is better. Women can work. Nothing is imposed by men. Everyone has his freedom." Another man from rural Afghanistan felt that things have improved for women since the conflict because "tyranny and violence have decreased and women's rights are given. Also, men don't come violently to women."

The more commonly held view by men was that women are prioritized over men and have received a disproportionate share of support, opportunities, and benefits — specifically from aid institutions. This perspective was shared by a wide variety of men, regardless of education, age, and marital status. Some of their responses were:

- Men's rights have gotten worse as women's get better. But I hope it will get better in the future.
- Men were not open minded to let their women work outside but since the Americans came and insisted on this, women are outside. Men only accept so they can solve their economic problems.
- Today women are more important than men. They can defend their rights against men.
- Now again women have their rights [as they did before the conflict] but this time men have lost their rights against women. And women are preferred over men.
- As a result of UN urgings, women want more rights than their own rights.
- The UN insists, and so women fight with their husbands for their rights. This is not correct.

Almost all the men interviewed felt that rights were being stripped from them to give to women. The following sentiments were reiterated by many. In the words of one man, international organizations' act of "taking the rights of men and giving them to women is something bad for men." Another added that "it is all because of international organizations that men are losing their rights." During a conversation with a married man from rural Afghanistan, he had the following to say:

> Why did you put your aim in this country as working with women and women's rights? Because something else is more important than these things.

> They created a women's affairs ministry here. If we are saying that men and
> women are equal, why don't we have a ministry for men?

Men interviewed frequently stated that their most important concern was the
overemphasis on women and their own resulting neglect. Men also explained
that the strong pushes for social change and transformation were too forceful
and too fast. The perception that these changes have been imported and imposed
(largely from Western countries) brings further resistance. Many men felt that
these changes could be perceived to be un–Islamic and ill-suited for Afghanistan. One young man with little education put it this way: "International organizations increased the level of freedom [for women] beyond its social limitations."

Men repeatedly shared concerns that they were not offered access to
opportunities "because all support and priorities are for women," as one man
explained. This was an oft-cited concern. A university-educated man elaborated that international efforts in Afghanistan thus far have demonstrated to
men "that these organizations cannot do anything for men and they are not
thinking of long-term change for the better in Afghanistan." A few men also
felt that the work that has been done for women has been hollow, such as this
young man from rural Afghanistan:

> International organizations have done very limited things for men. They
> haven't done anything important for men — and for women. Their works are
> just symbolic. They just say, not do.

These men felt that they were neglected in aid interventions. Indeed, men
believed that women were now better off than they were in the past, and better off than men are now. Women agreed that men had been neglected because
women had been given a disproportionate share of attention, and therefore
men's anger might be justified. Women recognized the imbalance in attention by the aid apparatus. However, they did not necessarily feel that they
were any better off. In fact, women generally felt disappointment because
promises made to them had not been delivered. The women themselves were
not comfortable with being in public eye as they would prefer to share opportunities and retain traditional parameters. However, this did not seem possible because the aid apparatus single-mindedly plowed forth with its political
project of transformation. Women also expressed concern that men felt that
their power was being stolen. They felt that this was inaccurate, especially as
the power they supposedly had only existed on paper. The aid apparatus had
not delivered on its promised transformation, and thus far such things were
only words. As one outcome of men's perception, some men prevented women
from taking advantage of available opportunities. For others, economic necessity compelled them. But the damage at home is already done.

The sentiments expressed in the preceding paragraphs cannot be divided along age, ethnic, or education lines. But there are patterns that can be discerned and that are worth noting. There is an overarching sentiment that men have been neglected in aid interventions. Both women and men share this view. There is a concern that violence is increasing — at home and in society. Finally, there is the sentiment that the influence of the aid apparatus is yet another variation on an occupying regime in Afghanistan, with its own ideas and impositions. This in-depth view of Afghan identities illustrates the depth and complexities in understanding identities when designing aid interventions. A nuanced understanding should entail emphasis on the context that animates gender roles and relations, as relayed by Afghan women and men themselves.

6

Maida, Maida[1]

I have hope, but I have no faith.
— Afghan woman on progress for women in Afghanistan

The voices in this section bring to the fore the perspectives of Afghan women and men to address the three strongest themes: the importance of honor, the denial of agency, and the dissatisfaction with aid — all connected to the neglect of men in aid interventions. Indeed, there has always been a strong link between women's rights and the fate of the nation. The weight of Afghanistan's honor rests squarely on women's shoulders. As a result, reforming gender relations has been met with resistance and is denounced by opponents as un–Islamic, and a challenge to faith and family.[2] Therefore, many women and men would counsel that such changes should be made slowly, with small steps. The Dari word *maida* describes this. In the central part of the country, however, *maida* can also be used to mean "broken."

The system of honor in Afghanistan plays such a prominent role that it merits special focus. Honor is the foundation of Afghan culture, manifested in the behavior of "one's women."[3] Afghanistan is a traditional and patriarchal society, within which the protection of society rests on the protection of women, and the honor of society is therefore reflected in the honor of women.[4] As a result, there is great weight placed on women's purity as the means by which to preserve honor.

Women's behavior is circumscribed, and they are very conscious of this responsibility. However, in the context of social and economic upheaval in the aftermath, women are obligated to meet the family's basic needs and are therefore compelled to transcend prescribed gender roles and social systems. When there is an opportunity for assistance, most women prefer to be aided within the context of the family. Regardless, most aid interventions overlooked this, actually provoking a retreat to more conservative measures. Women's status as keepers of family honor and identity becomes increasingly magnified — and *purdah* (restrictions on contact between men and women) more strictly enforced — when men lack economic and social autonomy, fundamental to their understanding of masculinity. The aid apparatus tended to view the reinforcement of *purdah* as a manifestation of Islamic intolerance. It more likely signified an attempt to preserve the family — and its dignity — in the context of rapid change beyond men's control.[5]

Thus, many Afghan men — and women — view women's employment as a reflection and reminder of their absolute poverty and destitution, an insult to men's dignity, and a questioning of men's ability to provide. An Afghan saying expresses this well: "While the rich can afford honor, the poor must 'eat shame.'"[6] Thus, the idea of honor is deeply embedded in Afghanistan.

Two women worry as they listen to an aid institution explain its plans, Kabul.

The primary scarce resources remain land, water, livestock, and — in a very real, but obviously different, sense — women. All four are vital, easily lost, and endlessly troublesome.... It is women, however, who are widely considered the most volatile cause for serious dispute.... With their sexuality generally considered unmanageable, women are secluded as much as possible from all but the narrowest circle of family males. Here they serve as the primal embodiments of masculine honor. A man may suffer the loss of material property and still keep the core of his self-respect intact. Mere suspicion, on the other hand, of illicit access to his women requires an overt response: immediate and extreme.[7]

Control over these resources thus forms the base of men's economic and political power — with women as the most politicized of these. Many women noted that men's honor was compromised in their inability to provide for the family. As a result, women viewed them as emasculated. Women frequently referred to the "special bravery of Afghan men," along with their strength and dignity. One married woman of rural origins expressed the concern of many when she said, "We don't want [our Afghan men] to stretch the hand of need to anyone in the world." She went on to explain that the new "occupying force" — namely the aid apparatus — has crippled Afghan men's ability to stand on their own.

Safeguarding Honor

To confirm findings, discussions were held with Pashtun women from different parts of Afghanistan — Kabul, other cities, and rural areas. The rationale behind isolating Pashtun women was to provide a context whereby the traditionally conservative ethnic group could share concerns they felt to be exclusive to their community. This was also done to determine if Pashtun women — as a group — expressed different ideas from those of the other ethnic groups.

Pashtun women are traditionally bound by the *Pashtunwali*, the unwritten legal code of their population. In this code, women play a symbolic role as the core of the society and therefore must be protected. The honor of the Pashtuns is therefore intimately linked with — and often entirely dependent on — women's honor. This results in circumscribed movements for women and limited — if any — contact with men. This restriction, known as *purdah*, sets clearly defined rules for women's interactions outside the domestic sphere.[8] The penalty of transgression of this unwritten code is worse than death: it is dishonor.[9] And death is the only viable alternative to loss of honor. Afghanistan's other ethnic groups have, at varying times throughout history, adopted measures that stem from the *Pashtunwali*. Inaccurate and facile analyses have been made connecting women's oppression to Islamic practices. However, contrary to common understandings of the role of women in Muslim contexts, norms governing women in Afghanistan are based more closely on tribal codes such as the *Pashtunwali*.

The women in this group did express what might be labeled as more conservative ideas and spent the bulk of the hour discussing the importance of religion and the concepts of *akl* and *namoos*, elaborated below. Although this finding might conform to the stereotype of the conservative Pashtun, I note that the label "conservative" is fluid — and relative — based on the current socio-political project in operation. *Akl* can be translated as "responsibility" in Dari, but has much deeper meanings. It refers to a code of accepted behavior, and reflects a combination of honor and shame with a notion of responsibility that together represents men's control of resources and includes men's control over women.[10] Women refer to *akl* in discussions of men's honor, and their responsibility in safeguarding it. *Akl* reflects their understanding of their role and the risks that betraying it may entail.

Namoos, pride, refers to the chastity of women, and implies the duty of men to protect and respect women. The term also refers to men's pride in safeguarding women's chastity. The women explained that they run risks of losing their chastity, or the *perception* that they have lost their chastity, with greater public exposure and the assuming of traditionally male roles. In Afghanistan, the worst insult for an Afghan man is to call his women *bi-namoos*, without chastity. This distinction reflects the Afghan tradition of strong divisions between the public and private sphere. *Namoos* can also be defined as shame. The term is used by men to exert control over women, by women to instill fear in other women, and by women to rationalize their role. The women in this focus group used these terms to explain the risks they take in participating in aid interventions and the desire they have to not step over these Afghan lines.

In a discussion of women's place, the women expressed strong desires to remain largely within traditional roles. The context of Islam and its view of gender roles was a frequent reference point. Women in this group generally viewed their roles as first within the household with their children. Family is indeed a prominent institution in Afghanistan, and motherhood the preferred role for Afghan women. Since Afghan women view themselves embedded within the family and society, it should be Afghan society as a whole — not isolated segments — that need to debate human rights in their contexts.[11]

These women also felt very strongly about men's role as provider for the family. They explained the connection between this traditionally male respon-sibility and men's honor. In short, a man with honor is one who is able to provide for his family. Conversely, a man without work is one who has no honor. Women explained that the control of resources in the language of honor and shame. A man's honor depends on his ability to manage and defend his chattel. A woman who has assumed these traditionally male responsibil-ities becomes like a man or literally, *nar shedza*, a "man-woman." To Afghans, "there are more important things than family or possessions, even than life" — honor.[12] Women repeatedly emphasized the importance of the dignity of Afghan men. One woman put it this way: "We don't want men to be unem-ployed and without dignity. Their dignity will also bring us more freedom."

This finding is reinforced by Nancy Hatch Dupree's study of the fam-ily as a social institution in different periods in Afghan history. She explained that when donors showed a distinct preference for women's employment, many men felt diminished and feared that their patriarchal status had eroded. They now depended on women for their survival. Women, in turn, assumed the role of primary breadwinner, "adding further to male sensitivities about their patriarchal prerogatives.... These role reversals required adjustments in relationships that were often the cause of considerable tension."[13] Women in this focus group preferred that the men have the responsibility of working and providing for the household and controlling the domestic resources. Women were conscious of the fact that they could bring shame on the family by assuming these roles. Women also recognize their role in defending and safeguarding male honor, as the "keeper of the family and the honor," as one woman explained. They understand that their actions could undermine male honor and result in serious repercussions. Paradoxically, women find much greater freedom to maneuver when they remain within the confines of these traditional roles. In fact, the women explained that they run the risk of being further restricted if they try to assume overly public lives as this negatively affects the public face of the family. Many Afghan men believe that work outside the home strips women of their dignity — thereby negatively affecting men's reputations.

Tales of *Ghayrat*

Afghan literature — in particular the short stories of Akram Osman and the *Landays* of Pashtun women — offers insight to these contradictions and present a creative interpretation of ground-level cultural and social realities.[14] Saira Shah, author of *The Storyteller's Daughter* and producer of the documentary *Behind the Veil*, expressed the importance of stories as a special window to understanding Afghanistan:

> Experiences follow patterns, which repeat themselves again and again. In our tradition, stories can help you recognize the shape of an experience, to make sense of and to deal with it.... What you may take for mere snippets of myth and legend encapsulate what you need to know to guide you on your way anywhere among Afghans.[15]

In an explanation of Akram Osman's main story, "Real Men Keep Their Word," Arley Loewen explains the meaning behind the term *marda ra qawl*. Loewen explains that this idiomatic expression literally means men keep their word, "but on a deeper level it refers to 'men of honour' who will stand by their word at all costs ... the highest virtue in traditional Afghan culture."[16] The term *ghayrat*, "the right to defend one's property and honor by force," can be used for this purpose.[17] Myriad Afghan expressions exist to depict the state of a man without work, and by extension without honor. In the story "From the Root of a Shrub," a character explains that "a man without a job either fools around or becomes sick," emphasizing need for man to have work as way to define himself.[18]

Lack of honor can also be manifested in two significant forms: dependence on external aid and Westernization. In "The Deceptive Object," (1971), one who eats bread without shame "refers to someone who can work but does not work, and eats and lives off others."[19] This sentiment has been expressed by men who feel a growing dependency on international aid, coupled with an inability to achieve self-sufficiency due to lack of opportunity. In "The Brains of the Family," the protagonist laments because "the atmosphere in [his] home became so Westernized that he felt [he] lost his honour, his dark, heavy dignified moustache seemed soiled."[20] Political leaders such as Muhammad Daud Khan linked honor to Afghan sovereignty. Daud is well known for his political poem using the eagle as a "symbol of freedom and indifference towards the dictates and politics of either the West or East."[21] The poem urged Afghans to be "free like eagles," to retain their dignity, and to cease their pleas for assistance from foreign powers.[22] This is significant in that many stories during the period of Soviet occupation (1979–1989) depicted the discourses of the day — replete with contradictions based on the tensions between Afghan and Western ideas.[23]

The *Landay*, or short poem, also offers insight to the prominence of honor in Afghan culture. The term *Landay*— literally meaning "the short one" in Pashto — is a brief poem of two verse lines of nine and thirteen syllables respectively. *Landays* "frequently punctuate conversations where it is used as a quote or a saying, lending support to a feeling or idea,"[24] and, in so doing, provide special insight into Afghan society in turmoil.[25] *Landays* can also be viewed as an act of resistance "because [the Pashtun woman's] melodies tirelessly glorify three themes that taste of blood ... love, honor, and death."[26] Of these three, emphasis rests on the honor code, and by extension the importance of adhering to traditional gender roles, particularly the role of men as protectors of the family and defenders of honor. These *landays* use battle as a metaphor to represent honor lost or gained:

> May you be found cut to pieces by a trenchant sword,
> But may news of your dishonor never reach my ears![27]

> May you be blackened by gunpowder and dyed in blood;
> But may you not return from the battlefield and in disgrace.[28]

> It is well that you are wounded in battle, my love!
> Now I shall walk proudly.[29]

Demonstrating Agency

Afghan women expressed confidence in their strength, demonstrating agency across all aspects of their lives. They recognized that they were being measured against standards that did little to reflect their realities. As a result, many felt anger at having been underestimated. Many others began to doubt their own abilities, judging themselves more harshly through the eyes of a critical world. These women were extremely vocal and articulate in discussions of agency. Many women — Afghan and non–Afghan — demonstrate their own agency in ways that outsiders cannot see — and therefore are not able to judge.

Most felt that the world sees them as weak, and they wanted an opportunity to correct this image. A few examples of this include:

- The world did not think well of Afghan women, that is why they wanted to help and save them. But Afghan women are stronger than outsiders know.

- They think Afghan women are weak. This image influenced work on women in Afghanistan.

- Afghan women are oppressed and weak! This is not accurate, but the world wants to see us this way.

- I don't think the image was good. They thought we could not struggle for our rights without their help. We are happy for help, but we want to direct the changes.

- The world thought Afghan women were prisoners. In a way this was true, but we are able to survive as we have over the years. We are not only victims.

In this context, the *chaddari* came up repeatedly as the Western symbol for their perceived weakness of Afghan women, and the source of Western pity. One woman explained that the world views Afghan women "just like animals in *bourkas*." Another said: "Foreigners always want to ask about *bourka*. It is the most important thing for them. Afghan women do not see the *bourka*. Foreigners only see *bourka*."

Afghan women articulated strongly that they want to be the ones to decide on the images. "One day we will have the power to change this image and people will listen!" one woman stated. These women felt strongly that the pervasive images were "through the eyes of other countries" and had little to do with Afghan priorities. "Their images are their own and we do not interfere," one woman explained. "But as we see it, they are far away from the truth." This image, many women explained, should be one that reflects who Afghan women are, what they want, and "how [they] would like to see [their] society." "We don't want our men to be owned by anyone," one woman stated. Many women expressed that they feel solidarity with their Afghan brothers and would prefer that women not be viewed as "in need of saving from Afghan men." Most women felt that they were artificially juxtaposed

A woman in her courtyard, Paghman.

against men. Facile analyses of women as unhappy victims and men as tyrants and terrorists were hard to combat.

On the part of the men, of the 31 who felt that their agency had been denied in the aid process, 71 pecent were of rural origins. Here the data differs slightly. For the other categories, married men appeared to be the most discontent. Regarding agency, men — and women — who were unmarried expressed the greatest concern (55 pecent and 44 pecent, respectively). Rural women comprised the majority (67 pecent). Most of the women in this category had no education (62 pecent), while the majority of men (71 pecent) were in the highest category of education. The distinction between rural and urban perspectives is likely a result of the displacement felt by those of rural origins. This group lacks the social safety net of community and kin that rural lives provide. Without such ties, the rural population's sense of disillusionment could be greater.

Afghan men articulated that they wanted to feel "as men" and they were actively denied this. Many cited a lack of respect and the perception that they were "under the authority of others." They also expressed a sense that interventions did not recognize men's and women's place and that they were imposing an alien world view on Afghanistan. "We want a free Afghanistan without the intervention of foreigners," one man explained. He was not alone in his opinion. Many Afghan men in this category felt strongly that they should be the ones to decide the direction of the new Afghanistan, and that the aid apparatus should adhere to their views.

These men expressed exasperation with the images they felt the world had of them. One man explained: "I think world image is that Afghan women are looked down upon. Oppressed and helpless. And men are tyrants, ignorant and bad persons." Another elaborated:

> World image is absolutely wrong and is not truth.... They think that Afghan woman lives as a slave in the society. They think Afghan man doesn't value Afghan woman, that man doesn't know her as a human. World image about Afghan man is also not correct. They know Afghan man as a tyrant, extremist, and supporter of terrorism and war but they support woman, peace and construction.

Another elaborated: "The image about Afghan women is completely far away from truth. They think woman is slave of man and it is man who always oppresses women and takes their rights." Another frequent response was the concern that the rest of the world did not want to support a free and stable Afghanistan, but was looking to occupy the country to meet their own needs. An elderly man had this to say: "I do not know [what image the world has] but somehow they think we are not good and this is why some of our freedoms are under their control." In this line of thinking, many men expressed concern that the world did not support or respect Islam as a religion. One young man expressed the views of many when he said "the world doesn't want a real Islamic regime in Afghanistan and also real Muslim men and women."

A young man of rural origins expressed frustration that media images and international organizations have resulted in pressure for social change. This pressure has not given room for Afghanistan to advance at its own pace and to foster change that is sustainable. Facile labels — such as "backwards" — erroneously referred to the perhaps slower pace of change that Afghans desired when compared to the fast-paced aid apparatus. He hoped that Afghanistan will be given the room it needs to make change on its own terms. He continued to say the following:

> It can be like a pressure when most of the countries of the world came here and they wanted us to do something regarding women's rights. Before five years a woman was like a machine to work at home and have children. Now it is changing. Of course it takes time. We are not in Europe. This is Afghanistan. Maybe men will say there is equality because they know that this is what they are expected to say. But they know it is not true.

Men were not opposed to changes, "as long as they are not against what Afghans want." And yet, no one had asked them what they want. They asked to be respected "as Afghans"— meaning within the context of their culture and religion. One man said: "Both 'gender' — man and woman — should have their own life." I noted the use of "gender" in this sense, particularly as it was used in English. Another man put it this way: "For Afghanistan I wish peace, safety, Islam, Afghan-ness, freedom. A complete free country which shouldn't be occupied by others." When asked about his hope for the future, one Afghan man said: "I am hoping to be optimistic, but men need some attention still. Changes are harder for them."

In the context of conflict and the aftermath, addressing gendered inequalities is best accomplished through a contextualized understanding of the situation. Working on gender issues (in the robust and genuine sense of the term) will ensure that men and women's needs are taken into account in a way that reflects their priorities, roles, and goals. These concepts need to be defined from within the country. In Afghanistan, perhaps country and context experts should outnumber conflict experts. It is far easier to learn the latter, but no knowledge of the latter can substitute for a lack of the former.

There is a notable difference in the data between the demographics of men and women regarding issues of agency. Men with generally higher levels of education felt that they had been misrepresented and denied agency in aid interventions, while the bulk of women who shared this view were those with no education. The same trend is true for dissatisfaction with aid interventions. Men who noted their dissatisfaction with aid interventions come from a largely better-educated group, while women who shared their sentiments generally had no education at all. This presents an interesting trend. It appears that men with higher levels of education are better able — or more willing — to articulate their dissatisfaction with the issues above than those with less education. The opposite is true for women. There appears to be an inverse relationship between women's levels of education and their levels of concern with the themes of aid and agency — and also with perceptions of violence. Women with no education are still able to articulate their needs and concerns, and demonstrate their own agency and a level of consciousness that one would not normally associate with uneducated women. These women also expressed concerns that they had been singled out for support because of the pervasive view from the aid apparatus that they were victims in need of saving. Facile analyses of women as victims and men as perpetrators serve only to alienate those men who are supporters and who could be mobilized for women's participation. It did not require any education at all for women to sense this.

One finding in the category of dissatisfaction with aid deserves particular attention. Of the 121 people interviewed, 104 (44 men and 60 women) clearly stated that their problems stemmed from the neglect of men in aid interventions. This is 86 percent of all of those interviewed — a significant majority. Based on the data, the significance of this oversight cannot be overstated.

A discussion group consisting of women of rural origins of varying ethnicities also expressed issues of agency. They all came to Kabul in order to benefit from aid activities and economic opportunities. The women explained that their perceptions of such opportunities in Kabul did not at all match their present realities. They felt disillusioned and not entirely confident that they will be able to become self-sufficient. Nonetheless, these women preferred to remain in Kabul as their village homes had nothing to offer them anymore. The women in this group shared stories and anecdotes to illustrate their conditions. They turned to me very early in the session and one of them asked me why other countries had abandoned Afghanistan "like they did before."[30]

One woman eloquently expressed sentiments that were echoed by other participants: "I think other countries pity us, pity Afghan women. You should tell them that if there had been peace in Afghanistan, our country and people would be just as educated and successful as any other." This was followed by another woman who said: "Tell the world that Afghan women are very strong and they will do anything for the future of their country and their children."

Despite their displays of strength, the women of this group then went on to share stories with each other of difficulties at home. They explained that their domestic lives had become increasingly strained in the last months, contrary to what they would have expected. The women in this group all have husbands or male family members who are not entirely supporters of their participation but feel that they have no choice but to send their women out to support the family.

One woman told of the negotiations she regularly undertook with her husband in order to have permission to attend trainings. She explained that, at first, he gave his permission because there was no other source of income for the family. But in recent months, his increased frustration and feelings of uselessness had taken a toll on her. She thus had made arrangements to split the little financial assistance she received from the institution with her husband in order to buy his compliance. She feared that this would not be sufficient for long as he has already started asking for more than half of the money, which would not leave enough to ensure the survival of the family.

Another woman in the group — a widow — shared her story. She explained that her 11-year-old son forbade her to leave the house, saying it would shame him if she were to be seen "wandering in the streets." She argued with him, explaining that there was no alternative and in order to support the family and provide food, she must take advantage of the only opportunity available to her. His response was: "If you want to leave the house, you'll have to kill me first." She respected his wishes and delayed her participation in the NGO program until her son was enrolled in school. Even then, many months into her participation, he did not think she left the house during the day.

Rethinking Aid

Afghan women and men frequently stated that they were not pleased with the progress made to date by aid institutions and many felt that the money could have been better spent and with farther-reaching effects. Afghans generally felt resentment for aid interventions. In one study, an Afghan man said: "We are really angry at all these foreign NGOs ... they conduct lots of surveys but nothing happens. There are more NGOs than people in Afghanistan. They should either work harder or ... go ... home."[31] Indeed, many of those interviewed shared this sentiment.

In Afghanistan motivation has been crippled by the expectation that aid interventions would provide for the people. It is important to view the dissatisfaction with interventions in the current context of overall hostility towards aid institutions. This frustration had been brewing in Afghanistan starting in late 2002 when Afghans began to articulate dissatisfaction with the army of international aid institutions — and their international standards of living — that were failing to make visible and sustainable changes in Afghanistan. This anger moved from the streets to the Afghan cabinet with the appointment of Dr. Ramazan Bashardost as Minister of Planning in 2004. Bashardost coined the now oft-cited term *NGO-ism* to describe the failure of the aid apparatus to assist Afghanistan, opting instead to foster corruption and increase their own wealth. Bashardost further accused NGOs of "economic terrorism" and blamed them for the misuse of the country's scant development funding.[32] This message played well to the Afghan public, particularly in Kabul, and was replayed during the riots in the summer of 2006.

Similar to Bashardost's view, many men felt that aid interventions had misused and withheld funds from Afghanistan. One older man put it this way: "We want those donations which the world is giving to Afghanistan today to be given to the people that are entitled to it, not to their agents." By agents, he was referring to aid institutions. "They only saw one layer of society," one man explained. It was therefore not a surprise that promised changes would not reach the people who needed them most. Indeed, the theme of empty promises was oft-repeated. One man expressed it this way: "They haven't done very good things yet, just promises of complete freedom. They prepared the opportunities for working. And now we wait. The rights which have to be given unfortunately haven't been given." Another added that aid institutions have "done their work hypocritically." Another stated that the Afghan government "should be based on its people, not on international organizations."

Many men also expressed their dissatisfaction with aid institutions through the lens of women. The general sentiment was that these institutions failed to understand what constitutes Afghan culture when it came to women. As a result, institutions abused women "by disrespecting their role and religion." Another man stated: "They haven't done anything necessary for women so far. They analyzed women's rights incorrectly. They have no respect for Afghan men and women." This discussion raised sensitivities, especially when the men blamed the aid apparatus for "unveiling our women" and for leading people away from Islam. One man put it this way: "As UN urges, women fight with their husbands for their rights. This is not correct."[33] It was not unusual for men to feel angered and emotional during this segment of the interview. Their frustration was apparent, particularly in the following line: "All women's activities ... just they talk about democracy and women's rights without any clear vision for changing." Another elaborated: "In the area of importing or bringing foreign culture and tradition, international organizations have bad effect on Afghan women."

· Women also believed that their participation in aid interventions "has created problems for women." These institutions, they explained, "tried to change the way men think," and they have failed. One woman explained that the agenda to "make men and women's rights equal" is not possible and is far too provocative for Afghanistan. And these institutions apparently contradicted themselves when they offered opportunities only for women. Many women explained that women are the only ones who are given opportunities for work and trainings, and therefore the survival of the family becomes their responsibility. One young woman from Kabul elaborated: "[These] acts have just increased the gap between men and women."

Many felt that aid progress was limited, and that promises have not been met. "They haven't done that much anyway," one elderly woman stated. "To make real progress will take much more time." The little that has been done "is only in a very symbolic way." One woman explained that if she measures against promises made, "the future is in ruin." Another elaborated that "women have opportunities presented like treats, but they cannot access them." One old woman of rural origins lamented: "I am told that we are equal now, but I am not sure yet." This sentiment was reinforced by another woman who asked: "Now women have rights on paper, but what do they do with them?" Other women expressed it this way:

- The organizations are established to help women, but then they work for their own promotion.

- There is a lot of attention to women on paper, but I am not sure if it is helping women in real life.

- Promises haven't been implemented. They trick both men and women of Afghanistan into believing that the world will come save them and change everything.

- What have they done yet for Afghan men and women? What good things could the future hold?

- We all fought for freedom, and now we are told to believe that there is freedom.

Many women also felt that their situation was an old issue and "the world does not want to know of Afghan women now." Another woman elaborated:

"I do not think the world cares about Afghanistan anymore. They are tired of saving them and now look elsewhere." These women generally agreed that the aid apparatus entered Afghanistan with much fanfare, re-arranged things, and subsequently made a swift exit. Many women felt that the hidden agenda of interventions was "to change what is Afghan culture" and to focus on "rights that are not in Islam." These women argued that their rights are in fact safe-guarded in Islam and that they are not for aid institutions to give.

A discussion with one group reinforced dissatisfaction with aid, emphasiz-ing the need to operate on Afghan terms. This group brought together the other ethnic groups—Hazara, Tajik, Uzbek, Nuristani, and so on—as these are gen-erally considered less conservative and have, at times, been more closely aligned with each other than with the Pashtun community.[34] This group was comprised of women who were originally from Kabul and other urban areas. Two of the women present were from Jalalabad, and three were Kabuli in origin.

The conversation in this group focused on pushing for progress, and the consequences of doing so. The women used examples from Afghan history to illustrate their sentiments and to demonstrate the Afghan population's reac-tion to strong pushes for social change. Below is a sample of the conversation and select quotes from the women in their discussion.

> SWEETA: In the Soviet time when they started to establish literacy classes for women in the villages, everyone reacted very strongly. Village leaders warned everyone not to have it, period.
>
> LIDA: I always insist on the fact that we cannot copy any other modernity to our country. We need to translate international ways into our own lan-guage, into our own context, and into our own culture.

The women also raised the subject of the word "gender" and its mean-ing. These women were not able to offer a concrete meaning of the word but did quickly share its strong associations with a foreign agenda. The women could not define gender, but they were cognizant that it was the right word to use in the presence of foreigners to signify progress.

The discussion continued:

> STORAI: People do not know what is this gender. My father is an educated man, but he sometimes asks me "What is this gender, gender, gender always you are talking about?" Even in educated families this is a new word. And in my family, we do not know what it means. Only that we hear it very much.
>
> SARA: I think it's not only a new word in Afghanistan, but in many other countries....
>
> HOMAIRA: But we are copying a model from outside. Copying is not the solution, I think.

STORAI: Men are saying that gender means taking the power from the men and giving it to the women.

SWEETA: My husband is angry with all of these trainings. He says: "Only training for you and nothing for me. And gender means I sit at home and you go out and do everything. And what are these international agencies doing? And it's a Western idea, and it's bad, and it doesn't respect our culture, and it's not Muslim."

LIDA: [International agencies] say that they cannot find any Afghan expert that knows about gender, so they have no choice but to bring someone from a different culture. What we should do is find those people who know Afghan culture, not another culture, and train them in gender: What does gender mean? What does gender want from the people? What is our responsibility to gender?

Indeed, researchers have noted that Afghans are currently feeling culturally displaced and are forced to renegotiate identities and gender roles. This sense of despair is in reality a frustration that while Afghans continue to struggle for physical survival, they risk being overridden by an aid apparatus that imposes hasty solutions before giving Afghans time to consider their role in the process.[35]

7

This Is Afghanistan

Both Afghan women and men feel lost in the new Afghanistan. They struggle to find new places in the gender order. For women, the sprinkling of seemingly liberated success stories appease the public, but these are few. In the words of one woman, the aid apparatus has "led one woman to a comfortable life and has led thousands of them to disaster." While this might seem extreme, it remains important to hear Afghan voices and views as it is their perceptions and experiences that will ultimately determine the success of this political project. To this end, it was essential to compare views of women and men from the same household to determine how things have changed and what effects they might have at that level. Analysis at the family level is relevant because it demonstrates the importance of not extracting women from their families and contexts.

Inja Afghanistan Ast[1]

The oft-repeated phrase, *Inja Afghanistan Ast* meaning "This is Afghanistan," was used both by men and women frequently to punctuate a phrase. Women used it in exasperation to rationalize "bad things" that happened to them. Men used this line to justify "the situation of women" and as a counter to strong pushes for change and importing alien ideologies. "This is Afghanistan," I was told on many occasions. "Those things just don't work here." Both women and men conveyed a sense that because "This is Afghanistan," things were not going to change — and certainly not in the way that the aid apparatus expected. It was therefore important to compare not only women and men as separate entities but also women and men from the same household in order to determine how they define what Afghanistan is within their own households. The profiles of couples reveal the differing dynamics between men and women animating each household.

A man with an Afghan flag greets the arrival of foreigners, Nuristan.

Couple 1: Fatima and Amanullah, Wife and Husband

Fatima is in her early 30s. She has had less than two years of education. Amanullah is 41 years old and has had seven years of education. The couple is originally from rural Afghanistan but they moved to Kabul two years ago to live with Amanullah's brother in hopes of finding work and providing for their three children. Fatima explained that Amanullah's brother, her brother-in-law, is bitter about the extensive focus on women. He is not happy that Fatima attends trainings and tries to convince Amanullah to prevent her from going out. Many fights have broken out in the household as a result. Amanullah is beginning to think that participating in trainings is not such a good idea. Neither Fatima nor Amanullah are particularly pleased with the efforts of the aid institutions. Amanullah is concerned that Fatima will start to respect him less with all these new ideas she is gaining from the training program. Fatima complained: "You tell me what my rights are, but what is the point if he won't give them to me? He should understand them first!"

Couple 2: Maryam and Alam, Wife and Husband

Alam is 37 years old and has had several years of education in Kabul. Maryam is 31 and has completed primary school. They have been married for 12 years. Maryam believes that, according to Afghan culture and traditions, women are respected and protected in Afghanistan, but that things have deteriorated in recent years. She believes that men are responsible for women and must provide for the family. Alam feels that it is a man's duty to guide women. "Women are innocent creatures," he said. "They need protection from other men. Men are in upper level [more] than women." Alam feels that institutions are undermining men's traditional role. He explained that aid institutions are changing "women's minds against their husbands and are encouraging them negatively." Alam further elaborated that the aid apparatus is interfering in family issues. Maryam is concerned because "not much is done for men." She feels that this could cause problems for her at home.

Couple 3: Zainab and Ahmadi, Wife and Husband

Zainab and Ahmadi are from central Afghanistan. Their livelihood was based on agriculture. They are not happy to be in Kabul and find that they do not like the direction Afghanistan is moving in in these new times. Zainab sees a lot of violence against women around her. She sees this as a new manifestation of an old struggle, but the difference today is that the "position of women is better than men in the society. Priority is given to women in every

Two young performers celebrate Afghan Independence Day (19 August), Kabul.

aspect of opportunities." Ahmadi is a day laborer and is able to bring home an irregular income. He is still hopeful that he will find more stable work. As long as he is working, he says that he is happy that Zainab is learning a new skill. He sees that other men are cruel and angry, and he does not think this will happen to him.

Couple 4: Storai and Hekmat, Daughter and Father

Storai is Hekmat's daughter. She is 21 years old and is not yet married. There are concerns that she is getting too old for marriage. Once she marries, she will have to stop studying and participating in trainings. Storai has witnessed how changing regimes have affected gender relations and have led to increased violence at home. It happens in her home. She does not want to get married, she says. Hekmat recognizes that there is more conflict and argument at home these days. He hopes for a day where men and women can return to their Afghan ways and respect their traditions and religion. He is not sure that day will come.

Couple 5: Lida and Fawad, Wife and Husband

Both Lida and Fawad are from the countryside. They have no education. Both feel very strongly that Islam provides the answers to managing changes that are taking place in Afghanistan today, particularly those between men and women. Fawad feels that it is his job to support his family and provide for them. He prefers that Lida stay at home. Unfortunately, Lida is participating in a vocational skills training program and he is at home. Although aid institutions provide his family with an opportunity to earn an income, he is not happy with this new international presence. He says that "they have done nothing for men" and he would prefer a return to "Afghan ways" and an Afghan pace of change. Fawad feels that Afghans are not in control of their country, and he is concerned.

Couple 6: Sweeta and Payman, Wife and Husband

Sweeta and Payman are in their 30s. She has had a few years of education. Payman has had nearly 10 years of education and is a teacher by trade, although currently unemployed. Sweeta feels that Payman's profession as a teacher has helped her to have greater access to education and training. But she knows that Payman is unhappy that he is not working. The aid apparatus has done nothing for men, she says. "My husband says that they make men angry when they do nothing for them and only offer opportunities to women. He is a teacher so he understands how people think about these things." Sweeta feels that recent changes have brought "uproar to families." Payman agrees that he has seen an increase in family conflict because women are no longer satisfied "with what men expected from them."

Couple 7: Sara and Waheed, Daughter and Father

Sara is 18 years old. She is not in school, and this upsets her. She says that women in Afghanistan still cannot study and work, despite what they are told to believe. Her father appears to be an advocate of education for women and men, but he does not think the current climate is conducive for Sara to go to school. He explained that "since the Americans came, we are told that men and women have freedom and can work outside and learn," but he feels that the situation is still unstable. Both Sara and Waheed feel that things were better for men and women "before the Americans came." Sara says that "some men think that women are being cared for more than men. But the reality is that both men and women suffer."

Couple 8: Masooda and Fayzal, Sister and Brother

Masooda lives with Fayzal, her older brother, and his family. She is concerned that men are not getting training and are therefore becoming much more rigid and traditional. Her brother is one of those men who could benefit from training "to become open-minded," she says. Fayzal thinks that a woman should be satisfied with her role as wife and mother and that women today are asking for too much. Aid institutions have encouraged women to leave the house, he explains. These institutions do nothing for men, he says, "only women get training but then they stay at home and it is useless." Women should stay inside for their own protection, he believes. Masooda is his responsibility, and she is getting too many ideas already.

Couple 9: Frozan and Waisuddin, Wife and Husband

Frozan is 35 years old. She is illiterate. Her husband, Waisuddin, is more than ten years her senior. He grew up in Jalalabad and attended six years of school. Frozan receives food aid that she hands over to Waisuddin to distribute to the family. Her job, she says, is to "make the society by raising good children." She would rather not be the only one bringing home food. Waisuddin has become more strict in recent years. "Women must obey what their husbands command," he says. Women are safer under the *chaddari*, he explained. He'd rather that the women in his family not leave the house at all, particularly his wife. Frozan's new role as the breadwinner has made her "stand in front of her husband," Waisuddin says.[2] He believes that this new influence is taking Afghans away from Islam. Aid institutions "keep people away from Islamic prayers since they give them money and they forget to pray."

Couple 10: Safia and Mirwais, Daughter and Father

Safia is 19 years old and has had three years of education. Her father, Mirwais, has had eight years of education. Safia sees violence in her family and feels that violence has always been a part of gender relations, but it takes different forms in the different periods of history. She explains that "women argue with their husbands because they are not allowed to go outside. That caused their husbands to beat them." Safia says that "the government has set some rules that men can't beat their wives and they no longer have power to be cruel" but she is not sure most men know about these rules. Mirwais thinks that the world does not have a good image of Afghan men. And he feels that aid institutions have not helped things at home because "most men think that organizations are creating distance between men and women by encouraging women negatively." He is not sure what the future of Afghanistan holds.

Dar be Dar: Including Men

Interviews conducted with Afghan women and men revealed a discontentment with the operations of aid institutions, and a sense that the social order had been disrupted in ways that have negative effects for women. Men recognize that they are not necessarily a focus of attention, and that the economic survival of the family now depends on the woman as she is offered greater opportunities. Women have noted that men are increasingly becoming angry and impatient as they continue to be denied the traditional role of provider in the family. A 20-year-old woman explained that "organizations provide opportunities only for women ... so the women have to step out of the house in order for the family to survive." A woman in her late 20s elaborated: "Women are allowed to work. Actually, there are *opportunities* for work. Allowing women to work is up to the husband. But if he cannot find work, he has no choice but to let his wife work."

Many women interviewed felt that the burden of supporting the family was placed on them and that many of them did not want it. These women expressed their preference for the male members of the family to work. Women explained that they took advantage of existing opportunities because there were

An old man with a piece of bread from a nearby picnic, Paghman.

no opportunities for men to earn a living, as stated above. Thus circumstance — not choice — drove these women. They did not necessarily feel empowered by this responsibility nor were they happy with their new freedom. In fact, they recognized the greater risks they faced in fulfilling traditionally male roles.

Almost all the men noted that women were prioritized in aid interventions. They generally agreed that aid institutions "did nothing" for them. While they complained to their wives, they were concerned about making more public complaints because their wives were bringing home money — which many of them were receiving. However, men expressed that they were offered very little in terms of services and support; therefore, they had no choice but to rely on their women to access training and economic opportunities and to share them with the rest of the family. This denied them their traditional role as provider and insulted their honor, many stated. One man described his situation as *Dar be Dar*, meaning being "door to door." This Afghan expression describes that of a man "in a state of desperation because all doors of opportunity are closed before him."[3] This sentiment characterizes the sense of desperation felt by many men, and the pervasive view that their honor has been insulted by reducing them to beggars. For many men, the insult to their honor came when their wives were able to find work and support the family and they were not. Indeed, this gets to the core of what it means to be a man in Afghanistan — and in most countries, in fact. There is a link between this aspect of male identity and violent behavior.

Men expressed concerns that aid institutions were encouraging women to speak out against their husbands and deliberately disrupting the household hierarchy. They also noted that women were promised dramatic life changes, but none of this has materialized. Expectations were raised, and commitments were not delivered. Many men also felt that aid institutions promoted change that was contrary to Islam. One man believed that institutions are "unveiling our women." Another man explained: "In the area of importing or bringing foreign culture and tradition, international organizations have bad effect on Afghan women." A man in his late 20s from Kabul elaborated that "sometimes [aid institutions] are pushing hard for change that is fast and big, and it is not sensible."

"Most men are not very satisfied with the organizations," a man explained, "they feel that these organizations are interfering in family issues." Another man felt that "organizations are creating distance between men and women by encouraging women negatively." Many men expressed concern with the influence aid institutions have had on Afghan culture. They felt that the interventions deliberately sought to enforce Western codes of culture as superior to Afghan ways. "Aid organizations inspired foreign culture on our men. They introduced Afghan man incorrectly. And also they brought down their role in the family and society, so it caused difficulties and violences between men and women," one man explained. Again, many men reiterated the notion that aid institutions were stripping men of their rights and giving them to women. This belief reinforces the view that the concept of rights is a zero-sum game and that more rights for women leave men without any rights at all. The following are select quotes from men to illustrate these points:

- They have paid their most attention to women and have forgotten men.
- They don't take care of our poor men.
- In lots of things, more focus is on women than on men.
- Every time first a position is given to women.
- Organizations are not loyal on their promises with men.
- International organizations pave the ground for working for women. And always women are the first, before men.

- They don't do what they say for men.
- In comparison with women, they have done less for men.
- They have done nothing for men, hardly mentioned them. International organizations haven't paid attention to men's rights.

While the Western focus on Afghan "gender apartheid" centered around women, the role of men has indeed been ignored. It is far too simplistic to juxtapose men as oppressors against women as victims. Men in Afghanistan are actually a key part of the solution. And men have suffered as well. No one would dispute the focus on Afghan women, but it is women themselves who highlight the suffering of Afghan men. One Afghan researcher put it this way: "The wound of abandonment runs deep in them. Afraid to be vulnerable, fiercely independent, they hide their wounds. This is the way they have coped with unspeakable hardship and loss."[4]

Many women articulated that they would enjoy greater freedom — and feel more comfortable with the opportunities they have been given — if men were also engaged and employed. In the words of one young woman from Kabul: "Organizations gave opportunities for women to work in NGOs and out of the home. Men need these opportunities also." These women explained that women would be "happier" and "more free" if men were working. "We want our men to have jobs also so that they can allow us to work," a married women of rural origins explained. Others said: "Men are not working, so women are also kept at home," and "if all men had wealth and jobs, they would not interfere with the women as much as they do." If liberating women was truly the objective, the aid apparatus would have done better to start with men first. Women elaborated:

- They have supported men indirectly by providing jobs and giving trainings to their wives.
- I do not know what opportunities men have. I see many of them without opportunities.
- No men are really involved.
- They have promised to help men also, but they have not done anything.
- Men need to have opportunities like women now so they can work and feel proud.
- Men are suffering more than women right now.
- Internationals want to create work opportunities for women, but women cannot take men's position.

- They have done nothing for men, my father says.

- They have made things unequal between men because those who have *wasita*[5] and know people have gotten good jobs and the rest have not.

- Men who know some big people have found a job in the international NGOs.

Women expressed concern that the lack of support for men has made them increasingly angry. Many women explained that they would prefer that their husbands were given equal opportunities to participate in aid interventions and elaborated that their lives would be easier as a result. Some women noted an increased gap between men and women, and many women mentioned increased levels of violence as outcomes of this frustration. One woman expressed her husband's dissatisfaction with inequalities between opportunities for men and women. He felt men were overlooked in the efforts to help women. Another elaborated:

> Men have become sensitive about women's organizations. They believe that these organizations train women to stand against the laws and their husbands. Of course this is not true. It is actually what men think.

This reinforces the importance of *perception* over reality. Another woman explained that men are becoming "more aggressive and angry to women because organizations do not give them any attention." Women preferred that men be engaged in aid efforts alongside women, with an emphasis on families — not individuals. Another woman reiterated the same point: "Men are angry with international organizations because they only care about women. Men feel that they have dark futures."

Research revealed that both women and men were concerned with the image the world had of them — an image that they believe has been used to justify aid interventions. The repeated themes included a concern that aid institutions artificially separated women and men — even in cases where they wanted to work together to rebuild the country. Further, there was an overarching perception that aid programs seek to change what is Afghan culture. Both women and men were concerned that men were constructed as the enemy, and women were victims needing to be saved from men by outsiders. An Afghan woman explained: "The world thinks that Afghan women need their help and they need to be saved from Afghan men." An Afghan man elaborated that "most people in other countries believe that Afghan men are the ones who have taken the women's rights from them."

An Afghan man stated that the world must have had a bad image of Afghanistan, or their freedoms would not be under foreign control. A woman elaborated: "I do not think the image was good. If it was good, we would not have so many foreigners coming to say they are helping us." Despite this, many women are happy with aid apparatus support, but also felt that they would like to direct the changes. Based on these views, Afghanistan is in the first phase of its engagement with men — near neglect.

This Road Leads to Turkestan

This phrase was used in an interview with a man who felt particularly frustrated by the lack of progress in Afghanistan and disappointed in the aid apparatus. It is a common Afghan proverb meaning that a certain action will lead nowhere, or is useless.[6]

The following table displays a triangulation of the data gathered from interviews with Afghan women and men based on three large themes that appeared frequently during discussions. *Agency* refers to a sense that the interviewees' identity was misrepresented. This also reflects a denial of agency and a lack of contextualized analysis that certain respondents believe characterized interventions. The theme *violence* refers to references — direct or indirect — that were made by interviewees regarding increased levels of violence in their lives, or the fear of increased violence. The category *aid* represents those interviewees who expressed a level of dissatisfaction with aid interventions. Concrete examples of dissatisfaction include excessive focus on women, mismanaged or misdirected aid, failure to deliver on promises, raised expectations. Neglect of men in aid interventions began as a component of dissatisfaction with *aid* but then emerged as its own category because of its significance to the interviewees.

The table offers a comparison between men and women across the above three themes and in three demographic categories. Women and men are analyzed based on their geographic origins (rural, urban, Kabul) and their marital status (single, married, widowed) and their education levels (none, 1–6 years, more than 7 years) to determine if there are trends within particular demographic groups. These themes are the ones that women and men identified as the most significant issues.

Comparison Between Women and Men Across Three Themes

	Agency	Violence	Aid
Total	76	47	70
Total %	63%	39%	58%
Men Total	**31**	**14**	**32**

		Agency	Violence	Aid
Region:	Kabul	8	3	6
	Rural	22	8	23
	Urban	1	3	3
Marital Status:	Single	17	6	13
	Married	14	8	19
	Widower	0	0	0
Education:	None	1	1	2
	1–6 years	8	4	11
	7+ years	22	9	19
Women Total		45	33	38
Region:	Kabul	13	11	11
	Rural	30	21	26
	Urban	2	1	1
Marital Status:	Single	20	11	14
	Married	18	20	18
	Widower	7	2	6
Education:	None	28	24	26
	1–6 years	7	6	5
	7+ years	10	3	7

Of those men who expressed dissatisfaction with aid programs and agencies, the majority are from rural areas (72 percent), married (59 percent), and have had seven or more years of education (59 percent). For women, the majority are also from rural areas (68 percent), and married (47 percent), but those with no education felt more strongly about aid issues (68 percent) than did those with increased education, as previously addressed.

In an office I frequently visited, three employees began an impromptu discussion in my presence, expressing curiosity about my research. Alam was a Pashtun man in his late 20s from Wardak with four years of education. He was married, and had recently become a father. When asked about the role of women in Afghanistan, he became visibly uncomfortable and said he did not want to answer. He was also not comfortable talking about his wife, but he did tell the group that his wife had six years of education. He laughed when the comment was made that his wife was more educated than he is. "My wife is not working," Alam said. "If she said she wanted to work, it would not be allowed according to tribal regulations. It is this way. I cannot explain it."

Alam's wife wears the *chaddari*. He emphasized that this is an important part of the Pashtun tradition. But then he went on to say this:

> The chaddari is not important, but what is important for a woman is modesty and reputation and to have a good character. If she decides tomorrow that she does not want to wear it, it's no problem for me.

The other men in the room snickered at this response. They did not believe him. They knew each other well and were able to recognize each other's dishonesty.

Aman was in his mid–20s, a Tajik. He worked as a driver. He spoke more freely of his wife: "She studied up to 8-class and is at home. She is not working. First she doesn't want to work. But if she wanted I would allow." The two other men in the room said that he did not answer honestly. They did not believe him. Aman smiled sheepishly. He continued to talk about the *chaddari*:

> My grandfather said my wife should use chaddari. My wife wasn't using chaddari before. He died three days ago and now I decide if she wears it or not. But she knows that she has to wear it out of respect for my grandfather.

Ahmadi was a 30-year-old Hazara man. He was the most vocal of the three, and also the most willing to talk about these delicate issues with a non–Afghan woman. He said:

> There is equality of rights between men and women. Woman is respectable and has a top position in our society because woman is mother and wife. There is a Dari saying: the second mother is our country. So this is how much we respect our women.

Ahmadi continued to talk about the role of religion in Afghanistan: "We are Muslim so we respect that. And also the customs of Afghanistan are important to us."

Ahmadi was the most comfortable talking about his wife:

> My wife is not working. But she doesn't want to work. She takes care of the children. Most of the women in this country want to have children. It's not a pressure from the husbands to have children. There is not any limitation on my wife. But she is from a conservative family. My wife was using chaddari before she married. But sometimes she doesn't wear chaddari, but only chador. If she doesn't want to wear it, I will decide at that time. In Afghanistan the joint family system is important. All sides must be respected. If an elder says that my wife must do something, she must do it.

These three men approached me of their own accord and began a discussion that appeared to be new to them. The questions stimulated much debate, thought, and even discomfort. The relevance of this conversation with men was that they took the initiative to raise these issues with me. While in some instances it was obvious that two of the men were trying to tell me what they thought I might want to hear, this was quickly corrected by the other participants. This group of men was also noteworthy because they represent three different ethnic groups and could have opposing opinions, particularly from the Pashtun man, and even more so when discussing women. Further, these men shared one important thing that none of the other men interviewed have — these men are all gainfully employed (as driver, guard, and "fixer"[7]). Regardless of type of employment, these men were all the authority figures at home because they were fulfilling their traditional roles. Their wives did not work, and none of them felt that they necessarily had any trouble at home. They agreed that they have unquestioned authority because they are male, and that they were fulfilling their obligations under that role.

The following table provides a comparison between Afghan men and women, non–Afghan policy-makers and policy implementers (referred to below as *aid*) and specialists, and Afghan policy-makers and policy implementers and specialists. The three themes that emerged from the data are compared based on their frequency. These themes emerged in all categories, demonstrating that there are large trends and patterns in opinions, regardless of people's particular groupings or affiliations.

Comparison Across Groups and Themes

	# Interviewed	Agency	Violence	Aid
Afghan Women & Men				
Total	121	76	47	70
Total %	100%	63%	39%	58%
Afghan Aid/ Specialists				
Total	25	19	14	25
Total %	100%	76%	59%	100%
Non-Afghan Aid/ Specialists				
Total	20	16	9	19
Total %	100%	78%	43%	95%

Of the 25 Afghan aid and specialists, 19 (76 percent) believed that men had been neglected in aid interventions. For the non–Afghan aid and specialists, 78 percent (16 of 20) believed that men's needs were neglected. Again, these findings resonate with the data from Afghan men and women — that the perception that men have been neglected is a powerful force that could be destabilizing aid interventions. This crude analysis serves a purpose. It presents us with a snapshot of the frequency of various perspectives. However, it is the voices themselves that should resonate most strongly in this case.

> International aid has a long and controversial record in Afghanistan. The wrong kinds of aid have at times created perverse incentives leading to renewed conflict. In the future, donors and aid agencies must be more self-critical and aware of these potentially negative effects.[8]

Working Drop by Drop

Qatra qatra darya mesha
Drop by drop, water becomes a river.

This Afghan expression has been employed as a saying used to advance the women's movement. It advocates slow, gradual change. In this vein, it is important to observe Afghan women drop by drop in order to better understand the significance of the changes in their lives over time.

The following are life stories from select women who were interviewed.[9] These women all felt the need to talk about their lives in order to contextualize their experiences. Many women began the interviews with stories of their past as a way to illustrate their unhappiness in the present and the extent to which their lives have not improved. "I want to tell you about my tragic life," one woman said. "I've spent days in hunger, nights in the darkness," added another. "Maybe you know about the life of an Afghan woman, filled with that much pain and difficulty that I'm not able to express it." There is more sadness that characterizes these stories, and noticeably less hope. There is also a hint of disappointment in the lack of changes in their lives in recent

A woman sits on the edge of Band-i-Amir, Bamiyan.

years. In fact, these women felt that their expectations were raised and now their hopes are further thwarted. These women are "wondering how to continue [their] life." One woman expressed her pain strongly: "I have a baby that I can't feed. There is no milk in my breasts." Their stories speak to these themes.

Zachaha

Our family consists of 12 people. We are four families who live in one house. We live in one room. Most of our family is women and small children. I am not literate. Because of the war, we moved from one side to another, so I couldn't study. With much difficulty we spent six months in Pakistan. We spent our time knitting rugs so we could provide a little food to keep us alive. I lost a daughter during the war, but now that we have peace in our country I want to live in peace and comfort. I've already suffered a lot.

Laila

During the fighting between parties, we moved to many different places to escape the violence. We were in Mazar-i-Sharif for about seven years, but we were not comfortable when the Taliban captured the city. They killed people, cut hands and legs, genocide and many more things happened. They also killed one of my sons. Then we secretly left Mazar and came to Kabul City. But unfortunately some other problems came into being ... the difficultly of paying for house rent, material, food. Prices got higher because people are coming back to their homeland. I live in one of my relatives' house for free. But life with them is difficult for me. I don't have a house of my own. I live in a room that doesn't have windows. This is only a small part of my painful story.

Habiba

I want to tell you a little about my life. I hope that you won't get tired of my life story. We have passed very difficult days and severity in Afghanistan. Maybe you have watched it on TV that how difficult was life in Afghanistan. We passed our life with poverty and didn't have anything to eat for many years. I have a son who lost his hand. We Afghan women suffered and passed our lives with many difficulties. Lots of Afghan women are illiterate or not literate enough. There is nobody to help us. I am wondering about the future. I am a woman with many problems in this time. There is no one now to help us, even God.

Dil Jan

I had a good and comfortable life, but all the fightings have destroyed my life. Afghanistan has been a country of war for many years, more than half of its population is living in crisis and poverty. I'm from the poor women of this part of the world. My husband cannot find work. My children are very young. I don't have any breadwinner at all. I need help to make my life better.

Nadera

During 23 years of war, the economic, social, and political situation was not good. We suffered a lot, and we had to live in difficult situation. Now in Kabul City, the situation is getting better, but not in other provinces. There are still warlords and gunmen in other provinces. My economic situation isn't good. I became a widow 16 years ago and my oldest child is 15 years old. I want my children to get educated and also find money to feed them and improve my economic situation so my children serve their country and society, not to destroy it and be away from education.

Sohila

I am a mother of four children and owner of nothing at all. My husband got lost during the cruel Taliban's regime. Except my four children I have to take care of my husband's old parents. I live only in the hope of my husband's return to home, but there is not any news of him recently. I actually don't know if he is alive or dead. Right now I am the only breadwinner for the family of seven people. Nowadays the rent of the house that I'm living in has increased, I can't afford it.

Rogull

Now let me tell you about my life. I got married when I was 15 years old, my husband was 25 years older than me. Now that 10 years has passed from my marriage, I haven't seen any good behavior from him. He puts a lot of pressure on me and my children. I am really tired of my life. My sons are seven-year-old twins and my daughter is nine years old. They are all very young. I don't know what to do. Since the day of my marriage I haven't had any comfortable day. I've always worked myself. I am not sure what to do with my life. My husband is very old now and I am 23 years old. I can't live alone now because of my young children. I have to suffer everything. I have a very painful life. He always insults my children. I don't have permission of anything inside my own home. I don't have any hope for a better life now. What should I do? How should I spend my life like this?

Shima

I want to tell you of my tragic stories that happened during the Taliban regime. Before the Taliban, I had a comfortable and peaceful life. I was always satisfied. Some months after the Taliban came, life was no longer easy in Kabul City. Every day they created a new policy for people to accept. We couldn't tolerate it so we left our home and went to Pakistan. We didn't have the comfortable life anymore, and we had to suffer being refugees. But after the Taliban's failure, we immigrated to our beautiful country. We had lost all our life. There was no house left, no things. During these years of war, houses of people were all destroyed. It has harmed people's economics. Since I was born, I have only seen fighting, bombing, destroying, and damaging, nothing else. I haven't felt happiness, peace of mind, and friendship ever. I don't know what it is like. I hope to find all these things in the future. I want to hold true friendship in my arms.

Abida

During 23 years of war, our country was destroyed and now American people are helping us to rebuild. All Afghan people spread to everywhere. Most of them went to other countries as refugees. Most of the women lost their husbands and became widows. Children lost their parents and became orphans. People have lots of economic problems. They have lost their homeland. I support my three children. I lived in a place where I could only hear the sound of bombs and rockets. I was very hopeless in life. I hated everyone. Now I know that there are good people living in this world, but in the past I've seen very cruel and bad people. We spend each night to face the day and each day to face the night only in hope of help and kindness. We wait for those who will take weak people's hands in order to help them.

Shekiba

I have suffered the war because of the ones who didn't want our country to be in peace. During these wars we couldn't escape from here too because we didn't have enough money to leave and stay in other countries, so we had to suffer and get burnt. I live in Qalai-Musa, a dirty and poor area of Kabul City which has destroyed streets, no electricity, and no water supply. Our house is made of mud and clay. The windows are covered with plastic paper instead of glass.

Roya

My 15-year-old son is handicapped. We don't have anyone to support and help us. Because of facing sorrow and sadness I can't see very well with my eyes. I was five years old when my father died. I lived with my aunt. When I was 13 years old, my aunt asked me to marry her son. After a few years, my husband left me and married someone else. He ignored my children too. Then, after some time I heard that he had died. Wars and fighting made our life more difficult. But now Allah has shown his kindness and has brought peace to our country. I would like you to convey to the peace-loving women there that Afghan people, particularly women, have faced many hardships. And now they are experiencing the very first freedom and they are learning to struggle for further rights.

Khatol

I am going to tell you about my life: I am responsible for providing my family expenses. There are five people in our family. I live in a house that has been destroyed by a rocket. I wash clothes to provide some food to feed my fatherless children in order to pass my life. This is the life of an Afghan woman that I am sharing with you.

Qandi

It will be a long time until all the women in pain in Afghanistan are able to live peaceful lives. During these past years we were left from everything. During the dark regime of the Taliban, women didn't have the right to go out of their houses. We were in debt and hungry. And we are still not able to pay the debts. I really want to forget all the past. I want to struggle for a better life. I believe that we are all women and we are able to help each other from anywhere around the world. I'm from a very poor family, but my spirit is always strong, not poor and weak.

Khalida

I am single and I live with my old father, two brothers, and one young sister. We are total five people in our family. I couldn't continue my education because of bad economical situation. I live in a rented house. We have a very simple and poor life. I myself sometimes wash clothes in houses to earn living. Now that I have enrolled myself in this organization, I am very happy that I get support. It is like a drop of water that a person pours into the mouth of another who is in a dry desert. That is the drop of water that is going to save her life.

Emergent themes from the profiles of couples resonate with those in women's life stories and histories. Firstly, both women and men feel that the focus on women has come at the expense of men. They feel that men's honor has been compromised by their neglect in aid interventions. Men and women largely agree that new elements of disagreement, conflict, and even violence have entered their lives. They feel that this is due in part to the perception that their values and socio-cultural systems have been compromised by an ideological occupation. Their differences and diversity — as Afghans — has not been recognized. It is problematic to refer to Afghan women as a homogenous group. Finally, they share a sense of disillusionment with the aid apparatus. These themes resonate with those that characterize this discussion: the centrality of honor, the denial of agency, the dissatisfaction with aid, and the exercise of agency through Afghan efforts to deal with these social changes on their own terms. It is this volatile combination that has brought about an unintended effect — increased violence against women.

8

Violence in the Aftermath[1]

> When poverty walks in through the door,
> happiness flies out through the window.
> —Afghan proverb indicating that poverty
> brings trouble and difficulties at home

While Afghanistan aspires to become a state that is pluralistic, Islamic, prosperous, and peace-loving, the challenges are great.[2] Afghanistan has some of the worst social indicators in the world, particularly for women. Many analysts and activists note that women remain oppressed, despite the oft-cited rhetoric of liberation of Afghan women. It has been said repeatedly that women are not yet able to enjoy their human rights. Women still suffer from deprivation and oppression, even several years after the conflict has ended. Women are still abused, prevented from accessing education and economic opportunities, and unable to participate in public life.[3] A former Minister of Women's Affairs was outspoken about the prevalence of violence against women. In a speech on women's rights and security in July 2005, she said:

> It has been more than three years since we embarked on a journey to peace and reconstruction. Our people have embraced peace ... but unfortunately this is not true for many of our women ... real peace has never entered their sphere of life. A different kind of conflict continues to haunt our women.... They live in constant fear of being beaten, harassed, abused verbally, discriminated, denied of rights, robbed of self respect and dignity, exchanged for material goods or for settling conflicts. War has never been over for them.[4]

In further conversations, the former Minister of Women's Affairs had the following to say about violence against women and the existing — and increasing — disparities between women and men:

> Even after years of attention to women, it has not succeeded in making women equal to men. In practical life, at the family and community level, power is still in men's hands. The economy of the home, the economy of the country, all this belongs to men. 100 percent. Still. So what have we given women?
>
> We have given them opportunities for education. But not for all of them.

141

Only those in urban areas. And even then not all of them. We can open up the gates of schools to them and take away all discriminatory laws — but even then it's not complete because that's only the Constitution and we have other discriminatory laws that are written and unwritten. And we have given them security, generally that has improved but still not fully. Work opportunities, those are limited. Only urban areas again. And we have given them opportunities in political life. We have a number of ministers in the cabinet. But still ... all this does not mean equality in their lives. Not at all.

The violence is still going on. It is increasing, even. There has been no positive impact on violence in the last years. It has not decreased, for sure. If we take deaths of women as an indicator, those deaths that have taken place in Herat and other places, self-burning and other things. This happens more than the media reports. I hear these things from the head of the Women's Unit in those places. If we take all this into account, it has increased. Forced marriages are going on, and more than before. Domestic violence is more than before. There is no change in terms of legal protection for women. Small interventions are taking place, but that has had no impact. So we need to do a lot. For a country where the load of centuries of discrimination is on the shoulders of women, with this little investment it is not possible to give them real equality and freedom and justice.

Afghan women today are still battered in the home, harassed in public places, married off without their consent, and traded and exchanged to resolve disputes.[5] This belief is reinforced by the *2004 Report of the UN Secretary General on the Situation of Women and Girls in Afghanistan* which states that "the volatile security situation and traditional social and cultural norms continue to limit women's and girls' role in public life and deny them the full enjoyment of their rights."[6] There is further evidence of violence against women in the private sphere. Studies on livelihoods of the urban poor in Kabul revealed a number of cases of violent conflict between men and women, due to economic deterioration. This deprivation and insecurity has psychological effects on Afghans, particularly those in Kabul who have come to the city seeking greater security and economic opportunity. Expectations were raised by promises of large amounts of aid. As a result, we cannot be surprised that many feel frustrated and angry about the absence of improvement in their daily lives — and their inability to access aid. This displacement of anger is not unusual, as Afghans can generally not point to any improvements in their own lives, and as a result, anger is directed "to the place where they feel they have dominance — their relations with women."[7]

In an article written in 2004, Nancy Hatch Dupree cautioned:

Hopefully, the aid community will heed the lessons learned over the past decades. Programs are needed to promote the integrity of the family, for one can ignore the family only at the cost of social stability.[8]

A woman remains inside while a crowd gathers outside her window, Logar.

Women are now paying the price of social instability. Their words and experiences reveal that violence against women is becoming an increasing concern. It remains difficult, however, to conduct research and access information on violence against women. Available understandings in Afghanistan are based largely on anecdotal evidence. Data are not yet widely available. In the few cases where figures are available, these may in fact underestimate reality. In Afghanistan, many refuse to acknowledge violence against women as an issue. In addition, women — and men — have different definitions of what constitutes violence. Violence against women in the context of intimacy is often not recognized and labeled as such. This is viewed by women as within the realm of normal gender relations and not assumed to be an abuse of women's human rights. In fact, there is a general perception among women that violence is a normal part of their lives and that it cannot be avoided. Many believe that this is what it means to be a woman in Afghanistan during these times.

Those women who are able to recognize violence against them are still not likely to change or address it. Such women recognize the added challenge this presents to gender relations, which could in turn provoke additional violence. Women may be reluctant to speak publicly about the violence they have feared, witnessed, or experienced for fear of being stigmatized. In addition, there is a perception that violence against women in the domestic sphere is a private affair that should be addressed within families and not revealed to outsiders. The concern is that such public admissions will bring shame to the family. Violence against women is often disguised and denied within the family to retain honor and standing within the community. In addition to the fear of social stigma and the blame they may receive, women are reluctant to report violence because existing institutions are not equipped to take action and protect them. Reporting the crime may place the woman at greater risk. The crime itself may not be recorded or classified as a crime by the institution. In Afghanistan, women's complaints of violence are often disregarded by national institutions, such as the Afghan National Police. Thus, women run the risk of exposing themselves to additional violence from the community, the institutions, and the state. It is difficult to measure rates of violence accurately, particularly when there is a social stigma attached. In a context of changing gender roles and relations, the space created for women may bring resentment and backlash, manifesting in a shift from public to private violence. When public violence turns private, it then becomes hidden from policy-makers and is beyond the purview of aid institution priorities.

The Revolutionary Association of the Women of Afghanistan (RAWA) states that officials estimate that at least half of all Afghan women have been forced into marriage, and that one in three have been beaten or abused.[9] The Afghan Independent Human Rights Commission registered over 1,650 cases of violence against women in 2006 — and many cases have gone unreported.[10] Afghans feel that violence against women will continue — and gender inequalities will increase — as long as Afghanistan is under occupation and as long as aid institutions and the Afghan government fail to make improvements in the lives of the majority of Afghans. A RAWA article explains:

> The Taliban used the "women's question" to enforce its own agenda. The imperialist occupation forces have also used the agenda of gender equality to ultimately pursue their own interests: the occupation of Afghanistan for strategic geo-political reasons. In the eyes of many people, the ministry of women is associated with the occupation.[11]

Indeed, the increased levels of violence against women are attributed largely to poverty, the ongoing occupation, and the failure of the aid apparatus to make real changes to women's lives. Backlashes against women in the aftermath are not unusual. There is worldwide evidence that violence against women predominates in situations of poverty, particularly where women gain economic independence while men remain unemployed. If such socioeconomic changes provoke violence against women, perhaps more caution could have been taken in design of gender interventions.

There are very few statistics to demonstrate violence against women in Afghanistan, and even fewer figures that are reliable. In the case of a drastic increase in statistics of violence in a given time, one cannot necessarily assume that rates of violence have increased. There might be other factors that contribute to the sudden change. Perhaps reporting procedures have become less arduous. Perhaps women are part of an organization or support group that is encouraging them to speak out. It is precisely these trends that make reporting on violence even more challenging. Statistics are unreliable, and quantitative data is difficult to obtain. But this effort requires more than just figures and statistics. Structural issues need to be identified and addressed. Patterns of abuse and discrimination need to be revealed and studied. And root causes of violence in Afghan society must be understood in context. In this vein, qualitative evidence that examines perceptions and experiences should be given significant weight.

Finally, it is worth briefly stating that not all Afghan women are victims, as discussed earlier. Not all Afghan men are perpetrators. Not all women are inherently peaceful. And not all men are bellicose. Such constructions reinforce patriarchal models of the gender order and negate patterns of violence practiced by women and patterns of peace practiced by men.[12] It is important to recognize that not all violence against women is at the hands of men.

There are various examples across cultures and histories to demonstrate that women have the capacity for violence against each other. This ranges from female genital cutting — where young girls are mutilated by the hands of older women — to the violence perpetrated on a new bride by her mother-in-law. While it is important to acknowledge such incidents, it is clear that in the majority of cases, women are primarily survivors of violence perpetrated by men. In Afghanistan, new brides can face abuse from their female in-laws, particularly if the marriage is the result of *Bad* (giving a female relative to the victim's family to settle a crime) or *Badal* (giving a female relative in marriage in return for a bride). If the bride remains childless, violence can also result. The forms of such violence perpetrated by women often entail abuse of power and could lead to psychological and physical abuse.

There is a nascent understanding that particular forms of violence against women — particularly domestic violence — increase after a conflict. In Afghanistan today, it is not unusual to hear women say that they felt "safer under the Taliban." Violence against women is believed to be pervasive in Afghanistan, sustained by a patriarchy that supports abuse and dehumanization of women. Violence against women also has significant economic and social costs, impairing women from actively and effectively participating in society and in their own — and ultimately Afghanistan's — development. The report of Yakin Erturk, the UN Special Rapporteur on Violence against Women, in July 2005 noted that violence against women continues to be pervasive in Afghanistan.[13] Erturk cites four reasons for the perpetuation of violence: (1) the traditional patriarchal gender order, (2) the erosion of protective social mechanisms, (3) the lack of rule of law, and (4) poverty and insecurity. Indeed, attempts to improve the status of women are linked with — and often superseded by — the multiple transitions underway in Afghan society.

In this case, it is possible to build on Erturk's work by adding a fifth element, the idea raised by many Afghan men and women that aid institutions are provoking a change in gender relations. New forms of violence are emerging as a result of women's increased visibility outside the home. Such violence is beyond social, ethnic, religious, tribal, or economic boundaries. The space created for women may bring resentment and backlash, driving violence further into the private domain.

Afghanistan's Millennium Development Goals Report for 2005 states that the silent epidemic of violence against women is due to the combination of their low status and years of conflict.[14] Violence against women in Afghanistan is widespread and ranges from deprivation of education to economic opportunities, through verbal and psychological violence, beatings, sexual violence and killings. Many acts of violence involve traditional practices including the betrothal of young girls in infancy, early marriage and crimes of honor, where a female is punished for having offended custom, tradition or honor.[15] Afghanistan's National Development Strategy — the government's overarching strategy for promoting growth, generating wealth and reducing poverty and vulnerability — also sees widespread inequalities for women.[16] The Constitution of Afghanistan guarantees gender equality; however, women lack legal awareness and many do not effectively enjoy the Constitutionally guaranteed equal protection of the law. Discriminatory provisions in laws and policies remain inconsistent with the Constitution.

According to Afghan tradition, females in the family are under the authority of the father or husband. They suffer restricted freedom of movement and nearly no control over the choices that govern their lives. Most women will not have the opportunity to assert economic and social independence, nor to enjoy their human rights. Girls are not given say over choice of husbands and find that they are abused and mistreated in the husband's home. Those who try to escape the abuse are stigmatized, isolated, and possibly imprisoned. Forced and underage marriages are also prevalent. Reports emerging from the United Nations Development Fund for Women (UNIFEM) and the Ministry of Women's Affairs indicate that approximately 60–80 percent of all marriages are forced, and occur frequently as payment for debt or to settle a feud.[17] A child marriage is by definition a forced marriage, because a child cannot have consented freely.[18] The selling and trafficking of women is increasing. Activists and specialists have expressed concern that domestic violence is widespread in Afghanistan and there remains little public awareness, prevention, or response. Cases are not reported, and in the rare cases where they are reported, they are not properly recorded. The Ministry of Women's Affairs Legal Department recorded 583 reported cases in 2004, and it is likely that many more cases remain unreported.[19] Violence against women and the absence of effective redress for survivors, whether through informal or formal justice mechanisms, is a pervasive human rights problem in Afghanistan.

Other forms of violence against women in Afghanistan include *Bad* and *Badal* (as previously mentioned), exchanging girls for cattle or material goods, and self-immolation. The latter entails women attempting suicide by setting themselves on fire. Reports indicate that the majority of self-immolation survivors sought death due to violence in the family. This phenomenon was first studied and publicized in Herat, but is prevalent all over Afghanistan. In fact, the common perception that self-immolation occurs with greater frequency in Herat is simply because that is where the incident was first exposed — and therefore where most journalists restricted their focus. Violence against women in Afghanistan can also include intimidation of women in the form of sexual or derogatory comments, harassment, and other means of drawing boundaries and delineating women's place in the gender order.

It is not unusual for men to use violence against women as a means of establishing and maintaining power relationships and structural inequalities. Indeed, all violence against women is caused by power inequality — and abuse of that power. Myriad reports have explained that there are consequences for women when, in the context of conflict and the aftermath, men perceive that they have lost their traditional roles. Women's marginalization and exclusion during conflict often motivates humanitarian organizations to focus on women's empowerment, further alienating men.[20] Instead of finding peaceful alternatives when traditional roles are threatened, many men seek to safeguard the present gender order and assert masculinity through violence against women. In cases where men employ such violence, women's choices, safety, and behavior are restricted as a result. There is a link between militarized masculinities, conflict, and gender oppression. It is not uncommon to see domestic violence as an unfortunate byproduct of the post-conflict culture of violence.

Having said all of this, it is worthwhile noting that violence against women is not exclusive to contexts such as Afghanistan. So-called third-world violence against women is viewed by those outside as a "death by culture."[21] It is important to think of the context that is lost — and the new one that is gained — when issues of violence against women cross borders and become part of a Western feminist agenda. These *other* issues of *other* women are subsequently adopted (read: hijacked) by academics and feminists and become part of what the West understands "third-world gender issues" to be. If these issues occur in Muslim countries, they then become "Muslim issues" and they continue to be misconstrued and de-contextualized with increasing publicity.[22]

Examples from other countries emerging from conflict seem to demonstrate that increased domestic violence forms an unfortunate component of the aftermath agenda. The UN Secretary-General's *Report on Women, Peace and Security 2002* states that domestic violence is one particular form that continues after the conflict.[23] In the aftermath, conditions for women risk further deterioration, violence tends to increase, and the potential for future conflict is likely. It is in this context that international attention and support begin to wane.[24] During the reconstruction process in the aftermath, violence against women is often ignored or viewed as a low priority compared with other concerns. Indeed, as previously mentioned, the absence of violence against women is not even a precursor for peace, according to the Peace Index as mentioned in Chapter 1.

The experience of women in Bosnia is an oft-cited case to demonstrate the trend of increased violence against women in post-conflict contexts. Violence was inflicted upon Bosnian women at the hands of demobilized soldiers in the form of domestic violence. Similarly, in Rwanda, women experienced increased violence following the conflict and became "soft" outlets for men's frustrations. Research on increased violence in post-conflict Guatemala notes that despite a decline in political violence, social violence was increasing.[25] In addition, there was a notable shift to increased urban-based violence coupled with a general sense of lawlessness and disorder. Afghanistan is experiencing a similar phenomenon. Manifestations of the current crisis of poverty and vulnerability in urban areas includes domestic violence and social breakdown alongside increased crime rates.[26] Similarly, in Angola, many men were left unemployed following the conflict. Research revealed that men felt undermined by the fact that they were unable to contribute to the household and that instead women were supporting the families. As a result, men's frustrations led to increased violence against women, coupled with greater drug and alcohol use.[27]

Research in the Lukole Refugee Camp in Tanzania revealed striking similarities to Afghanistan. It was noted that United Nations High Commissioner for Refugees (UNHCR) efforts to empower women through aid interventions had negative effects, with men feeling threatened by the perceived loss of their position as breadwinners and figures of authority. In short, they felt as if UNCHR was "taking their authority and their women from them."[28] Feelings of loss following a conflict — particularly feelings of social and moral decay — are interpreted in terms of gender relations, which are, in turn, projected as resentment toward the institution that is attempting to take their women and their masculinity.[29] Further, women in so-called empowerment programs were not able to exercise it at home. Many women gave half of their financial support from the agency to their husbands so as not to antagonize them. I noted the same trend in Afghanistan where women are cautious to present cash and in-kind earnings to male members of the family to appease them and to secure their continued participation in aid programs.

While not in conflict or the aftermath, research in Atzompa, Mexico, also bears resemblance to Afghanistan. In Atzompa, women felt compelled to accept increased male violence as a reaction to men's own sense of displacement as women are granted greater economic opportunities. When women's economic benefits are offset by increased patriarchal violence, the whole concept of development is thrown into question, "since material 'progress' entails a regression — an escalation in male violence."[30]

Increased violence against women in the aftermath is not just a phenomenon of the developing world. In fact, research in the United States following Hurricane Katrina in 2005 revealed that American men are also susceptible to violence in times of uncertainty:

> Especially when so much is out of their control in Katrina's aftermath, men without jobs ... may feel unmasked and unmanly.... Some men will cope through drugs, alcohol, physical aggression or all three, hurting themselves and putting the women and girls around them at risk. We can count on increased reports of violence against women as this is so common in U.S. and international disasters.[31]

Evidence of Unintended Effects

Interviews with policy-makers, policy implementers, NGO leaders, and Afghan specialists reinforced the views above on increased violence — specifically domestic violence — for reasons that include the continued availability of weapons, violence that male family members have experienced or meted out, trauma, frustration, and men's inability to access trainings and economic opportunities. Afghan history demonstrates that this is not unusual. The United Nations Research Institute for Social Development (UNRISD) explains that attacks on women's newly assumed rights and behaviors constitute a post-war backlash against women.[32] Afghanistan is cited as a case in point. An Afghan woman working on gender issues with an aid institution explained:

> I think that the communities are not ready to accept the new changes in women's situation. They think women expect too much. One way to not give [women] what they want is to use violence against them.

An Afghan NGO leader elaborated:

> Men and women are not ready to accept the extent of freedom that Westerners are asking for in their programs in Afghanistan. People become sensitive to the fact that Afghan women are expected to dress in Western style — if they are "liberated" — and to work very closely with men and foreigners. That is the reason violence against women has increased. If the status quo continues, there will be more violence against women. Instead, it should change to a more Afghan — more slow — pace. Change doesn't need to be revolutionary for it to work.

Another gender specialist shared her experience:

> There were several cases known to me where women were being abused by their husbands for taking classes and participating in women's workshops.

Some women became scared and stopped attending. Fathers, brothers, husbands were never involved in any of the programming activities.

Some policy-makers and policy implementers attributed the perceived increase in violence against women to a general sense of lawlessness and disorder that characterizes countries in the aftermath. A gender advisor continued:

If in fact violence has increased, my guess at the main reason would be a growing insecurity toward the position of women in the home and community and the fear of Westernization. In short, a backlash against various trends — some good and some decidedly bad — that have come due to Afghanistan opening up to the West, not to mention the sudden and dramatic increase of Western individuals and organizations.... If we compare to other post-conflict countries, it's possible to predict that violence against women is greater here because of the increased power of the mafias and warlords, exacerbated income disparities, the continuously unstable situation, and trauma in men that leads to violence.

Indeed, contributing factors to violence against women include erosion of livelihoods, poverty, lawlessness, insecurity, which have in turn eroded social safety nets. The gender officer for an international organization put it this way:

There are hardly any reports focusing especially on violence against women from different periods during the conflict. However, I would not be surprised if there was a rise in domestic violence as part of post-conflict developments. There seems to have been an increase in kidnappings and trafficking.

Most of those interviewed, however, could not confirm an increase in violence against women, per se, but certainly suspected that this was the case. Many cited concerns of an imminent backlash, or the possibility that the backlash was already underway. An Afghan woman policy-maker in an aid institution had the following to say:

There is a kind of negative idea among the people on gender that has to be corrected. And some people think that too much goes to women. The communities are sometimes not ready to accept the changes in women's situation. For them it is too much and too fast. One way for men is to use violence. There is a backlash at the speed of change and the focus of foreign aid, women being the focus.

During the interviews, participants were not asked specifically about violence. Instead, they were given the opportunity to share their own perceptions of how gender roles and relations are changing and how they are at present. In so doing, it was not assumed *a priori* that violence would be an important issue. Instead violence emerged from the interviewees themselves when they found it to be an issue that was relevant to the discussion.

Of the 14 (out of 50) men who expressed concern that violence was increasing, the majority were from rural origins (57 percent), married (57 percent), and had a high level of education (64 percent). The majority of women who reported incidents of violence or fear of violence were from rural origins, married, and with no education. Of the 33 (out of 71) women who believed that violence was increasing, the majority were also rural (64 percent) and married (61 percent). However, regarding education levels, the majority of women who expressed concern that violence was increasing come from the category that had no education (73 percent). In terms of level of education, this is opposite to the men in that men in the highest education category were more conscious of increased violence than those with less education.

Interviewees — particularly women — alluded to violence without specifically stating it. Examples include referring to increased verbal abuse, decreased mobility, increased fighting in the family, and statements such as "he makes things more difficult for me now." Terms to connote increased violence include "danger" and "fighting." In Dari, the term for violence, *tashadud*, generally refers to political conflict and violence on a large scale, unless *tashadud aley-he zanaan* — violence against women — is referred to specifically. The more common term for violence against women in the form of domestic violence is *khshoonat aley-he zanaan*. The term for conflict, *kash-ma-kash*, was generally not employed for the home. Women used *nezaa* — fighting — more frequently along with words that connote "family problems" or "family concerns." Women also expressed the fear — *tarsidah* — of increased violence in the future and the sense that this was to be anticipated as a result of present status. For both men and women, a mention of violence did not always mean that they are personally facing violence in the home. Violence in the home should also be put in the context of a general sense of frustration, lawlessness, and disorder. This is particularly relevant given recent incidents of public violence and the increasing tension in Afghanistan.

Afghan men who addressed issues of increased violence did not do so directly, but implied that conflicts at home were becoming an increasing part of their lives. For instance, one man explained that "relations between men and women have gotten worse than in previous periods." Another stated that "fear still exists" between men and women and that "relations are not so good like before." Men referred to difficulties at home and increased pressure. One man even said: "I wish that men should give up irrational discrimination and violence against women." An Afghan man in his late 20s from Kabul put it this way:

The international community came here and want to work only for women. And they don't want to improve the status of Afghan men. Therefore Afghan men start making problems for their sister, their mother, their wife. They start making problems.

Men who referred to violence expressed that they felt "anger" against their wives when, after men acquiesced to women's participation in a training program, the women failed to find gainful employment and were unable to provide support to the family. Many men explained that there had been much debate and argument in the house in order for the wife to convince the husband that she should participate in aid interventions — particularly when they entail income generation — as this could question the man's role as provider. Economic necessity trumped all other concerns, and certain men agreed to let their wives leave the house. When these said trainings failed to yield significant economic support, these men felt that their wives were "useless" (and also told their wives this) and that they were let out of the house "for nothing." This also bred resentment with the intervention itself, which was also labeled "useless" and accused of using women to fill some kind of quota without offering substantive training. Men alluded to raised expectations that wives would be able to support the family. Yet when they failed to do so, the outcome generally seemed to be increased verbal and psychological violence. Women's self-esteem suffered as a result, and

A girl invites us into her home in Khairkhana, where most live in partial tents along a wall, Kabul.

they felt less likely to take risks or make unconventional demands in the future. Many women articulated that they would feel more comfortable accessing their opportunities if men were not neglected.

Similarly with women, most discussions about violence were implicit, but many were also able to refer to violence directly. Most of the discussions on violence centered around men's frustrations and inabilities to access opportunities. Women saw this as an explanation for the violence that was newly directed towards them. One elderly woman explained: "My husband didn't have good behavior during the Taliban regime. He was angry because he didn't have a job, so he left me forever." Another was more direct, stating that "men should stop abusing women because of their opportunities." She felt that her husband resented her ability to bring home an income, however meager, and that she would prefer that he work. Some women expressed this new violence as a result of men's insulted honor. A married woman in her late 20s put it this way: "We don't want our men to be backed by any other man in the world. It is this that causes violence." She elaborated to explain that Afghan men are feeling dependent on others and as a result their dignity was under question. Both men and women expressed a strong desire for men to be able to stand on their own feet, without the support of others. Another woman reinforced this point, explaining that "men are more aggressive and angry" because they lack employment. A few women were vocal in their blame of aid institutions and their focus on women. One said: "They increased violence between men and women and it will increase more." An Afghan woman elaborated: "The men, they have become more angry, more violent. Much more violent."

A few men, and many women, shared the view that violence against women has increased in the aftermath. Some felt that this is a continuation of wartime violence, such as this man from rural Afghanistan with no education who said: "Still men are the same. Most men are cruel to their wives and daughters. It might be a cause of the war." Another man blamed the enforced changes in gender relations for increased violence and hostility, explaining that "fundamentalist ideas have developed because many people feel that the changes happening with gender are obligatory and they are resisting them." Women from varied ages and backgrounds expressed more strongly worded concerns. Below are a few examples:

- I think that violence is increasing against women because men are angry.
- Apparently men and women's rights are equally distributed but still the violence against women has increased. This talk of rights has just increased the gap between men and women.

- Relations between men and women are getting worse because women are trying to have a new life and men don't want it.
- I think relations are not based on equality. Women are trying to gain power and men do not want to allow it.
- I think that women are fighting with men to secure their rights, and men are resisting the changes.
- Men and women's rights are not equal yet. Men are more aggressive and angry.
- Apparently men and women have equal rights — but violence against women has increased.

Most of the women interviewed did not refer to violence directly, but used other words such as anger, hostility, and tension. Some examples are:

- Some women's organizations have reflected wrong things about women, which has made men very angry.
- They do not support men directly. It makes the men angry.
- All bad things happen when men are not educated and literate.
- In some places, men have become sensitive about women's organizations. They believe that these organizations train women to stand against the laws and their husbands. Of course this is not true. It is actually what men think.
- Men know that they are not involved. And they are angry as a result.
- We want dignity for our men, and then they will treat us better.
- An imposed war has bad influence on men and women's relationship.
- Relations between men and women are getting worse because women are trying to have a new life and men don't want it.
- Relations seem good, but nothing is as it appears.
- Relations are changing and in many ways it is worse.

I Am Caged in This Corner...

In Afghanistan, women are being increasingly castigated for being Western-influenced. Strong pushes for women's rights run the risk of being undermined because these are perceived to be linked with the agenda of foreign occupation. The risk is even greater when women are working for foreigners. Even the perception that women might be working towards a

"Western agenda" could undermine efforts and put their personal safety at risk. Women may jeopardize their own safety and standing in the community by aligning themselves with foreigners. The perception that an Afghan woman is promoting a foreign agenda could lead to the belief that she is contaminated by her association with outsiders.[33] In associating with foreigners, it is believed that she has betrayed the trust of the community and thereby undermined her own — and men's — honor.

Indeed, these unintended consequences of interventions are only just coming to the fore. However, identification of these problems will not necessarily bring solutions. A leader of an aid institution for women suggested that the aid apparatus should work with Afghan women to help them recognize possible negative implications and to see "whether they are prepared to take on that fight. At the end, if they are not prepared, nothing is going to happen." Those interviewed noted a need for increased sensitivity to program design, and to promises made, as well as an increased understanding of the impact a foreign presence might have in Afghanistan regarding violence against women.

Afghan women's groups have expressed repeated concern about the increased levels of violence — both at the public and private levels. As one example, in May 2005, three Afghan women were found raped and strangled in Baghlan Province. It is believed that these women were murdered for their involvement with international non-governmental organizations. This comes from a note that was left pinned to the women's bodies blaming their fate on their involvement with NGOs and its resulting "whoredom." As a result, hundreds of women protested in Kabul. Soon after, another woman was stoned in Badakhshan Province. This prompted a reaction from Afghan

A girl completes a cultural performance to celebrate the opening of a new NGO, Kabul.

women resulting in the Declaration of Afghan Women's NGOs of 5 May 2005 urging for investigations that will bring the perpetrators to justice and asking for increased security for all Afghan citizens. And yet, security remains precarious in Afghanistan. Nearly every document, speech, and report on Afghanistan — by Afghan and non–Afghan alike — has highlighted the need for improved security. No political or social process can be successful or sustainable without a commitment to provide genuine, sustainable security — particularly including women. There is no need to belabor this point. Many have said it, yet it continues to fall on deaf ears.

The demands for security further prompted plans for a protest and an email entitled "What you can do about the Backlash," listing the following as one of the action items:

> Contact your country representative/embassy in Afghanistan and ask for accountability on how your tax dollars are being spent in Afghanistan. No more empty rhetoric on "national programs and policy" — what are the results on the ground?[34]

A few days afterwards, *Daily Outlook*, Afghanistan's English language newspaper, noted the increase in violence against women in several front-page

A woman speculates on why greater changes have not been made since "liberation," Paghman.

articles.[35] On the following pages, there was an article about the Minister of Women's Affairs' work program, including support for widows and disabled women. She also expressed concern with the increase in domestic violence and the lack of mechanisms to bring perpetrators to court. The adjacent article reported a 16-year-old girl who was raped and killed in Kabul. The *Kabul Weekly*—in English and Dari—ran several articles during that week also. The front page article stated that violence against women continues while the aid apparatus "looks on." A subheading of the article stated that the incident revealed "a village uncomfortable with outside interference."

A few months later, Afghanistan was shocked at the murder of Nadia Anjuman, a famed Afghan poet, by her husband. She was 25 years old. According to friends and family, Anjuman was seen as a disgrace to her family due to her poetry, which described the oppression of Afghan women:

> I am caged in this corner, full of melancholy and sorrow
> My wings are closed and I cannot fly
> I am an Afghan woman and I must wail

Her tragic death was a public example of the violence that Afghan women still face and an indication that — many years into reconstruction — the Afghan government and the aid apparatus had failed to address issues of domestic violence. Anjuman's poem, "Soundless Cries," is one of the few that is available in English in its entirety.[36]

> I hear the green paces of the rain
> Here they are coming
> A thirsty few who have come
> With their dusty outfits on
> With their breaths soiled with the
> Deception of mirages
> Paces, dry and dusty
> They arrive here now
> Girls, grown up with hurting soul
> And wounded bodies
> Happiness has escaped their faces
> Hearts, old and cracked
> The word of a smile never written
> In the book of their lips
> Not even a drop of tear can come out
> The dried rivers of their eyes.
> Oh dear God!
> I do not know if their soundless cries
> Reach the clouds, The skies?
> I hear the green paces of the rain.

Unfortunately, we still know far too little about the interactions between aid and the dynamics of violence — in both the public and private spheres. Other research has documented men's sense of frustration with their inability to meet the household's basic needs and the violence that they mete out as a result. Research on urban vulnerability highlights this quote from a 35-year-old man as an illustration of the negative impacts insufficient income have on intra-household relations:

> When I had a job, everything was fine; we had good relations in our house. But it was only temporary, and now I am at home and everything gets on my nerves. I am not able to feed my family, and I am angry about that and then I am beating my wife, because she is complaining about that. What can I do? Give me a job, then everything will be good again.[37]

Such accounts are not unusual. Social assets are scarce. Gender roles are changing. Gender relations are strained. Traditional social safety nets are deteriorating. And violence against women is increasing.

Roles, Relations, and Opportunities

But is this not all part of the possible growing pains associated with breaking into new gender roles in the aftermath? Indeed, there is a burgeoning literature on changes in women's roles in conflict and its aftermath. In this context, an examination of the gender order is particularly relevant as Afghan society is undergoing processes of socio-political transformation, one result of which is the fluctuation of gender identities. Conflict compels individuals, households, and communities to fundamentally rethink and restructure their ways and beliefs. A part of this restructuring is played out on gender roles, and subsequently on gender relations. And yet, no consensus exists on whether these new gender roles are advantageous to women or sustainable in the long term. Despite new roles, opportunities, and responsibilities, women may easily be marginalized in the reconstruction process. Further, many theorists have argued that any expansion of women's roles in war is only temporary and fails to sustain itself when the war ends, likely provoking a retreat to more conservative gender roles. A woman working with an Afghan woman's NGO explained:

> Conflict certainly seemed to create some opportunities for women in a position to work in NGOs or international agencies or even to start their own organizations, but I'm not sure to what extent it created opportunities outside the sphere of work — especially within the household where it seems the real power is.

Afghan women have received inconsistent signals from above during the course of history: at one time enforced modernizations and at another a reversion to traditionalism — with little time to negotiate these opposing changes. Today, they have lost the clarity that comes with traditional roles, yet they lack the resources to seize so-called modern opportunities. Aid interventions added their gender-focused messages to the series of political and social experiments in Afghanistan, granting women rights from above and then subsequently stripping them away. And yet, some women have gained strength through these vacillating initiatives, others as a result of economic necessity. Most Afghan women, however, cannot find their place amidst the new rhetoric that enforces yet another model for women to follow. Afghan men's experiences, on the other hand, appear to be less varied. As they move beyond the business of warring, they find themselves lost in the new Afghanistan. Those who are unable to find work are feeling threatened by the loss of authority that came with their role as breadwinner. They are further diminished when women assume this traditionally male role.

Aid interventions, particularly in the aftermath of conflict, are often conflated with radical social change. However, these interventions do not often challenge gender power relations, and even run the risk of doing a disservice to women by implementing programs and policies that have not taken all possible repercussions into account.[38] Aid interventions aiming to empower women may in fact place women at increased risk. This is particularly relevant in the case of Afghanistan, where the rhetoric used to justify aid interventions stemmed from the language used to justify the ousting of the Taliban — a military intervention. And yet, eight years later, one could argue that Afghan women are neither liberated nor empowered. Interventions that raise expectations of empowerment encourage women to step outside pre-existing gender roles. In so doing, gender and power relations are challenged. Women face greater risk if the environment for social change is seen to be an external imposition. On such shaky ground, advancing women's rights cannot find a solid foundation.

Women may suffer further when gender-focused interventions fail to take *gender* issues into account, focusing only on women. Men's perceptions that they are neglected could result in a backlash for women. Social change and transformation are not simply introduced by aid interventions, but are longer-term processes operating at a structural level to address gender inequalities — on women's own terms. Such processes are contextual and local. It is not unwise to ask if an international aid-imposed agenda of social change is really the right approach. Further, Afghan women felt that they were not sufficiently consulted on the direction and pace of social change. This demonstrates a denial of women's agency and of their ability to act on their own behalf and achieve gains. Theorists have elaborated on this point, arguing that the possibility of a backlash against women confirms that aid interventions should be designed by women participants. Empowerment is not a technical tool that can be handed to women. Instead, it must be generated by the women it is meant to serve.[39] It is crucial to support and advocate a contextualized approach that recognizes Afghan history and Afghan pace and patterns of social change. To this end, interventions must aim to understand definitions and dynamics of empowerment and gender equality in local contexts. This entails congruence with Islam and other social frameworks within which Afghans choose to operate.

An advocate for context is not necessarily an apologist for culture. Culture is one of many dynamic factors that can provide a better understanding of Afghanistan — and better interventions as a result. An understanding of culture might reveal that interventions should be cognizant of the images used and the resulting perceptions that emerge. The perception of an imposed Western agenda coupled with the image of Afghan women as downtrodden creatures beneath *chaddaris* does little to advance the cause of Afghan women, particularly in the context of the Western world's current climate of fear/fascination with women in Islam. Women's rights activists advise caution in order to avoid backlash from the conservative elements of Afghan society.

Shifts in the gender order are largely indigenous, yet they can be supported or hindered by external interventions. There is little consensus on how to sustain positive changes. This is particularly relevant in the context of Afghanistan, "where you open doors for women, showing them another reality. And if you don't also work with men ... you close the doors again and she goes back home and probably is less satisfied and less compliant than she was before," a senior gender advisor explained. Aid interventions in the context of conflict and the aftermath may create additional dependency because the agenda is not within their control. While women may benefit from the increased emphasis placed on them by aid institutions, men tend to feel emasculated as a result. Failing to take gender dynamics into consideration could result in increased inequalities, as respondents have frequently stated. This perspective is reinforced by studies that show that ignoring the needs of men and focusing exclusively on women's participation can create additional challenges such as male resistance, token female participation, and the continuation of male domination.[40]

Aid interventions that do not take gender dimensions into account may be exacerbating violence against women. Domestic violence — and even the fear of violence — is a key factor in limiting women's participation in aid interventions.[41] In fact, women are well aware that their active involvement in aid interventions may present challenges to men's roles. There may be tensions if women's newly assumed roles are not viewed in line with traditional social structures. This backlash could return women to their pre-war roles, or perhaps leave women worse off than they were before the war. Even if gender *roles* change in conflict, gender *relations* may not change.[42] However, it is possible to emphasize women's centrality to reconstruction efforts and aid interventions without marginalizing men. Working with men in gender programming as participants and as advocates and supporters could help change male perceptions of women and help to overcome practices which restrict women's rights. This is integral to combating violence against women and to pushing the progression of engagement with men to the fifth phase — working with men in their own right.

9

Insecurities and Ideological Occupations

It is essential to let Afghan voices speak for themselves as these voices are often rendered silent in international policy circles. Indeed, I have been the fortunate recipient of many of these voices through my long experience in Afghanistan and my conscious presence of existing on both sides, so to speak, with Afghan women's issues. I do not use this as an imposition of binary oppositions, but simply to mean that I have been both active participant and researcher in this context. There are challenges when we study the communities to which we belong. I write about the aid apparatus in Afghanistan with the full knowledge of having been part of this community. Therefore, this is an exercise of self-reflection in addition to an observation of particular dynamics in a historical moment.

This work was part of an iterative process spanning four years, and an interest spanning twelve years. During the course of my research, I received the following emails from Afghanistan and gender specialists, policy-makers and policy implementers, and interested others sharing their views. As a member of the aid apparatus during this moment, I felt that my work would have been incomplete if I did not invite comment from those who shared this particular experience. Findings are further reinforced when those who have the capacity to object are actually in agreement.[1] It is in this vein that the following feedback was obtained.

A researcher, professor, and specialist on Afghan women had the following to say:

> The main thing that struck me is that men thought many women hear about "women's rights" through international channels but they do not know what that means or how they should go about getting rights within the Afghan context ... and this creates conflict and they believe that for some of the self-immolation victims this was part of the cause ... a clash between the discourse of women's rights without the understanding of the definition of rights in Afghanistan.

An independent gender specialist and published author on Afghan women came across the precursor to this work and sent the following email in March 2006:

I think you would probably see the same dilemmas I do as I think about how to "translate" many of the Western notions that underlie the field into something that is progressive and possible and built from indigenous Afghan thought. I've been of really mixed opinions as to how this might work and in whose image.

I just thought your report was great and raised so many important issues that are exactly what I'm trying to figure out and the questions of relativity and respect and empowerment and shared language, or lack thereof....

Women's resilience may be negatively impacted by liberation from above, which I suspect destroys the sense of agency, empowerment and community control by and for women that was found at the grassroots level. While some women have seen improvement, many have seen none and others have lost informal, community opportunities for agency as elites, "experts," and government and international controls are put in place.

...Very challenging work given the escalation in backlash against women and others that appears to be in the works.

A leader of an international NGO in Afghanistan working very closely with women had the following to say:

The West is trying to push its own kind of thinking on programs such as women in parliament. I think we are way too ahead of the past here and we are all guilty ... we all come here with our own preconceived notions, experiences and so on and try to structure programs according to what we did in other countries. It is obvious from the way the West arrived here in 2001 to today. Just look at the "hearts and minds" effort by the armies — they don't learn any lessons, even recent lessons from other countries where it didn't work — the promise of a better future, a better tomorrow by the West if you adopt democracy or "our way" without explaining the context that it is going to take years and years and will not happen overnight, the consequent disappointment, disillusionment of Afghans because the pace of change to improve their daily existence is too slow, their expectations are dashed, their security is not improved, the cost of living rises and salaries do not, lack of jobs. Where is the leadership to explain that things take time, to help people understand? But then you have the massive corruption, the drugs, warlords, criminals and those involved in the most awful atrocities back inside the circle of power. Is it any wonder people are skeptical? Who explains to them why it may be necessary to keep your enemies close to your side ... and anyway have they really changed, are they really going to adapt to a new system or are they already planning the downfall of this government? There is so much to be done and already the corruption is massive, and women naturally are the ones who have to deal with the consequences of all this every day. Men frustrated, young lads with no prospects of work, the arranged marriages and the bridal price. Well, I better not go on ... there is fault on all sides but I find it hard to believe that for most women life has not changed much but the West will still proclaim "freedom for women" ... I wish it were so.

The gender representative of a contracting agency shared the following feedback after having read an earlier report, and following extensive discussions on the subject:

> [The data] definitely resonated with the experiences, difficulties and challenges I have faced in my work. I felt myself nodding in agreement in various places throughout the report. I think you managed to fairly represent what was happening, and how it differed from what people, both national and international, felt should be happening. I especially liked your point about the lessons learned but not applied — I think that is definitely true. When I started the micro-enterprise program, we planned to include men in the training, however for various reasons that did not happen. I think it is a weakness in our program that I hope will be addressed in the future. Taking more time to create and plan for both the technical and logistical aspects of program implementation would help improve the impact, but we need to work more with our donors to ensure we have the space to do so.

> I very much agree that "gender" has really meant "women" in terms of programs. The concept of gender, and creating gender equality or equity seems difficult to relate to this environment and cultural context. It seems like it just gets confused with women's issues and rights, and is perceived to be favoritism to women. Even though my staff understand that gender is about both men and women, in our work it is hard to translate that into effective inclusion of men.

> We had an interesting meeting with the chancellor of the university the other day. We were talking about some of our programs for women, and he was very upset that we were setting a bad example by creating segregated programs that would favor women. He encouraged us to not leave out the boys. It was unclear whether he just wanted to make sure

A man who sells fish on the edge of a lake, Bamiyan.

the men had more opportunities, or if he genuinely felt that there should be more equal interaction. My immediate reaction was that he didn't want the boys to be excluded from opportunities for them to be making money, but I also think it may provide a good opportunity to encourage that kind of mixing at the university — if it can be done appropriately in a way that both girls and boys are comfortable.

I find the lack of contextualized analysis to be very true among the international staff. Early after I arrived I actually read a book about women and politics and development in Afghanistan that clearly outlined how difficult it has been to make change in the past, and how negative the reaction was by the Afghans when they felt the changes were being imposed too quickly. It really made me aware of the need to work within the culture and to expect slow change, and only when it was initiated by the community. However, our donor requires more immediate outputs and numbers. So even knowing the history, I often feel that we have to push things a little bit to meet the requirements of our donor. That often means that our monitoring is at a very superficial level — so many women trained, so much money disbursed — and thus does not reflect any potential meaningful change that will continue after our program ends.

There is also a lot of frustration by the men that they cannot find work, which I think leads to resentment when their wives are selected for training. Women around the world struggle with the issues that arise when their husbands earn less, are not working, or feel otherwise inferior — it is not unique to Afghanistan. However, here there are much more violent repercussions against women as the resentment by individual men feeds into a larger group within a cultural context where women are supposed to be taken care of, not supporting the family, and where the culture allows for much more violence in general, and specifically against women. In a gender training that we held for our own staff the men commented that they would have no problem with women working, as long as jobs for all the men were found first.

An Afghanistan and gender specialist had the following to say on the concern that the term "gender" has become conflated with "women":

I have found when interviewing and talking with international aid workers about gender mainstreaming that that really means mainstreaming women into various projects and programs. Why can't we just say mainstreaming women? Gender mainstreaming seems misleading.

Gender is a Western concept for sure ... but also note that it is also a flexible, overused, and misused term in the West as well. Perhaps addressing issues of masculinity and femininity in both the local and international context would make more sense. Also for example U.S./Western conceptions of femininity and being a successful female in society vary greatly from Afghan conceptions of womanhood, femininity and the success of a woman in society — even in the public sphere. Conceptions of gender when implemented as a focus of aid — this is what I getting from your study — bring with them all of the complicated and contradictory definitions of gender within a Western context and then try to map that onto local/Afghan context without a clear and consistent understanding of that context and how much it has shifted/been altered by war, conflict, and dramatic changes in gender norms, codes, and expected behavior for men in women in various social, political and family contexts. In addition to the neglect of men, there is also the neglect of the family and family relationships as a central focus of Afghan life for both men and women.

There have been several local indigenous movements towards women's rights: the women's party, RAWA, locally based women's NGOs, women's operations of secret schools, and facilities for women both during the civil war and Taliban. There have been women consistently working on altering the social and political fabric of their lives, and they need assistance. But it seems that no one or very few of those in international gender development are seeking out these existing relationships because they have their own agendas or programs or ways of "doing gender."

She also shared with me an email that she received in July 2006 in response to her request for information on Afghan women's leadership. The author is a long-time Afghanistan specialist and analyst, and was also a participant in my study:

Special plea: Take it easy, at least publicly, on "Afghan women's leadership." The whole country is on the brink of collapse in a manner not altogether unlike what happened in the late 1920s and late 1980s. The main attack comes from ultra-conservatives. I worry that post–9/11 gains for Afghan women could be reversed as happened after the fall of Amanullah and then Najibullah. Foregrounding women's issues at the moment risks severe backlash.

Lessons from a Backlash

An Afghan activist and leader of an NGO for women said the following:

This study is valid especially for the international aid players in Afghanistan but I hope that they learned from the lessons that you remind them. From my point of view, lack of a clear agenda and appointing of unprofessional staff for the position of experts in Afghanistan caused that only women be considered gender in programs, therefore most people think that gender is empowerment of women. In Afghanistan, any word which is not part of the patriarchal terminology and is perceived as a Western term and having Western value — even if this word be part of other Islamic concepts and terminologies — still Afghans will considered strange and anti-culture and will not be accepted by the majority of people. Gender concept is always strange for the Afghan patriarchal society. And, there is no interest in understanding these things about Afghanistan. This is a fact, and I think the international community/aid organizations are not interested in the fundamental social and political changes in Afghanistan otherwise they should already have passed the process of analyzing the social institutions and their backgrounds and histories for better ways to make changes. Backlash has resulted but we also should not expect that a great social change in values and norms in a traditional and patriarchal society be warmly welcomed by the society.

In a group discussion, Afghan women NGO leaders had the following to say:

> ORZALA: People in Afghanistan — and especially the women in Afghanistan — were not given the time and space to sit a little bit and evaluate what they wanted to do. I can give you my own experience. I established an organization in January of 1999. I started the organization by my own opportunities and possibilities. And I started this organization in an emergency context. And I remember very well from that day up until this time that I am talking to you, I am running, running, running.... For people like me, and the majority of us, it's very important to be given some chances to look at what we're doing.... In the West, people plan their year. Here we plan our day. We cannot look beyond the day. This causes lack of coordination and this causes why we just run behind opportunities. We don't have our own strategies. Unfortunately, we run after anything. There is no cultural-sensitive and context-specific strategy for this country, taking into account its culture and history and very specific situation. A strategy that can take into consideration men as well as women.

Indeed, the absence of a strategy for women and men was an oft-repeated concern. The discussion continued to address the neglect of men in aid interventions as a key to understanding possible increases in violence against women:

> FARIBA: I do agree with you that this does create some problems and does increase violence against women. Just as an example — we established a computer course for girls from poor families. A free course. And then we were faced with boys. They said "If your priority is really for poor families, I am also the son of a poor person, so why am I not counted?"
>
> NAJIA: I think there is a need for positive discrimination for women. When we say that it should be gender-sensitive and only focusing on women, perhaps the reason why it is too much focused on women is because the positive discrimination is important because of the difference in men's opportunity and women's opportunity. But we should never, ever forget men's participation. Because as soon as you forget men's participation this will not be balanced, but it will actually be worse. The balance will be totally broken.
>
> ORZALA: We don't want to have educated and professional women and yet illiterate men. At the same time it should be equal.
>
> ROYA: If you say that being gender sensitive and the aid we get for it perpetuates sensitivity of men toward this issue and perpetuates violence against

women more, I would say it is true that men are getting uneasy about it and thinking that this gender focus is not going well. Violence increases when people don't have opportunities. It happens everywhere in the world, not just Afghanistan. But in Afghanistan and other third world countries, the women tend to be more domestic. That is the difference. So if they are not given an opportunity to work outside or earn their money, it's not affecting them as much as it would affect a man. And when a woman gets that opportunity and a man doesn't, he becomes frustrated. That is true. And I think it would be true all over the world, not only Afghanistan. Because he cannot work and the woman does. It is a natural thing ... or rather let me say that it is a "nurture-al" thing that men have the ego and sense of being in power and control. So when they see this, they feel that they lose their confidence and they don't feel good about it. And this frustration certainly contributes to the violence against women.

LAILA: Absolutely I think you are right. This is a pattern that we have seen everywhere in the world, and especially in most post-conflict countries, when men are in war and then there is no more war and what do they do? And they are very tense and frustrated and violent. They are influenced by the violence they have seen and they are unable to access economic opportunities and so they become increasingly frustrated. But what is different about Afghanistan from Bosnia and other cases is that yes, probably violence against women has increased for those kinds of reasons. But we can't even begin to say that we can prove it. There are no numbers at all. We can't show numbers to demonstrate this, to prove that this is really the case. The only thing we can go by are people's stories, which I think are much more powerful than the numbers anyway. It's the stories of the individual women that are a good measure. That's how I would measure. So the difference here from a Bosnia, for example, is that there was such a high profile placed on women and the intervention on behalf of women that disrupted the social dynamic in the house. What I heard over and over again is that "if there is no training for my husband, I can't come here. If there is no job for my brother, I can't keep coming here to this center. I can't do this anymore." And very often they said that they would prefer that he works, and not her. But everything was coming for her and not for him. So when you come in as a development organization and you don't know how things work in Afghanistan, how Afghans think ... and you put women on one side and men on the other side, like cattle. And you distribute benefits unequally, that's not a very smart thing to do.

In June 2006, a large meeting of gender and women's groups and interested individuals was convened in Kabul. An email group was created prior to the meeting, and the discussion of the agenda yielded many interesting comments, such as the following, taken directly from emails received as part of the discussion:

- There are many well-meaning initiatives, but few of these seem sustainable.
- We had a lot of gender meetings in the past.
- Gender mainstreaming and economic empowerment for women of Afghanistan ... is not as easy and simple like people think.
- Development agents often pose a barrier to progress in that they take on all the responsibility and decision making forgetting to pass the baton to the "developees" ... giving up control is not easy to do ... allowing people to make mistakes in your presence is even harder ... it is so much easier to just tell people what to do!!
- The current and seemingly deteriorating situation in Afghanistan makes the gender discussion even more critical. We do so much relatively high profile work with women, I've begun to be concerned about what kind of negative attention we could be in for in the future.
- After the terrible incident when three female Action Aid staff were killed in Jawzjan, we probably have to rethink gender and how we understand and facilitate it in the communities.
- In doing gender work in areas of high insecurity, am I jeopardizing the women that I work with?

The thematic working group Post-Conflict and Negative Attention, comprised of representatives from international and Afghan organizations, debated appropriate approaches to ensuring community acceptance in Afghanistan. Participants agreed that there were some fundamental flaws in the aid apparatus, starting with a resistance to genuine promotion of gender issues on the part of aid institutions. The lack of coordination, funding difficulties, short-term focus, and desire for "quick-fix solutions" were also cited as problems. The group raised the importance of understanding people's perceptions and the impact of rhetoric, particularly that stemming from the U.S. discourse of liberation that animated interventions in Afghanistan. Such language is problematic, it was agreed. It raises expectations and results in unmet promises and disillusioned people. Further, it comes with the assumption that a savior is going to deliver liberation. One woman continued that "we were not at all prepared to deliver on what we're saying, and if we don't, we are creating new tensions." This rhetoric may have stemmed from a particular discourse, but it was heard by all, particularly Afghans. As a result, a rhetoric fatigue has set in, coupled with a renewed dislike for foreign occupation that brings its own short-lived enthusiasms for alien ideologies.

Afghan participants in the working group felt that it was a convenient excuse to blame Afghan culture for resistance to gender-focused approaches, but this only reflected a failure in the apparatus to adequately understand Afghan society. One participant put it this way: "We don't spend enough time understanding. We need to build trust, we didn't do that. Go back to history and see what went wrong. They went out aggressively to bring reform with women, whatever regime it is — Soviet, American, and so on." The group emphasized the importance of understanding Afghan history and the ways in which social change has been resisted or received. A contextualized analysis, one Afghan woman explained, could have revealed that in the 1920s, for instance, the women's issue brought down a monarchy, resulting in many years of silence and regressions in terms of women's rights. This was the result of an aggressive program for social change led by an urban minority with little relation to the rural communities. She elaborated that "we need a more in-depth analysis and we need to look at what we're doing and turn it around before a backlash becomes inevitable."

An analysis of Afghan contexts, members of the group explained, could have revealed the gaps and errors in our assumptions. One Afghan woman explained that the aid apparatus assumes that Afghan women's voices are not heard, "but maybe they are not heard by *us*." The few voices that might be heard are not the ones that are representative of women in Afghanistan. She advocated a more thorough understanding of Afghan culture and society before starting operations, including knowledge of power and decision-making structures in the home. In so doing, efforts for empowerment could be better guided and not destabilize the family. Indeed, the pervasive feeling in the group was that in these last four years, the aid apparatus has nearly failed Afghan women. It started with flawed policies, and continued to accumulate flaws from there. One woman elaborated: "It was clear that the policy that was set for the U.S. to free Afghanistan was to 'liberate' Afghan women from the *bourka*. No Afghan is going to align themselves with that."

The Afghan woman continued: "I've been pushed a lot to work with women and women only but you can't work with just women. The more you work with women the more the men get annoyed." Participants reported that, in their organizations, Afghan male staff felt strongly that men's needs should be met first. "Find jobs for men first and then we'll talk about women," one man stated. It was agreed that the discourse employed for the gender agenda was hollow — and yet contagious. Even men use the language of gender and empowerment, no matter what they really believe, one woman said. "They think it's what we need to hear."

And yet there are repercussions. "Why are girls' schools being burned? Are we facing a situation that is creating new tensions?" one woman asked. There is a backlash, another woman explained, to what we — the aid apparatus — believed was the appropriate response to the gender-and-women issue. It was agreed that this environment never was post-conflict — firstly because the tensions never really subsided, and now "because new tensions have been created."

Later, a discussion of so-called women's leadership programs ensued. This was part of the language that followed the recent intervention trends that have moved from income generation to rights to leadership, amongst other short-lived aid fads. These shifts generally occur faster than many institutions can follow, and certainly too fast for participants, leaving Afghan men and women no time to consider their roles in the process and no opportunities to set the direction of the interventions. One Afghan woman specialist had the following to say:

> The title ["women's leadership programs"] itself creates so much resentment. Gender relations in Afghanistan are complementary and not juxtaposed men against women. This juxtaposition from aid agencies reflects individual rights and a Western capitalist context. This isn't applicable in Afghanistan because traditionally there is coexistence.

One of the non–Afghan specialists expressed her sentiments this way:

> There have been reports that women themselves are not happy about having so much focus upon them, numerous women's projects, freedom from the *bourka*, etc. Although, of course, they need so much, focusing exclusively on women is sometimes having a negative effect.... The kind of negative effects can be, for example, upsetting the dynamic within communities by giving more to women than men who are also very needy, causing tensions. Women themselves feel uncomfortable about this.

And finally, an American woman and women's rights activist had the following to say about the situation:

> Sadly, what we've seen is that U.S. rhetoric on "liberating Afghan women" was completely devoid of substance. We saw this from the beginning with the willingness of the U.S. to cooperate with the *Mujahideen* groups whose gender ideology was just as restrictive as the Taliban's. Reports from Afghanistan are uniformly bad on women's rights issues; violence against women is still common and women are still being intimidated out of participating in public life. In my opinion, the Bush administration used Afghan women — used them by focusing on their real suffering under the Taliban to get what they wanted (support for U.S. military action against Afghanistan), and then never putting in any real effort towards improving their lives. You ask if there have been any unexpected outcomes — I'm sorry to say that I expected this outcome from the beginning.

Are lessons learned — as we like to say?[2] The term is a peculiar piece of development lingo. We know the lessons, but we neither learn nor apply them. The idea of lessons learned is therefore a misnomer. Perhaps we can hope to do no harm, or possibly do *less* harm by learning from past efforts. We cannot claim ignorance — and yet we fail to make changes to practice. Even following unsuccessful interventions, the resulting consensus on what ought to be done has not led to change. "We don't learn, we just repeat," an Afghan human rights activist explained. "When we talk about women in Afghanistan, there is a list of important things showing what we did wrong. And we are still doing it. And we have not learned ... yet."

Interventions, Implications, and Occupations

The gender agenda in Afghanistan is lost in a desert that lacks context and history. It is a desert that failed to recognize what Afghan history aptly demonstrates: the deep and pervasive dislike of foreign intervention. Indeed, there exists an invisible corrective to foreign engagement in Afghanistan — a force of nature, dragging Afghanistan back to its roots.[3] Most Afghans believed that the aid community saw the problem of women in Afghanistan on simple terms and with a simple solution — on their own terms. Afghans will not embrace changes — particularly those involving women — as long as they are believed to be aligned with foreign interests.

Afghan history has also demonstrated that the most powerful means by which to destabilize agendas for social change is to label them un–Islamic. Understandings of Afghan socio-cultural contexts inevitably entail recognition of the value and significance of religion in the lives of Afghans. Every Afghan interviewed — woman or man — highlighted the importance of achieving gains within the context of Islam. Among discussions with non–Afghan policy-makers and policy implementers, the importance of Islam was often overlooked. Many Afghan members of aid institutions urged that interventions "should do everything with respect to Afghan and Islamic culture," in the words of one Afghan woman NGO leader. An inability to engage meaningfully with Islam prevents social change from penetrating the surface, particularly when dealing with gender issues.

Researchers have noted a cultural dissonance between changes within Afghan contexts and the values advocated by Western aid.[4] For example, many Afghan women have argued that the traditional division between public and private worlds does not necessarily mean that they have no decision-making power. These women prefer to view changes within the contexts of their traditions and religion. Many of those interviewed, particularly Afghan women, expressed strong sentiments against using radical language and tactics for fear of a backlash. This also includes adopting a seemingly Western approach to working with women. Another Afghan woman with an aid institution advocated that "gender experts should follow a gender perspective in Afghanistan *through Afghan eyes*. This means taking into consideration the prevailing customs and traditions."

An understanding of Afghan history, as previously illustrated, demonstrates that backlashes are not new. Attempts to force women's rights have resulted in violent backlashes, leaving women worse off than they were before. In light of the above, an understanding of the Afghan historical trajectory — particularly regarding gender politics — could illuminate patterns and problems that might pose obstacles in present attempts to restructure gender relations. Experts council against taking shortcuts to historically and sociologically informed analyses of the context and transformations of Afghan society.[5] This is the foundation for understanding gender issues in Afghanistan. More profound analyses of and engagement with Afghan society could prevent women from being addressed in a social and historical vacuum, thereby creating interventions that complement women's realities.

An interview with an Afghan woman named Zohra in the book *Women of Afghanistan Under the Taliban* expressed the sentiments of many:

> Of what I have read in history ... and what I have experienced in 46 years of my life, one thing has been confirmed to be right, that if there is foreign handling of our affairs, our people will never see a progressing Afghanistan. And I must say that our people throughout history have proved their opposition to the foreigner and never have accepted any kind of slavery. I have a piece of advice for U.S., Pakistan, Iran and Saudi Arabia that before taking any decision on Afghanistan, spend a few minutes and flick through the pages of Afghanistan's history, I am sure they would find some useful materials. The 20 years of wars have struck our innocent nation severe blows that they are incapable to speak out against the external and internal aggressors, but a time will come when our people will stand on their feet and sweep out the enemies of Afghanistan.[6]

An Afghan woman working as a policy implementer with an aid institution expressed strong sentiments about the push to import and impose foreign concepts in Afghanistan, as history has demonstrated the repeated failure of this strategy:

> I do not need to remind you that imposing an idea on Afghans is impossible. You know this. To bring positive change, the idea should be fixed in an Afghan cultural framework. Gender is the most valid example of this. We should have started by focusing on men because they are the ones traditionally with more power. When men understand the meaning of gender and its importance — and how it benefits them — women will immediately gain what

they deserve. But we have not yet learned from history and we still try to do things the wrong way. Backwards.

It is problematic to note the trend emerging from data that parallels the "regime" of the aid apparatus to previous occupiers in Afghanistan's history. Again, this is not new. Aid has long been a means by which outsiders gain influence in Afghanistan.[7] To Afghans, this looks not unlike history repeating. Understanding Afghanistan's legacy of occupation might explain present-day resistance to outside interference. This repeated cultural imperialism fueled Afghan perceptions that "outsiders, no matter how well-intentioned, sit poised, ready to engulf the nation with new sets of foreign values."[8] It is said that the one thing that repeatedly unites a very divisive Afghanistan is the need to drive out occupiers. This opposition to imperialism is voiced most strongly when it relates to women. Specifically, it is assumed that the corruption and degradation of Afghan women is a fundamental part of the Western cultural imperialism agenda.[9]

This degradation also manifests itself in the form of parties, pornography, and alcohol — a direct onslaught on Afghan values.[10] This can be demonstrated by the "no Afghan" door policy in Kabul restaurants that serve alcohol — or the myriad brothels masquerading as restaurants. These recreational activities appear — to Afghans — to be an attack against their *Afghaniyat*, or sense of Afghan identity. Indeed, this ideological occupation has taken the form of perceived imposition of an alien culture. This imposition, coupled with the lack of meaningful changes in the lives of Afghans, has resulted in Afghans adopting more conservative views.[11]

The present-day project of perceived cultural imperialism is one that stems from experiments in social engineering led by the aid apparatus. At several periods of interface in Afghanistan's history, the hostility toward this project was led by those largely in rural areas against a government or military apparatus. The current interface is now also experiencing open clashes in urban areas. The urban population has increased dramatically since 2002 as refugees and internally displaced persons are lured to Kabul and other Afghan cities to access the perceived opportunities of urban life and the perceived benefits of aid apparatus.

The failure of development efforts and women's rights is not simply due to a contradiction between modernity and tradition. It is in fact a widening of the gap between the urban elite and the rural majority.[12] This is, firstly, because the aid apparatus is centered in urban areas. And, even more noteworthy, the rural population has been displaced to the cities. It is in the cities that the dramatic social changes have been received or resisted. And it is in the cities where, historically, Afghan women have been both delivered and stripped of their rights. The old urban elite who applauded strong pushes for social change in the past have largely left Afghanistan. Today, the population of Kabul is predominantly comprised of Afghans of rural origins. Once a liberal urban center, Kabul has become a site of violence in the supposed aftermath — and therefore an interface where a more rigid gender order is enforced. Forces of change have been played out in the cities, and the first discussions of women's rights and roles began in Kabul and continue to transpire largely in the capital. Thus, urban women face a particular challenge — even if they only comprise a small percentage of Afghan women.

In the recent increase of violence, many have documented the Afghan perception of their occupation. Former Afghan president Professor Burhanuddin Rabbani[13] has become an outspoken critic of Western cultural imperialism, arguing that it has come to corrupt Islam and obstruct Afghanistan's development as an independent country. He put his views this way:

> We consider this a conspiracy against our religion, our freedom and security. They talk about women's issues, while thousands of women die, and nobody

Zia Gul, also known as Khala-jan (Dear Auntie), waits for lunch during a picnic, Paghman.

cares for them. But that does not stop them from talking about "moral corruption." They haven't come here for the reconstruction of Afghanistan, but they have come here to corrupt us.... The regime that rules our country stands against the wishes of the entire nation.... In Afghanistan, our policies should be defined by our nation, not by any foreign country. The current Afghan government's policies are not acceptable to the Afghan people. We must protect our freedom. If a foreign country gives aid, that should be without any strings attached. If the donors put conditions, we should not accept such aid.[14]

His influence over Afghan public opinion should not be underestimated, nor should his understanding of it. Rabbani's thoughts might appear to be provocative, but his words speak for many in Afghanistan. In May 2005, an article in *Kabul Weekly* — a paper written in English and Dari by Afghan authors — also reinforced this point.[15] It is relevant that the authors were Afghan and the text was English because the messages conveyed were geared to the aid apparatus. The article "NGO-Union Founded to Create Self-Sustainability: NGOs in Afghanistan Take a Step Towards Ending Reliance on International Funds" told the story of Afghan NGOs wanting to dictate their own agenda and end their "dependence." The subheading read, "Afghan NGOs seeking to rid themselves of international funds" and elaborated that foreign organizations are "attempting to project the values and norms of foreign civil societies on Afghanistan ... [bringing] negative results." The article also stated that "experts believe that NGOs' activities are not useful unless they find national financial sources and organize their programs according to the priorities of the nation's needs." One Afghan NGO-Union member said: "Their meetings and activities are commanded by foreigners, who are of no use to Afghanistan." He continued to say that NGOs should be free of foreign donors so that they can be allowed to implement projects in line with the values of Afghanistan; "Only then can they release themselves from the bondage of strangers."

The significance of the Afghan perception of being occupied by yet another regime cannot be overstated. It is expressed most clearly in this "Open Letter to Expatriates in Afghanistan," written by Sanjar Qiam and sent to various distribution lists in 2006. Segments of this letter follow:

The historical irony of this phenomenon never ceases to amaze me. Both post and pre Taliban eras are marked by oligarchic order: warlordism rooted out whatever was left of state infrastructure and committed all sorts of atrocities. The post Taliban period is marked by Expatlordism — a new type of oligarchy.... There is an increasing concentration of the means of communication at the top, this is due to communication culture, instruments, language and tendencies in foreign organization.... Organizational oligarchy has brought about societal oligarchy. Just like everything else a society can absorb certain dose of foreigners over a certain period of time. Afghanistan can take a very small dosage of foreigners as they are allergic to them. Every page of history witnesses the low "absorption capacity"—if I may borrow the term from EU.... I am making a reference to the history of a proud and individualistic man who defends his way of life.... My point is for one reason or another we are all protective. Except the difference is in your network everyone should play by your rules, which is fine. But you play by your rules in my network too. You don't have the faintest idea of my network and you even don't try to acquire some. You never think of shifting your stand, and redesigning your aims and your way of work. You tend to make Afghanistan feel like home. But Afghanistan is not your home. The more you try to live "your life" the more Afghans would hate you.

    Yours truly, Sanjar

On 24 June 2006, BBC aired a special report entitled "Afghanistan: Losing the Aid Game." This report was quite timely as it coincided with the first writing of this work and, more importantly, took place within a discouraging political climate in Afghanistan where frustrations and disillusionment appeared to be the order of the day. This report was aired a few short weeks after the riots in Kabul, the worst demonstration of violence in so-called post-conflict Afghanistan since the ousting of the Taliban in late 2001.

On 29 May 2006, riots erupted in Kabul, ignited by a traffic accident between Afghan vehicles and a U.S. military convoy, leaving over 14 people dead and nearly 150 injured. A volcanic reservoir of discontent overflowed into the city, directed at those who — in principle — are in Afghanistan to help. Myriad news articles reported on the sense of frustration felt by Afghans at the lack of progress in their country. "Underlying it all is the fact that young men have not seen any tangible change in their lives in terms of either jobs or basic services," explained an international aid worker.[16] Another article quoted an Afghan security officer who said: "Many people hate the NGOs because they see all this money coming into the country and they have not been able to get jobs. They were waiting for a day like today."[17]

These riots followed the killing of four Afghan aid workers with an international NGO in Jawzjan Province. Each year is progressively more brutal for aid workers in Afghanistan. The year 2009 appears to be the worst yet. Human Rights Watch presents a comparison of aid workers killed since 2003[18]:

12 aid workers killed in 2003
24 aid workers killed in 2004
31 aid workers killed in 2005
27 aid workers killed in 2006

17 aid workers killed in 2007
38 aid workers killed in 2008

The sense among the aid apparatus is that the situation will continue to deteriorate. Many have speculated that Afghanistan will once again be plunged into war. A June 2006 BBC report stated that "international development is failing one of its biggest challenges" in Afghanistan.[19] The report explained that people are disillusioned with the government and the aid apparatus, and that, as a result, a revival of conflict is likely. Afghanistan's semblance of freedom is fragile, the report explained. An array of reputable guests addressed the discrepancy between so-called peace and the absence of prosperity in Afghanistan. One of these guests was Ramazan Bashardost, the infamous former Minister of Planning whose critique of "NGO-ism" was previously discussed. Bashardost referred to the aid apparatus as a mafia who have "killed a golden and historic chance to foster cooperation between a Muslim country and a Western country." The report demonstrated that in many parts of Afghanistan, the conditions are so poor it appears "as if an emergency had just hit." One would never believe that Afghanistan is eight years into so-called post-conflict. Afghanistan is an example of what was called "the law of unintended consequences," and yet the country could have been a positive example of what a concerted international effort can accomplish. The report concluded that good intentions and solid plans did not translate on the ground and that there has been an absence of action, despite the abundance of consultants.

In a personal email communication from a colleague following the riots and reports, she wrote:

> There are reports circulating on internet groups of the anger amongst Kabulis when they hear and see international lavish parties and self-congratulatory news of their contribution to the development effort when the city and the country as a whole is still teeming with a half-starved, ill-serviced, growing population.

Back to the Beginning

To conclude, it is worthwhile going back to the beginning to gauge progress. The following excerpt was written in March 2003, in the relatively early days of Afghanistan's aftermath. During this time, there was hope that Afghanistan — and the much-touted cause of Afghan women — was on the path to victory. Since the writing of this piece, the situation in Afghanistan has suffered myriad evasions and rewritings, so much that the original aim has been lost in a haze of rhetoric. "The world's attention turned elsewhere, and Afghanistan, we were told, was now OK."[20] Perhaps the following passage on women will serve as a good measure to judge how "OK" Afghanistan really is:

> Afghan women cannot be disaggregated from the communities in which they live. Past attempts ... failed in part because they did not enjoy a base of community support; they drew instead on poorly understood models that were not adapted to the political and social realities of Afghanistan. There is a risk that today's reform will prove equally ephemeral. The international community's approach to gender has been guided not so much by Afghan history and its own accumulated experience in community development, but by a desire for immediate, visible signs of progress in women's education and economic empowerment.[21]

I argued at the beginning of this writing that Afghan women have been wrongly used as the barometer to measure social change in Afghanistan. However, as this case of Afghan women has demonstrated, the relative success or failure of the situation of Afghan women can surely be a barometer to measure the success or failure of the aid apparatus in Afghanistan. Indeed, the rights agenda — most directly applied to Afghan women — is the barometer by which the aid apparatus will finally assess its own success — or not. If the rights agenda is indeed the ultimate benchmark, what could be said about present-day developments in Afghanistan?

This work should not be taken as a judgment on whether a particular type of intervention has succeeded or failed. Success or failure is really not the point. Even a failed intervention can accomplish a strategic task and have particular outcomes. This attempt at a political task — restructuring the gender order — through a technical aid intervention has actually served to destabilize the gender order as the complexities of this task have been underestimated. The current gender order in Afghanistan is therefore far from settled as Afghan men perceive a challenge to their entrenched patriarchy through aid institutions. These institutions come in good faith but with a flawed understanding, and an inability to see indigenous challenges to the gender order that were already underway. As one effect, violence against women has appeared as the mechanism by which the gender order is defended when it is challenged.

It is important, however, to place this particular analysis in the context of increased violence and conflict, and a deteriorating political and economic situation. The existing measures of countries-in-conflict confirm this. For instance, the World Bank uses a nine-point checklist to indicate countries that could be approaching conflict[22]:

1. Violent conflict in the past ten years
2. Low per capita gross national income
3. High dependence on primary commodities exports
4. Political instability, including transformation of the state structure and a breakdown in law and order
5. Restricted civil and political rights
6. Militarization
7. Ethnic dominance
8. Active regional conflicts
9. High youth unemployment

One might argue that present-day Afghanistan qualifies for all of these points. To balance this, the UNDP Human Development Report lists seven elements that are necessary for long-term human security and a sustainable development process in Afghanistan[23]:

1. Security and safety
2. A responsible state and an accountable state-building process
3. Inclusive and empowering institutions and policies
4. Genuine participation
5. Balanced development (specifically in terms of focusing equally on rural areas and ensuring women's participation)
6. A supportive international community
7. Peaceful and cooperative regional agendas

One might further argue that given the recent escalation of violence, the inability of the central government to exercise authority over many provinces, the continued marginalization of Afghan civil society groups, the further deterioration of social indicators in rural areas, the decreased funding and focus from the aid apparatus, the continued tensions with Pakistan, and the possible increase of violence against women, Afghanistan in fact meets all of the World Bank's conflict indicators and none of the UNDP's elements of success. How Afghanistan will fare in the future remains to be seen.

The Gendered Interface

Similar to any aid activities, gender interventions may produce significant unintended consequences for women and for the gender order. Enforced social transformations can magnify inequalities. These are battles of politics and power. Aid interventions add a further complication as they are non-linear, socially constructed and negotiated processes with unintended consequences. These add a new layer to an ongoing battle for social space and cultural boundaries.[24] As a result, the effects may be in no measure what was intended or anticipated — and the end result may be significant enough to overwhelm the original intent.[25]

There are several interfaces at play in Afghanistan. In turn, these interfaces can yield unanticipated effects. One such unanticipated effect can emerge from gender-focused interventions when they fail to address *gender* issues, focusing only on women. The neglect of men in aid programming is an area of concern as transforming the gender order entails a focus on both women and men. Local gender ideologies are already on unstable ground in the aftermath of conflict — gender interventions notwithstanding. Gender interventions could further exacerbate this instability, presenting a challenge to Afghan forms of patriarchy. It is in this vein that I argue for a re-animation of gender in the Afghan context.

Interventions deny Afghan women's agency by promoting the discourse of externally driven transformation. The assumption is that Afghan women are unable to act on their own behalf. Facile analyses of women as "vulnerable individuals living in a vacuum may eventually isolate rather than reintegrate women."[26] Despite the discourse, this investigation revealed the manifestations of Afghan agency — both women and men.

Creating an artificial divide between technical and political interventions could result in unexpected social outcomes. It is difficult to isolate factors and determine which aspect of implementation produced particular effects. The separation of aid intervention into implementation and effects is an oversimplification of a highly complex set of processes that can only be understood in context. It is possible only to illuminate the different paths that may have led to certain effects. Aid policy-makers and policy implementers therefore have a key role to play, not only in how they interpret women's needs and interests, but also in the ways in which they choose to bring these needs and interests to fruition through programs.

There is no agreed-upon measure of transformation or progress for women in Afghanistan. From the perspective of the international media, the *chaddari* has often taken on a symbolic role as the barometer of social change. Yet the *chaddari*, or any act of veiling, must not be confused with, or made to stand for, lack of women's agency.[27] "With a veil on her head, no Afghan woman has ever stopped herself from letting her voice be heard, and frequently is it she who has the last word."[28] In current discussions on Afghanistan, generalizations on the situation of women often refer unconstructively to visible transformations — prevalence of veil or *chaddari*, or meetings of men and women — over institutional changes such as laws and improvement in status.[29] Conversations with Afghan women suggest that gender inequalities have not been rectified by engagement in aid activities as they had expected, based on aid rhetoric. The promise of transformation, as it were, did not materialize. In fact, these women were quite vocal about what they saw as a deteriorating situation regarding gender equality. They expressed concern about the high-profile focus from aid agencies and the media, and felt that facile analyses regarding the *chaddari* and their low social status were misguided and did not reflect Afghan realities.

Gender is a highly charged and politicized project in Afghanistan. Definitions and perspectives reflect a particular political power, revealing a lack of consensus about the primary goal at the strategic level. Aid interventions saw no political implications of their actions. And yet, as Afghan history demonstrates, gender issues (and their affiliated interventions) continue to be a highly charged sphere of Afghan life. As a result, aid institutions are political actors "whose actions have political impacts whether they like it or not."[30]

Unexpected effects have emerged from gender interventions because the creation of a particular discourse encouraged the formulation of a particular type of policy that was then not implemented in practice. There are therefore several probable paths — or a combination of all — that have led to these unanticipated outcomes. It is important to recognize that these are only partial effects; it is not possible to determine all factors that contribute to a certain outcome. Research can reveal select factors that may play a significant role in altering the gender order. Gender-focused international aid can possibly have positive effects on the gender order. This could be achieved in recognizing women's agency in a gender analysis that is historically and socially embedded. Ideally, this entails a focus on both strategic interests and practical needs in gender planning. Effects may be neutral if interventions maintain the status quo and do not disrupt the gender order. Negative effects are likely when interventions extract women from their historical and political realities and undermine women's agency.

Thus, at one end of the spectrum, interventions can offer the possibility for more public roles for women in the aftermath, including leadership positions in organizations and government, at the other end, violence against women is a possible negative effect which prevents women from accessing opportunities presented by their engagement in aid activities. In analyses of the effects of aid interventions, the positive effects — more public in nature —

tend to obfuscate potential negative effects, and are often used as measures of social change. The combination of positive and negative effects could therefore hinder transformation for women.

Violence against women can increase in the aftermath. I recognize the difficulties in demonstrating that increased violence against women may have been a possible negative effect, however it is possible that aid interventions created an enabling environment for such effects. Based on data, Afghan perceptions reveal that aid interventions may have played a role in producing these effects.

It is worthwhile restating what has been emphasized throughout this work and myriad others. Women's rights are the stage on which internal and external tensions have played out in Afghan history. Women's issues are used by political groups to rally support one way or another, and by foreign occupiers to interfere in Afghan politics. An Afghan lawyer and leader put it this way:

> When foreign intervention or influences are seen as the catalyst for reform in women's rights, rather than allowing the reforms to grow from within, the changes are not long-lasting. Conservatives and traditionalists inevitably use the issue of women's rights to link the ruling government with foreign interests or to accuse the government of running counter to Afghan culture or tribal customs. These accusations are then used to build popular support against the government and its reforms. In many cases, these foreign interests have been successful in hampering developments in women's rights.... If the issue of women's rights is regarded solely as an agenda to appease pro–Western influences, conservative groups are likely to use the issue to build popular support against the government that brings about such changes.[31]

The idea of a brewing backlash and negative effects for women is therefore not a secret. Even the UN has articulated their concern, stating that Afghan history repeatedly demonstrates that "efforts to strengthen women's status inherently carry the danger of a backlash."[32]

In a discussion of the failure of redistributive reforms in Soviet-occupied Afghanistan, Barnett Rubin, a leading authority on Afghanistan, cites four lines of argument that could easily be applied to present-day attempts to restructure the gender order[33]:

1. The reforms failed because the reformers had insufficient knowledge of the society they were trying to reform.

2. The Afghan state did not have the capacity to carry out the reforms.

3. According to the government itself, external intervention deprived it of the chance to correct its "mistakes."

4. Finally ... the reforms failed because the government that carried them out lacked legitimacy.

These four lines of argument fit well with the four presuppositions with which I began this discussion. Indeed, Rubin's analysis confirms that a robust understanding of the Afghan context is lacking. For these purposes, it is therefore likely that policy formulation reflected a discourse on women that was not socially and historically contextualized. Rubin continues to address issues of capacity. This is relevant to aid institutions because their intent, based on policy, was to transform women's position, yet the discourse on transformation denied women's agency. In short, meeting political concerns with technical responses does put capacity into question. Rubin further states that external intervention debilitated the Afghan government from implementing policies. In this case, the technical nature of implementation would contribute to achieving the stated goal of transformation. Thus the aid apparatus in fact debilitated itself. This is linked to Rubin's fourth point, that the apparatus lacked legitimacy. In fact, it continuously fed its lack of legitimacy, leaving Afghans with little belief that the aid apparatus can actually achieve the political project it set out for itself. Finally, to extend Rubin's argument one step further, I have argued that the combination of these lines of argument has produced significant unintended effects, including increased violence against women — a direct counter to the one vociferous goal the apparatus set for itself.

Extending James Ferguson's anti-politics framework to gender-focused aid interventions in Afghanistan might further illuminate Rubin's lines of argument. Ferguson might argue that the aid apparatus portrayed Afghan women as eager candidates for the political project of liberation — manifesting itself in the rights and empowerment discourse. Yet, the aid apparatus was not equipped to take on this political project, so they responded in the ways that they were able — through a standardized package of technical responses. In so doing, however, the aid apparatus further fueled the political game within which they found themselves. It is not possible to de-politicize women in Afghanistan — the most dangerously political project of all. The aid apparatus naively believed that advancing the gender agenda would be a safe issue (who can say no to a little women's liberation, after all?) and a guaranteed success. But if success is measured by the perceptions of those who are its supposed beneficiaries, the evidence is less clear. Ferguson puts it this way, illuminating:

> the fundamental contradiction in the role "development agencies" are
> intended to play. On the one hand, they are supposed to bring about "social
> change," sometimes of a dramatic and far-reaching sort. At the same time,
> they are not supposed to "get involved in politics" — and in fact have a strong
> de-politicizing function. But any real effort at "social change" cannot help

but have powerful political implications, which a "development project" is constitutionally unfit to deal with. To do what it is set up to do (bring about socio-economic transformations), a "development" project must attempt what it is set up not to be able to do (involve itself in political struggles).[34]

Free from the Inside?[35]

The personal is still political — perhaps even more true when it comes to gender issues in Afghanistan. It is worthwhile advocating for a renewed understanding of the connection between personal and political — particularly as this plays out in aid interventions. This reconnection could fuse an Afghan feminism and a contextualized politics presenting opportunities for advancement grounded in human rights and gender justice. But this has not been the path taken.

Gender policies do not operate in a socio-political vacuum. Afghan history demonstrates that externally enforced social reforms have been resisted time and again. Attempts at engineering a social transformation will continue to have serious repercussions for women as long as their agency is denied in the process.

One year after the fall of the Taliban, *Malalai*,[36] the women's magazine,

Masooda, Sarah, and Khatera celebrate International Women's Day, wearing traditional clothing made by a small women's business, Kabul.

asked what has changed for Afghan women one year on. The lead article, entitled "Freedom for Women: Only Words" argued that "the freedom which now exists for women is a freedom with little meaning."[37] A "flame of hope has been kept alive ... [though] endless speeches about the tragic lives of women and the importance of paying attention to them," but Afghan women and men alike are increasingly disillusioned with the reconstruction process and believe that it is indeed only words.

"We need more than words," I wrote in a statement on International Women's Day (8 March) in 2003, issued by a consortium of women's NGOs in Afghanistan:

> We must follow through with action. But we must also be prepared to be patient. This will not be a "quick impact project." What is needed is social evolution. Just a glance at the history of Afghanistan shows that rapid social change has resulted in serious consequences. Efforts to improve women's lives will be worthwhile in the long term if we remain sensitive to the culture and history of the country and if we operate with a clear sense of where Afghan women themselves want their future to be. Essential to starting this process is recognition and awareness that women are essential to the rebuilding of Afghanistan and should be given an active role in all development efforts. Women across Afghanistan want to participate meaningfully in the reconstruction of their community.[38]

While an array of theories and perspectives have been presented, the important lesson is that well-intended efforts and interventions may in fact produce unexpected outcomes for women. Violence against women is not exclusive to Afghanistan, to developing countries, or to conflict and aftermath countries. It is an epidemic that affects women worldwide and knows no social, cultural, or religious boundaries. It would do a great disservice to women in Afghanistan to isolate their suffering and label it an Afghan problem. This reveals that a more profound understanding of the gender order in the aftermath is needed.

The Dari word for transition, *gozargah*, represents a place people pass through, a point of transition, and an historic location in Kabul where nomads sought respite. Afghanistan's *gozargah* is neither the beginning of the journey nor the end. This story of an aid intervention represents a historical snapshot of an ongoing institutional and social process. This is also a highly political process — with political outcomes. The aid apparatus depoliticized what is likely the most political discourse of all in Afghanistan — women. Such reinventions cannot but have political ramifications. There are side effects from an attempt to engineer social transformation. Neglect of the politicization of the women issue has only served to feed the political fire. And women are increasingly burned by those flames.

The story began with a contextualized understanding of women and men in Afghanistan to reveal its incompatibility with the discourses that surrounded them. It is a story that argues for agency of both women and men — and demonstrates that it always existed in Afghanistan. The primary argument reveals the disconnects between the pervasive discourses and the realities of Afghan lives. It also exposes the disconnects between policy formulation, intent, interpretation, and implementation. As one result, it exposes the effects of such disconnects — namely that aid interventions have possibly made life more difficult for women. It is through the voices of Afghan women and men that this *gozargah*, this juncture in Afghanistan's transition, is understood. It is also through these voices that understandings of freedom are imagined. At last we begin to understand that freedom is indeed only won from the inside.

Dari Terminology

Afghaniyat. Afghan national identity

Akl. Responsibility

Bad. Offering women as brides in reparation for offenses

Badal. Offering women as brides in exchange for another bride

Bi-namoos. Without chastity

Bourka. Full body covering for women

Chador. Women's veil

Chaddari. Full body covering for women

Dari. Persian dialect spoken in Afghanistan

Ghayrat. Right to defend one's honor by force

Gozargah. Transition, juncture

Hijab. Women's veil

Imam. One who leads prayers, also head of Islamic community

Jihad. Holy war

Jirga. Tribal council

Jinsiyat. Sexuality

Kash-ma-kash. Conflict

Kharab. Bad

Khariji. Foreigner

Khshoonat aley-he zanaan. Domestic violence

Landay. Short poem

Loya Jirga. Grand Assembly

Mamus. Men's duty to protect and respect women

Mujahideen. Fighters in the holy war (plural)

Mullah. Religious official of small community

Namoos. Pride

Nang. Honor

Nar-shedza. Man-woman

Nezaa. Fighting

Nufus-dar. Having people, belonging

Pashto. Language spoken in Afghanistan

Pashtun. Afghan ethnic group, Pashto speakers

Pashtunwali. Pashtun tribal code

Purdah. Restricted movements for women

Shabnam. Night letters

Talib. Student of religion

Taliban. (plural)

Tarsidah. Fear

Tashadud. Violence

Tashadud aley-he zanaan. Violence against women

Wasita. Having special contacts and access

Wolesi Jirga. House of the People

Zan. Woman

Zanaan. Women

Acronyms and Abbreviations

ACBAR	Agency Coordinating Body for Afghan Relief
AIHRC	Afghanistan Independent Human Rights Commission
ANDS	Afghanistan National Development Strategy
CEDAW	Convention on the Elimination of All Forms of Discrimination Against Women
CSO	Civil Society Organization
GAD	Gender and Development
GoA	Government of Afghanistan
I-ANDS	Interim Afghanistan National Development Strategy
ISAF	International Security Assistance Force
MoWA	Ministry of Women's Affairs
NDF	National Development Framework
NGO	Non-Governmental Organization
RAWA	Revolutionary Association of the Women of Afghanistan
SAF	Securing Afghanistan's Future
UN	United Nations
UNAMA	United Nations Assistance Mission in Afghanistan
UNDP	United Nations Development Programme
UNHCR	United Nations High Commissioner for Refugees
UNIFEM	United Nations Development Fund for Women
UNRISD	United Nations Research Institute for Social Development
WID	Women in Development

Chapter Notes

Chapter 1

1. I have elected to employ the term "aid" to encompass both relief and development work as the lines between them are often indistinct in the context of conflict and the aftermath. I have employed the term "development" to a lesser extent as I believe, in line with Ferguson, that the concept (in quotations) is one that needs to be problematized in and of itself and is subject to varying definitions. Both aid and development as concepts are employed as interpretive grids through which we come to understand the contexts of poverty. I do not assume that there are uniform interpretations of this grid — or of its varying outcomes. J. Ferguson. (1994). *The anti-politics machine: "Development," depoliticization, and bureaucratic power in Lesotho.* Minneapolis: University of Minnesota Press.

2. The period of conflict in Afghanistan began with Soviet occupation in 1979, ending with the fall of the Taliban in late 2001. In using this periodization I am aware that conflict persists beyond the end of formal warfare.

3. For this study, I use the term "participants" to represent those who might be more commonly known as "beneficiaries" of aid interventions. The designation beneficiary is passive and falls short as it does not fully convey the depth and complexity of the relationship between actors.

4. I define discourse as "a *system* of language which draws on a particular terminology and encodes specific forms of knowledge." F. Tonkiss. (1988). Analysing discourse. C. Seale (Ed.). *Researching society and culture.* Thousand Oaks, CA: Sage Publications.

5. For these purposes, aid institutions include international relief and development organizations (such as those of UN agencies and international NGOs). The term does not include local Afghan organizations unless specified.

6. For these purposes, aid interventions refer to the policies and programs of aid institutions.

7. Similar to Kensinger, I use the terms "West" and "Western" to loosely define the European and American hegemonic constructions of culture, ideas, and politics. This should not be taken as an assumption that the "Western"

perspective is a uniform one; rather it is perceived as uniform from the perspective of Afghans. L. Kensinger. (2003). Plugged in praxis: Critical reflections on U.S. feminism, internet activism, and solidarity with women in Afghanistan. *Journal of International Women's Studies,* 5(1). Building on this, I employ Robinson's use of the terms not intending to make broad geographic divisions but because there is a lack of other terms that could reframe the discussion to challenge power imbalances. J. Robinson. (2002). *Development and Displacement.* Oxford: Oxford University Press.

8. J. Ferguson. (1994). *The anti-politics machine: "Development," depoliticization, and bureaucratic power in Lesotho.* Minneapolis: University of Minnesota Press.

9. For these purposes, the aid apparatus refers to aid institutions, aid interventions, and the discourses surrounding them.

10. I define institutions as the rules that govern behavior in economic, social, and political systems and organizations at the local, national, and international levels. Crisis States Programme (2001). *Crisis States Programme concepts and research agenda.* London: London School of Economics Development Research Center.

11. United Nations Development Programme & Islamic Republic of Afghanistan. (2004). *Afghanistan national human development report 2004: Security with a human face: Challenges and responsibilities.* Kabul: United Nations Development Programme.

12. The *chaddari* is a full-body form of covering traditionally worn by Pashtun women in Afghanistan to mark the symbolic segregation between men's and women's spheres. Amongst non-Afghans, it is more commonly known as *bourka.* However, *bourka* is the Arabic/Urdu term, while Afghans use the Dari/Persian term *chaddari.* See S. Barakat. (2004). Setting the scene for Afghanistan's reconstruction: The challenges and critical dilemmas. In S. Barakat (Ed.). *Reconstructing war-torn societies: Afghanistan.* Hampshire, Eng.: Palgrave Macmillan. I use the term *bourka* when it has been used by respondents, but prefer the term that is more common to Afghans.

13. N. H. Dupree. (1985). Women in Afghanistan: A brief 1985 update. In F. Rahimi (Ed.). *Women in Afghanistan*. Kabul: Paul Bucherer-Dietschi, p. 14.

14. F. Rahimi. (1977). *Women in Afghanistan*. Kabul: Paul Bucherer-Dietschi, p. 36.

15. A. Hans. (2004). Escaping conflict: Afghan women in transit. In W. Giles and J. Hyndman (Eds.). *Sites of violence: Gender and conflict zones*. Berkeley: University of California Press.

16. For further information, see H. Emadi. (2002). *Repression, resistance, and women in Afghanistan*. Westport, CT: Praeger.

17. D. Ellis. (2000). *Women of the Afghan War*. Westport, CT: Greenwood; P. McAllister. (1991). *This River of Courage: Generations of women's resistance and action*. Philadelphia: New Society Publishers.

18. P. McAllister. (1991). *This River of Courage: Generations of women's resistance and action*. Philadelphia: New Society Publishers.

19. N. H. Dupree. (1985). Women in Afghanistan: A brief 1985 update. In F. Rahimi (Ed.). *Women in Afghanistan*. Kabul: Paul Bucherer-Dietschi.

20. R. Skaine. (2002). *The women of Afghanistan under the Taliban*. Jefferson, NC: McFarland and Co., p. 18–19.

21. A. Hans. (2004). Escaping conflict: Afghan women in transit. In W. Giles & J. Hyndman (Eds.). *Sites of violence: Gender and conflict zones*. Berkeley: University of California Press. p. 235.

22. N. H. Dupree. (2004). Cultural heritage and national identity in Afghanistan. In S. Barakat (Ed.). *Reconstructing war-torn societies: Afghanistan*. Hampshire, Eng.: Palgrave Macmillan, p. 317.

23. R. Skaine. (2002). *The women of Afghanistan under the Taliban*. Jefferson, NC: McFarland and Co., p. 17.

24. M. Weiner & A. Banuazizi. (Eds.). (1994). *The politics of social transformation in Afghanistan, Iran, and Pakistan*. Syracuse: Syracuse University Press, p. 25.

25. H. Ahmed-Ghosh. (2003). A history of women in Afghanistan: Lessons learnt for the future *or* yesterdays and tomorrow: Women in Afghanistan. *Journal of International Women's Studies*, 4(3).

26. R. Skaine. (2002*). The women of Afghanistan under the Taliban*. Jefferson, NC: McFarland and Co., p. 30.

27. V. M. Moghadam. (1999). Revolution, religion, and gender politics: Iran and Afghanistan compared. *Journal of Women's History*, 10 (4), 172–195.

28. D. Kandiyoti (Ed.). (1991). *Women, Islam and the state*. Philadelphia: Temple University Press, p. 8.

29. For these purposes, the "international community" refers to the aid apparatus. I limit use of the term in that it appears to be a misnomer, assuming uniformity of opinion and behavior, in the way one might imagine of a community. Regarding Afghanistan's official entry into the international community, the country gained membership to the United Nations on 19 November 1946.

30. J. Benjamin. (2000). Afghanistan: Women survivors of war under the Taliban. In J. Mertus (Ed.). *War's offensive on women: The humanitarian challenge in Bosnia, Kosovo, and Afghanistan*. West Hartford, Eng.: Kumarian Press.

31. S. Barakat & G. Wardell. (2004). Exploited by whom? An alternative perspective on humanitarian assistance to Afghan women. In S. Barakat (Ed.). *Reconstructing war-torn societies: Afghanistan*. Hampshire, Eng.: Palgrave Macmillan.

32. W. Giles & J. Hyndman (Eds.). (2004). *Sites of violence: Gender and conflict zones*. Berkeley: University of California Press.

33. N. H. Dupree. (2004). Cultural heritage and national identity in Afghanistan. In S. Barakat (Ed.). *Reconstructing war-torn societies: Afghanistan*. Hampshire, Eng.: Palgrave Macmillan, p. 323–324.

34. N. Niland. (2004). Justice postponed: The marginalization of human rights in Afghanistan. In A. Donini, N. Niland, & K. Wermester (Eds.). *Nation-building unraveled? Aid, peace and justice in Afghanistan*. Bloomfield, CT: Kumarian Press, p. 79.

35. I. Smillie & L. Minear. (2004). *The charity of nations: Humanitarian action in a calculating world*. Bloomfield: Kumarian Press, p. 102.

36. Oxfam. (2008). Afghanistan: Development and humanitarian priorities. Kabul: Oxfam International, Afghanistan, p. 2.

37. C. Johnson & J. Leslie (2004). *Afghanistan: The mirage of peace*. London: Zed Books, p. 207.

38. J. Ferguson. (1994). *The anti-politics machine: "Development," depoliticization, and bureaucratic power in Lesotho*. Minneapolis: University of Minnesota Press, p. 259.

39. C. Johnson & J. Leslie (2004). *Afghanistan: The mirage of peace*. London: Zed Books, p. 76.

40. These aid individuals, along with war reporters, were often referred to as "emergency junkies" based on their careers built on moving from one emergency context to another. Many of these saw Afghanistan as an extension of their previous country assignments and were therefore able to revive previous professional relationships and programs with little regard for whether they were valid in the new context.

41. J. Benjamin. (2000). Afghanistan: Women survivors of war under the Taliban. In J. Mertus (Ed.). *War's offensive on women: The humanitarian challenge in Bosnia, Kosovo, and Afghanistan.* West Hartford, Eng.: Kumarian Press.

42. L. Abirafeh. (2004, October). Burqa politics: The plights of women in Afghanistan. *Chronogram,* http://www.chronogram.com/issue/2004/10/news/burqa.php.

43. United Nations Inter-Agency Network on Women and Gender Equality, OECD/DAC Network on Gender Equality, et al. (2003). Retrieved from http://www.un.org/womenwatch/ianwge/collaboration.htm, p.7.

44. H. Karzai, Japan, United States, European Union, & Saudi Arabia. (2002, January 21–22). Co-chairs' Summary of conclusions: The international conference on reconstruction assistance to Afghanistan. *Bonn agreement.* Tokyo, Japan.

45. Islamic Republic of Afghanistan (2002). *National development framework: Draft: Version 2.* Kabul: Islamic Republic of Afghanistan.

46. D. Kandiyoti. (2005). The politics of gender and reconstruction in Afghanistan. *Occasional Paper.* Geneva: United Nations Research Institute for Social Development, p. 20.

47. Islamic Republic of Afghanistan (2004). *Securing Afghanistan's future: Accomplishments and the strategic path forward.* Kabul: A Government/International Agency Report: Islamic Republic of Afghanistan, Asian Development Bank, United Nations Assistance Mission to Afghanistan, United Nations Development Program, The World Bank Group.

48. This statement is problematic as women were in fact harassed at the *Loya Jirga.*

49. C. Robichaud. (2006). Remember Afghanistan? A glass half full, on the *Titanic. World Policy Journal,* 23(1), 17.

50. Human Rights Watch (2006). *Lessons in terror: Attacks on education in Afghanistan.* Kabul: Human Rights Watch, p. 9–10.

51. For more information see http://www.rhrealitycheck.org/blog/2007/07/30/violence-against-women-not-included-in-peace-index.

52. S. G. Jones. (2006). Averting failure in Afghanistan. *Survival,* 48, 111–128.

53. CARE International in Afghanistan: Policy brief. (2003). Kabul, CARE International.

54. C. Robichaud. (2006). Remember Afghanistan? A glass half full, on the *Titanic. World Policy Journal,* 23(1).

55. CARE International in Afghanistan: Policy brief. (2003). Kabul, CARE International, p. 4.

56. Security and Peace Initiative (2005). *American attitudes toward national security, foreign policy and the war on terror.* Washington, D.C.: Security and Peace Initiative.

57. W. Byrd. (2007). *Responding to Afghanistan's development challenges: An assessment of experience during 2002–2007 and issues and priorities for the future.* Kabul: World Bank.

58. United Nations Population Fund. (UNFPA). (2005). The promise of equality: Gender equity, reproductive health and the millennium development goals. *The state of world population report.* New York: United Nations Population Fund.

59. United Nations. (2005). *World population prospects: The 2004 revision — Highlights.* New York: Department of Economic and Social Affairs of the UN Secretariat.

60. United Nations Development Programme & Islamic Republic of Afghanistan. (2004). *Afghanistan national human development report 2004: Security with a human face: Challenges and responsibilities.* Kabul: United Nations Development Programme.

61. Islamic Republic of Afghanistan. (2005). *Vision 2020—Afghanistan millennium development goals report 2005.* Kabul: United Nations Development Programme.

62. E. Rostami-Povey. (2007a). *Afghan women: Identity and invasion.* London: Zed Books.

63. Information on urban livelihoods in this section is taken from J. Beall & S. Schutte. (2006). Urban livelihoods in Afghanistan. Issues Paper Series. Kabul: Afghanistan Research and Evaluation Unit.

64. E. Rostami-Povey. (2005). Women and work in Iran. *State of Nature,* Autumn, 75.

65. The term "aftermath" is based on S. Meintjes, M. Turshen, & A. Pillay. (Eds.). (2001). *The aftermath: Women in post-conflict transformation.* London: Zed Books.

66. M. B. Anderson & P. J. Woodrow (1998). *Rising from the ashes: Development strategies in times of disaster.* Paris: UNESCO.

67. M. Duffield. (2005). Human security: Linking development and security in an age of terror. *General Conference of the EADI.* Bonn, Ger.: n.p., p. 15.

68. For further information on this concept, see J. Ross, S. Maxwell, & M. Buchanan-Smith. (1994). *Linking relief and development.* Brighton: Institute of Development Studies.

69. J. P. Lederach. (1997). *Building peace: Sustainable reconciliation in divided societies.* Washington, D.C.: United States Institute of Peace Press.

70. S. Meintjes, M. Turshen, & A. Pillay, (Eds.). (2001). *The aftermath: Women in post-conflict transformation.* London: Zed Books, p. 152.

71. D. Kandiyoti. (2003). *Integrating gender analysis into socio-economic needs assessment in Afghanistan.* Kabul: United Nations Development Fund for Women.

72. Sylvia Walby defines patriarchy as a "system of social structures and practices in which men dominate, oppress and exploit women." S. Walby. (1990). *Theorizing patriarchy.* Oxford: Blackwell. I agree with Walby in that it is important to note that all men are not dominant, just as all women are not subordinate.

73. M. H. Kamali. (2003). *Islam, pernicious custom, and women's rights in Afghanistan.* Malaysia: International Islamic University.

74. D. Kandiyoti (Ed.). (1991). *Women, Islam and the state.* Philadelphia: Temple, p. 14.

75. In this case, socio-cultural factors refer to mobility and ability to work and earn income, amongst others. These factors depend on age, ethnicity, economic status, etc.

76. S. Walby. (1988). Gender politics and social theory. *Sociology,* 22(2), 215–232.

77. D. Hilhorst. (2003). *The real world of NGOs: Discourses, diversity and development.* London: Zed Books.

78. J. Beall & D. Esser. (2005). Shaping urban futures: Challenges to governing and managing Afghan cities. Issues Paper Series. Kabul: Afghanistan Research and Evaluation Unit (AREU).

79. I use the term "transformation" also to represent the array of aid-agency terms that have come to have similar meanings. "Empowerment" is one such term. I do not intent to imply that the two are synonymous, but they are used in similar ways in development rhetoric.

80. J. Ferguson. (1994). *The anti-politics machine: "Development," depoliticization, and bureaucratic power in Lesotho.* Minneapolis: University of Minnesota Press, p. 281.

81. M. Villarreal. (1992). The Poverty of practice: Power, gender and intervention from an actor-oriented perspective. In A. Long & N. Long (Eds.). *Battlefields of knowledge: The interlocking of theory and practice in social research and development.* London: Routledge, p. 264.

82. For more information, see http://www.oneworld.net and http://democracyinaction.org.

83. For more information, see www.boxer.senate.gov.

84. N. Kabeer. (1994). *Reversed realities: Gender hierarchies in development thought.* London: Verso, p. 224.

85. A. Cornwall & K. Brock. (2005). Beyond Buzzwords: "Poverty reduction," "participation" and "empowerment" in development policy. Overarching Concerns Programme Paper Number 10. Geneva: United Nations Research Institute for Social Development, p. iii.

86. Molyneux and Lazar present a thorough evolution of the "rights-based" discourse, explaining its origins in the 1990s as an effort to re-politicize the rights discourse for women, representing the difference between proclaiming rights and actually exercising them. For more information, see M. Molyneux & S. Lazar. (2003). *Doing the rights thing: Rights-based development and Latin American NGOs.* London: ITDG Publishing.

87. M. Molyneux & S. Lazar. (2003). *Doing the rights thing: Rights-based development and Latin American NGOs.* London: ITDG Publishing, p. 2.

88. V. Ware. (2006). *Info-war and the politics of feminist curiosity: Exploring new frameworks for feminist intercultural studies.* London: Gender Institute, London School of Economics.

89. I borrow this term from D. Hilhorst. (2003). *The real world of NGOs: Discourses, diversity and development.* London: Zed Books. The hegemonic geopolitical discourse on Afghanistan has been primarily American. It can be argued that images of Afghan women as victims serve various political projects such as the American offensive against the Taliban, and the aid apparatus' quest for funding — and legitimacy.

90. J. Ferguson,. (1994). *The anti-politics machine: "Development," depoliticization, and bureaucratic power in Lesotho.* Minneapolis: University of Minnesota Press, p. 58.

91. D. Kandiyoti (Ed.). (1991). *Women, Islam and the state.* Philadelphia: Temple.

92. This term was first coined by Edward Said. E. W. Said. (1979). *Orientalism.* New York: Vintage.

93. I have elected to avoid use of the WID/GAD collection of acronyms, opting instead for less loaded terminology. However, they deserve a brief explanation here as they present relevant background to the evolution of the discourse. The focus on WID can be credited to its founding mother, Esther Boserup, in her 1970 work that brings women into economic development. E. Boserup. (1970). *Woman's role in economic development.* New York: St. Martin's Press.

94. W. Harcourt. (2005). The body politic in global development discourse: A woman and the politics of place perspective. In W. Harcourt & A. Escobar (Eds.). *Women and the politics of place.* Bloomfield, CT: Kumarian Press, p. 43.

95. J. Ferguson. (1994). *The anti-politics machine: "Development," depoliticization, and bureaucratic power in Lesotho.* Minneapolis: University of Minnesota Press.

96. N. Kabeer. (1994). *Reversed realities: Gender hierarchies in development thought.* London: Verso, p. 91.

Chapter 2

1. Segments of this chapter will be published in L. Abirafeh (forthcoming). Discourses on *chaddari* politics: Translating perceptions into policy and practice. In J. Heath & A. Zahedi (Eds.). *Women of Afghanistan in the post 9/11 era: Paths to empowerment*. California: University of California Press.

2. E. Rostami-Povey. (2007a). Afghan women: Identity and invasion. London: Zed Books, p. 138.

3. Gender policy-makers are heads of aid institutions, gender/women focal points, senior gender advisors, etc. None of these senior people were Afghan at the time of my research. Gender policy implementers are gender/women program implementers, heads of Afghan women's NGOs, and others — the frontline workers who interface directly with those whom the programs aim to serve. Policy-makers are significant as they create gender policies, while implementers translate policies into action, often based on their own interpretations.

4. N. Long. (2000). Exploring local/global transformations: A view from anthropology. In N. Long & A. Acre (Eds.). *Anthropology, development and modernities: Exploring discourses, counter-tendencies and violence*. London: Routledge, p. 191.

5. N. Long. (1977). *An introduction to the sociology of rural development*. London: Tavistock Publications, p. 183–184.

6. B. Ehrenreich. (2003). Veiled threat. In A. Joseph & K. Sharma (Eds.) *Terror, counterterror: Women speak out*. London: Zed Books. p. 77.

7. For more information, please see: http://urbanlegends.about.com/library/blafghan.htm.

8. M. Sultan. (2005). *From rhetoric to reality: Afghan women on the agenda for peace*. Washington, D.C.: Women Waging Peace Policy Commission, p. 31.

9. J. Goodwin. (2003). *Price of honor: Muslim women lift the veil of silence on the Islamic world*. New York: Plume.

10. S. Azarbaijani-Moghaddam. (2004). Afghan women on the margins of the twenty-first century. In A. Donini, N. Niland, & K. Wermester (Eds.). *Nation-building unraveled? Aid, peace and justice in Afghanistan*. Bloomfield, CT: Kumarian Press, p. 100.

11. For more information on the "Gender Apartheid" campaign, see Feminist Majority at www.feministmajority.org. I do not dispute that the situation of Afghan women at that time was dire. Despite criticism, I credit Jan Goodwin and Feminist Majority for bringing to light the situation of Afghan women and for serving as strong advocates to raise awareness and funding in the U.S. Kandiyoti writes that "Feminist Majority's "Campaign to stop gender apartheid in Afghanistan" scored some U.S. political victories for Afghan women's rights. Through a series of petitions and lobbying activities, they played a significant role in 1998 in persuading the UN and the U.S. to reject formal recognition of the Taliban. They also put pressure on U.S. energy company Unocal to back out of a $3 billion venture to put a pipeline through Afghanistan that would have given the Taliban $100 million royalties." D. Kandiyoti. (2005). The politics of gender and reconstruction in Afghanistan. *Occasional Paper*. Geneva: United Nations Research Institute for Social Development.

12. J. Benjamin. (2000). Afghanistan: Women survivors of war under the Taliban. In J. Mertus (Ed.). *War's offensive on women: The humanitarian challenge in Bosnia, Kosovo, and Afghanistan*. West Hartford, Eng.: Kumarian Press.

13. A. M. Jaggar. (1998). Globalizing feminist ethics. *Hypatia*, 13(2), p. 8–9.

14. S. Wali, S. (2002). Afghanistan: Truth and mythology. In S. Mehta (Ed.). *Women for Afghan women: Shattering myths and claiming the future*. New York: Palgrave Macmillan, p. 1.

15. G. Dorronsoro. (2005). *Revolution unending: Afghanistan: 1979 to the present*. New York: Columbia University Press, p. 291–292.

16. A. M. Jaggar. (1998). Globalizing feminist ethics. *Hypatia*, 13(2), p. 10.

17. I was invited to speak on the issue of Afghan women at the Women as Global Leaders Conference in Dubai, United Arab Emirates. At that point I had already been working in Afghanistan for nearly three years. I used the conference as an opportunity to gauge public opinion on the situation of Afghan women more than three years after their "liberation" and their virtual disappearance from the media. The audience was comprised of forty female participants, mostly American. They were conference participants who elected to attend my session on Afghanistan. Ages ranged from fifteen to sixty-eight and included students, academics, and development practitioners. At the beginning of the two-hour session, I circulated a questionnaire to the participants and asked that they complete it immediately. The answers then served as the starting point for the discussion on images of Afghan women.

18. While most of the participants mentioned the *chaddari*, it is important to note that all of them used the word *bourka*. In fact, none of them were familiar at all with the word *chaddari*.

19. Nancy Hatch Dupree is one of the foremost authorities on Afghanistan. She has di-

rected the ACBAR (Agency Coordinating Body for Afghan Relief) Resource and Information Centre in Peshawar since 1989. She is the author of six guidebooks on Afghanistan and has published over 150 articles on Afghanistan. Her husband, the late Louis Dupree, was a prominent anthropologist and Afghanistan specialist. No research on Afghanistan is complete without referencing the Duprees' work. N. H. Dupree. (1985). Women in Afghanistan: A brief 1985 update. In F. Rahimi (Ed.). *Women in Afghanistan.* Kabul: Paul Bucherer-Dietschi, p. 14.

20. United Nations Secretary General (1997). *The situation in Afghanistan and its implications for international peace and security.* New York: United Nations General Assembly Security Council.

21. G. Whitlock. (2005). The skin of the *bourka*: Recent life narratives from Afghanistan. *Biography,* 28(1), p. 57.

22. R. Skaine. (2002). *The women of Afghanistan under the Taliban.* Jefferson: McFarland and Co., p. 29.

23. It should be noted that the Taliban also did their part to pit men against women by requiring that men enforce the edict that "their women" wear the *chaddari*. Failure to do this would result in severe punishment. "In this way, the Taliban accomplish control over both men and women. They not only obliterate women's presence but also by usurping what was the purview of the family, they put to shame the men of the family, thus rendering them disempowered." N. Gross. (2000). The messy side of globalization: Women in Afghanistan. *Symposium on Globalization and Women in Muslim Societies.* Washington, D.C.: Library of Congress.

24. L. Abirafeh. (2004, October). Burqa politics: The plights of women in Afghanistan. *Chronogram,* http://www.chronogram.com/issue/2004/10/news/burqa.php.

25. U. Narayan. (1997). *Dislocating cultures: Identities, traditions, and third world feminism.* New York: Routledge.

26. These women's stories were previously published in R. Skaine. (2008). *Women of Afghanistan in the post–Taliban era: How lives have changed and where they stand today.* Jefferson: McFarland and Co.

27. N. H. Dupree. (1996). *The women of Afghanistan.* Stockholm: Swedish Committee for Afghanistan, p. 15.

28. F. Cleaver (Ed.). (2002). *Masculinities matter! Men, gender and development.* London: Zed Books.

29. *Ibid.,* p. 1.

30. J. Ferguson. (1994). *The anti-politics machine: "Development," depoliticization, and bureaucratic power in Lesotho.* Minneapolis: University of Minnesota Press.

Chapter 3

1. Segments of this chapter were previously published. See L. Abirafeh. (2004, October). Burqa politics: The plights of women in Afghanistan. *Chronogram,* http://www.chronogram.com/issue/2004/10/news/burqa.php; and L. Abirafeh. (2005). Lessons from gender-focused international aid in post-conflict Afghanistan ... learned? In A. Wieland-Karimi. *Gender in international cooperation.* Bonn: Friedrich-Ebert-Stiftung.

2. S. Azarbaijani-Moghaddam. (2004). Afghan women on the margins of the twenty-first century. In A. Donini, N. Niland, & K. Wermester (Eds.). *Nation-building unraveled? Aid, peace and justice in Afghanistan.* Bloomfield, CT: Kumarian Press.

3. K. Staudt. (2002). Dismantling the master's house with the master's tools? Gender work in and with powerful bureaucracies. In K. Saunders (Ed.). *Feminist post-development thought: Rethinking modernity, post-colonialism and representation.* London: Zed Books, p. 57.

4. C. Johnson & J. Leslie. (2004). *Afghanistan: The mirage of peace.* London: Zed Books, p. 77.

5. E. Rostami-Povey. (2007). *Afghan women: Identity and invasion.* London: Zed Books.

6. I use "masculinities" to define the various socially constructed definitions for being a man. These are dynamic concepts that can vary over time and in different contexts. The term conveys the idea that there are perceived notions and ideals about how men are expected to behave in a given context. Women's Commission for Refugee Women and Children (2005). *Masculinities: Male roles and male involvement in the promotion of gender equality.* New York: Women's Commission for Refugee Women and Children.

7. T. Bouta, G. Frerks, & I. Bannon. (2005). *Gender, conflict, and development.* Washington, D.C.: International Bank for Reconstruction and Development, p. 91.

8. F. Cleaver (Ed.). (2002). *Masculinities matter! Men, gender and development.* London: Zed Books, p. 24.

9. P. Paci. (2002). *Gender in transition.* Washington, D.C.: World Bank.

10. F. Cleaver (Ed.). (2002). *Masculinities matter! Men, gender and development.* London: Zed Books, p. 81–82.

11. M. Range. (2005, June 20). Gender equality as a driving force for achieving the MDGs. *Monday Developments.*

12. I borrow "the Myth of Liberation" from a section heading in a report by Jean-Paul Faguet. J.-P. Faguet. (2004). Democracy in the

desert: Civil society, nation-building and empire. Crisis States Programme Discussion Paper. London: London School of Economics Development Research Centre. Faguet refers to what he sees as the fallacy of liberation, namely that "external intervention can be used to lift the constraints that oppress society, allowing it to spring forth and democracy to flourish." Successful economies and effective governments have, in the past, only been built on a foundation that includes social organizations, strong traditions, civic interaction, and an institutional framework. "The flower of democracy will not thrive in such a desert." The "desert" that Faguet refers to in this case — Iraq — could easily be extended to apply to gender interventions in Afghanistan.

13. *Bourka* was the preferred spelling of the publisher. *Chaddari* was not a well-known term and would not illicit the same response in the article.

14. S. Mehta (Ed.). (2002). *Women for Afghan women: Shattering myths and claiming the future.* New York: Palgrave Macmillan. p. 142.

15. *Shalwar Kameez* is one name that is used to refer to the traditional male garment in Afghanistan.

16. K. Hunt. (2002). The strategic co-optation of women's rights: Discourse in the "war on terrorism." *International Feminist Journal of Politics*, 4(1), 116–121.

17. C. Johnson & J. Leslie (2004). *Afghanistan: The mirage of peace.* London: Zed Books, p. 23.

18. R. Hassan. (2002). Muslim women's rights: A contemporary debate. In S. Mehta (Ed.). *Women for Afghan women: Shattering myths and claiming the future.* New York: Palgrave Macmillan, p. 137.

19. B. McCaffrey. (2006). *Academic report— Trip to Afghanistan and Pakistan.* New York: United States Military Academy, West Point.

20. J. Ferguson. (1994). *The anti-politics machine: "Development," depoliticization, and bureaucratic power in Lesotho.* Minneapolis: University of Minnesota Press.

21. N. Stockton. (2004). Afghanistan, war, aid, and international order. In A. Donini, N. Niland, & K. Wermester (Eds.). *Nation-building unraveled? Aid, peace and justice in Afghanistan.* Bloomfield: Kumarian Press, p. 30.

22. A. Costy. (2004). The dilemma of humanitarianism in the post–Taliban transition. In A. Donini, N. Niland, & K. Wermester (Eds.). *Nation-building unraveled? Aid, peace and justice in Afghanistan.* Bloomfield, CT: Kumarian Press, p. 162.

23. C. Johnson & J. Leslie (2004). *Afghanistan: The mirage of peace.* London: Zed Books., p. 157.

24. S. Azarbaijani-Moghaddam. (2004).

Afghan women on the margins of the twenty-first century. In A. Donini, N. Niland, & K. Wermester (Eds.). *Nation-building unraveled? Aid, peace and justice in Afghanistan.* Bloomfield, CT: Kumarian Press, p. 101.

25. *Ibid.*, p. 104.

26. D. Mosse. (2005). *Cultivating development: An ethnography of aid policy and practice.* London: Pluto Press, p. 91.

27. Watkins explains that "only poorer classes, usually Hazaras, ever permitted their women to work as maids, so servants were and to a large extent still are males," thus it is not even appropriate for most Afghan women to work in houses. For more information, see M. B. Watkins. (1963). *Afghanistan: Land in transition.* Princeton: D. Van Nostrand Co.

28. United Nations Development Programme & Islamic Republic of Afghanistan. (2004). *Afghanistan national human development report 2004: Security with a human face: Challenges and responsibilities.* Kabul: United Nations Development Programme.

29. The Human Development Report explains that aid strategies for Afghanistan were presented to Afghans as a *fait accompli.* United Nations Development Programme & Islamic Republic of Afghanistan. (2004). *Afghanistan national human development report 2004: Security with a human face: Challenges and responsibilities.* Kabul: United Nations Development Programme.

30. D. Kandiyoti. (2005). The politics of gender and reconstruction in Afghanistan. *Occasional Paper.* Geneva: United Nations Research Institute for Social Development, p. vii.

31. F. Cleaver (Ed.). (2002). *Masculinities matter! Men, gender and development.* London: Zed Books, p. 8.

Chapter 4

1. C. Johnson & J. Leslie. (2004). *Afghanistan: The mirage of peace.* London: Zed Books.

2. *Ibid.*, p. 63.

3. A. Sen. (2006). *Identity and violence: The illusion of destiny.* London: Penguin Books, p. 84.

4. Women and Children Legal Research Foundation. (2004). *Impact of traditional practices on women.* Kabul: Afghan Women Leaders Connect, p. 60.

5. R. H. Magnus & E. Naby. (1998). *Afghanistan: Mullah, Marx, and Mujahid.* Boulder: Westview Press, p. 22–23.

6. A. Wieland-Karimi. (2005). *Afghanistan: Looking back on 2004, looking forward to 2005.* Kabul: Friedrich-Ebert-Stiftung, p. 6.

7. L. Abirafeh. (2004, October). Burqa pol-

itics: The plights of women in Afghanistan. *Chronogram*, http://www.chronogram.com/issue/2004/10/news/burqa.php.

8. M. E. Greenberg & E. Zuckerman. (2006). The gender dimensions of post-conflict reconstruction: The challenges of development aid. Helsinki: UNU-WIDER, p. 3.

9. T. Bouta, G. Frerks, & I. Bannon. (2005). *Gender, conflict, and development.* Washington, D.C.: International Bank for Reconstruction and Development, p. 131–132.

10. C. Johnson & J. Leslie. (2004). *Afghanistan: The mirage of peace.* London: Zed Books, p. 169.

11. *Ibid.*, p. 174.

12. A. B. Saeed. (2005). *Dangers of running for office in Afghanistan.* Kabul: Institute for War and Peace Reporting.

13. Afghan Independent Human Rights Commission–United Nations Assistance Mission in Afghanistan. (2005a). Joint verification of political rights, first report, 19 April–3 June 2005. Kabul: Afghan Independent Human Rights Commission.

14. Afghan Independent Human Rights Commission–United Nations Assistance Mission in Afghanistan. (2005b). Joint verification of political rights, second report, 4 June–16 August 2005. Kabul: Afghan Independent Human Rights Commission.

15. *Sharia* is the Islamic code of law, based on the Koran.

16. Afghan Independent Human Rights Commission–United Nations Assistance Mission in Afghanistan. (2005c). Joint verification of political rights, third report, 17 August–13 September 2005. Kabul: Afghan Independent Human Rights Commission.

17. Human Rights Watch. (2005). *Campaigning against fear: Women's participation in Afghanistan's 2005 elections.* New York: Human Rights Watch, p.15.

18. E. Rubin. (2005). Women's work. *New York Times Magazine*, p. 6.

19. J. G. Swank, Jr. (2005). Success for females in Afghanistan. *Canada Free Press*, http://www.canadafreepress.com/2005/swank090205.htm.

20. Women and Children Legal Research Foundation. (2005). *Report on women political participation in Afghanistan.* Kabul: Open Society Institute, p. 52.

21. T. Coghlan. (2005). Election hopes of Afghan women. *BBC News.* Qalat.

22. *Ibid.*

23. S. Biswas. (2005). Campaign climax in Afghanistan. *BBC News.* Kabul.

24. A. Wilder. (2005). *A house divided? Analysing the 2005 Afghan elections.* Kabul: Afghanistan Research and Evaluation Unit, p. 35.

25. L. Dupree. (1980). *Afghanistan* (3rd ed.). Princeton: Princeton University Press, p. 587.

26. Human Rights Watch. (2006). *Lessons in terror: Attacks on education in Afghanistan.* Kabul: Human Rights Watch, p. 14.

27. L. S. Noory. (2006). Where have all the women gone? *The Examiner.* Retrieved 23 June 2006, from http://www.examiner.com/a-1580 37-Lida_Sahar_Noory__Where_have_all_the_women_gone_.html.

28. Communication from distribution list to select members, 28 March 2006.

29. Human Rights Watch. (2006). *Lessons in terror: Attacks on education in Afghanistan.* Kabul: Human Rights Watch, p. 50.

30. *Ibid.*, p. 5.

31. *Ibid.*, p. 125.

32. *Ibid.*, p. 79.

33. *Ibid.*, p. 98.

34. *Ibid.*, p. 46.

Chapter 5

1. Segments of this chapter were previously published in L. Abirafeh (forthcoming). Discourses on *chaddari* politics: Translating perceptions into policy and practice. In J. Heath & A. Zahedi (Eds.). *Women of Afghanistan in the post 9/11 era: Paths to empowerment.* California: University of California Press.

2. R. Winthrop. (2003). Reflections on working in post-conflict Afghanistan: Local vs. international perspectives on gender relations. *Women's Studies Quarterly*, 31 (3–4).

3. S. Walby. (1997). *Gender transformations.* London: Routledge.

4. United Nations Development Programme & Islamic Republic of Afghanistan. (2004). *Afghanistan national human development report 2004: Security with a human face: Challenges and responsibilities.* Kabul: United Nations Development Programme, p. 11.

5. C. Johnson & J. Leslie. (2004). *Afghanistan: The mirage of peace.* London: Zed Books.

6. United Nations Development Programme & Islamic Republic of Afghanistan. (2004). *Afghanistan national human development report 2004: Security with a human face: Challenges and responsibilities.* Kabul: United Nations Development Programme, p. 216–217.

7. N. H. Dupree. (2004). The family during crisis in Afghanistan. *Journal of Comparative Family Studies*, 32(2), 311–332.

8. Ethnic groups in Afghanistan include Pashtun, Tajik, Uzbek, Hazara, Aymaq, Turkmen, Baluchi, Nuristani, and Pashai.

9. In this context, she is referring to my previous publications including the FES report,

amongst others. FES is Friedrich-Ebert-Stiftung, the German foundation to support the social democrat party. L. Abirafeh. (2005). *Lessons from gender-focused international aid in post-conflict Afghanistan... learned?* In A. Wieland-Karimi (Ed.). *Gender in international cooperation*. Bonn: Friedrich-Ebert-Stiftung.

10. C. Johnson & J. Leslie. (2004). *Afghanistan: The mirage of peace*. London: Zed Books, p. 37.

11. The concept of "do no harm" expands on this, arguing in favor of a contextualized understanding so that aid interventions avoid additional damage to those they are trying to assist. M. B. Anderson. (1999). *Do no harm: How aid can support peace — or war*. Boulder: Lynne Rienner Publishers.

12. It is generally assumed that Pashtuns are the more conservative ethnic group. This leads to facile analyses assuming that all things "traditional" emanate from this particular group. Such an example reinforces the importance of not taking ethnic identity at face value. For more information, see C. Johnson & J. Leslie. (2004). *Afghanistan: The mirage of peace*. London: Zed Books.

13. United Nations Development Programme & Islamic Republic of Afghanistan. (2004). *Afghanistan national human development report 2004: Security with a human face: Challenges and responsibilities*. Kabul: United Nations Development Programme, p. 101.

14. C. Johnson & J. Leslie (2004). *Afghanistan: The mirage of peace*. London: Zed Books, p. 52.

15. A. Sen. (2006). *Identity and violence: The illusion of destiny*. London: Penguin Books.

16. The rationale behind this exercise was to come to a better understanding of how Afghans value particular aspects of their identities. Asking respondents to prioritize one identity as the most important does not intend to negate the existence of multiple identities simultaneously, nor does it ignore the fact that identities and affiliations change in time and in different contexts. This aspect of the research simply demonstrates that the artificial divisions in programming based on sex might not have been valid for some participants. It might have, in fact, extracted women and men from their social roles and challenged their other, perhaps stronger, affiliations.

17. Segments of this section were previously published. L. Abirafeh. (2003). The role of religion in the lives of women in the new Afghanistan. *Critical Half*, 1(1), 36–37.

18. Allusions to the "other culture" that has altered Islam generally refer to the Wahhabi version of Islam, originating in Saudi Arabia.

19. S. Shah. (2003). *The storyteller's daughter*. London: Penguin.

20. W. G. Azoy. (2003). *Buzkashi: Game and power in Afghanistan* (2nd ed.). Prospect Heights, Ill: Waveland Press.

Chapter 6

1. *Maida, Maida* is also the name of a famous Afghan wedding song.

2. World Bank. (2004). *Afghanistan: State building, sustaining growth, and reducing poverty: A country economic report*. Kabul: World Bank, p. 80.

3. H. Nassery. (2004). *The gender issue in Afghanistan*. Kabul: United Nations Development Programme, p. 6.

4. R. Skaine. (2002). *The women of Afghanistan under the Taliban*. Jefferson: McFarland and Co., p. 24.

5. M. Centlivres-Demont. (1994). Afghan women in peace, war, and exile. In M. Weiner & A. Banuazizi (Eds.). *The politics of social transformation in Afghanistan, Iran, and Pakistan*. Syracuse, NY: Syracuse University Press, p. 358.

6. World Bank. (2005). *National reconstruction and poverty reduction: The role of women in Afghanistan's future*. Kabul: World Bank, p. 80.

7. W. G. Azoy. (2003). *Buzkashi: Game and power in Afghanistan* (2nd ed.). Prospect Heights, Ill: Waveland Press, p. 30.

8. *Purdah* refers to the Islamic practice of seclusion of women. More information can be found in P. Marsden. (1998). *The Taliban: War, religion, and the new order in Afghanistan*. London: Zed Books.

9. S. Shah. (2003). *The storyteller's daughter*. London: Penguin, p. 118.

10. For more information, see N. Tapper. (1991). *Bartered brides: Politics, gender and marriage in an Afghan tribal society*. Cambridge: Cambridge University Press.

11. R. Skaine. (2002). *The women of Afghanistan under the Taliban*. Jefferson: McFarland and Co., p. 142.

12. S. Shah. (2003). *The storyteller's daughter*. London: Penguin, p. 29.

13. N. H. Dupree. (2004). The family during crisis in Afghanistan. *Journal of Comparative Family Studies*, 32(2), 311–332.

14. For more information, see A. Osman & A. Loewen. (2005). *Real men keep their word: Tales from Kabul, Afghanistan: A selection of Akram Osman's Dari short stories*. Oxford: Oxford University Press; S. B. Majrouh. (1994). Songs of love and war: Afghan women's poetry. New York: Other Press.

15. S. Shah. (2003). *The storyteller's daughter*. London: Penguin, p. 8.

16. A. Osman & A. Loewen. (2005). *Real*

men keep their word: Tales from Kabul, Afghanistan: A selection of Akram Osman's Dari short stories. Oxford: Oxford University Press, p. xxxi.

17. S. Shah. (2003). *The storyteller's daughter.* London: Penguin.

18. A. Osman & A. Loewen. (2005). *Real men keep their word: Tales from Kabul, Afghanistan: A selection of Akram Osman's Dari short stories.* Oxford: Oxford University Press, p. 101.

19. *Ibid.*, p. 173.

20. *Ibid.*, p. 140.

21. *Ibid.*, p. 204.

22. Afghan literature, particularly the short stories of Akram Osman, can be used as social comment. Following Muhammad Daud Khan, Osman employed the symbol of the eagle as a metaphor to criticize foreign influence in Afghanistan. An excerpt from his story entitled "The Blind Eagle" expresses this sentiment: "Here, immersed in a realm free from the dictates of the East and the West, the eagle lost himself in a burning desire of unknown love" (Osman, 2005, p. 201). A. Osman & A. Loewen. (2005). *Real men keep their word: Tales from Kabul, Afghanistan: A selection of Akram Osman's Dari short stories.* Oxford: Oxford University Press.

23. *Ibid.*, p. xiii.

24. S. B. Majrouh. (1994). *Songs of love and war: Afghan women's poetry.* New York: Other Press, p. xi.

25. N. H. Dupree. (1990). A socio-cultural dimension: Afghan women refugees in Pakistan. In E. W. Anderson & N. H. Dupree. *The cultural basis of Afghan nationalism.* London: Pinter Publishers, p. 128.

26. S. B. Majrouh. (1994). *Songs of love and war: Afghan women's poetry.* New York: Other Press, p. xvi.

27. *Ibid.*

28. Dupree, N. H. (1990). A Socio-Cultural Dimension: Afghan Women Refugees in Pakistan. The Cultural Basis of Afghan Nationalism. E. W. Anderson and N. H. Dupree. London, Pinter Publishers.

29. *Ibid.*

30. History documents the Afghan legacy of abandonment following the end of Soviet occupation. The country fell into civil war and plunged into international anonymity. All this changed with the Taliban and 11 September 2001.

31. J. Beall & D. Esser. (2005). Shaping urban futures: Challenges to governing and managing Afghan cities. Issues Paper Series. Kabul: Afghanistan Research and Evaluation Unit (AREU), p. 27.

32. B. J. Stapleton. (2006). Security and reconstruction in Afghanistan: Shortcomings and mid-term prospects. Karachi: University of Karachi, p. 6.

33. In this case, the UN is used to represent the international community as a whole.

34. This is particularly relevant in the battle between the Northern Alliance (various ethnic groups) and the Taliban (largely Pashtun).

35. United Nations Development Programme & Islamic Republic of Afghanistan. (2004). *Afghanistan national human development report 2004: Security with a human face: Challenges and responsibilities.* Kabul: United Nations Development Programme, p. 218.

Chapter 7

1. Some of these stories of couples were previously published in R. Skaine. (2008). *Women of Afghanistan in the Post-Taliban Era: How Lives Have Changed and Where They Stand Today.* (pp. 123–150). Jefferson, NC: McFarland and Co.

2. By this he means Frozan is confronting her husband, or facing him with new confidence.

3. A. Osman & A. Loewen. (2005). *Real men keep their word: Tales from Kabul, Afghanistan: A selection of Akram Osman's Dari short stories.* Oxford: Oxford University Press, p. 85.

4. M. Sultan. (2002). Hope in Afghanistan. In S. Mehta. *Women for Afghan women: Shattering myths and claiming the future.* New York: Palgrave Macmillan, p. 202.

5. *Wasita* is a Dari term that describes the situation of having special contacts and access.

6. Akram Osman's (2005) short stories provide a good definition of the use of the proverb: "In colloquial Dari, Turkestan is often used as the place where someone who is misdirected ends up" (p. 39).

7. A "fixer" is defined as one who arranges logistics, handles procurement of goods and services, and generally runs errands for the institution.

8. United Nations Development Programme & Islamic Republic of Afghanistan. (2004). *Afghanistan national human development report 2004: Security with a human face: Challenges and responsibilities.* Kabul: United Nations Development Programme, p. 219.

9. Some of these women's stories were previously published in R. Skaine. (2008). *Women of Afghanistan in the Post-Taliban Era: How Lives Have Changed and Where They Stand Today.* (pp. 123–150). Jefferson, NC: McFarland and Co.

Chapter 8

1. Segments of this section were published in an edited book on domestic violence though the Peaceful Families Project: L. Abirafeh (2007a). Freedom is only won from the inside: Domestic violence in post-conflict Afghanistan. In M. Alkhateeb & S. E. Abugideiri (Eds.). *Change from within: Diverse perspectives on domestic violence in Muslim communities.* Washington, D.C.: Peaceful Families Project.

2. Islamic Republic of Afghanistan. (2006). *Afghanistan national development strategy.* Kabul: Islamic Republic of Afghanistan.

3. M. Safa. (2005, 13 September). Women, defense and security. *Deputy Minister for Technical and Policy Concerns.* Afghanistan: Ministry of Women's Affairs.

4. M. Jalal. (2005, June 27). *Accelerating national peace and reconstruction by safeguarding women's rights and security.* Afghanistan: Ministry of Women's Affairs.

5. M. Safa. (2005, 13 September). Women, defense and security. *Deputy Minister for Technical and Policy Concerns.* Afghanistan: Ministry of Women's Affairs.

6. United Nations. (2003). *The situation of women and girls in Afghanistan: Report of the secretary-general.* Commission on the Status of Women. New York: United Nations Economic and Social Council.

7. C. Johnson & J. Leslie. (2004). *Afghanistan: The mirage of peace.* London: Zed Books, p. 23.

8. N. H. Dupree. (2004). The family during crisis in Afghanistan. *Journal of Comparative Family Studies,* 32(2), 311–332.

9. RAWA, the Revolutionary Association of the Women of Afghanistan, is an oft-cited example of an Afghan feminist movement (www.rawa.org), although there are many others.

10. See www.rawa.org/temp/runews/2007/03/08/afghanistan-women-s-hopes-for-equality-fade.htm.

11. www.rawa.org/temp/runews/2007/03/03/afghanistan-no-gender-equality-under-occupation.htm

12. Women's Commission for Refugee Women and Children. (2005). *Masculinities: Male roles and male involvement in the promotion of gender equality.* New York: Women's Commission for Refugee Women and Children.

13. Y. Erturk. (2005). Integration of the human rights of women and a gender perspective: Violence against women. New York: United Nations, p. 2.

14. Islamic Republic of Afghanistan and UNDP. (2005). *Millennium development goals: Islamic Republic of Afghanistan country report 2005: Vision 2020.* Kabul: Islamic Republic of Afghanistan and UNDP.

15. Amnesty International. (2005). Afghanistan: Women still under attack — A systematic failure to protect. http://web.amnesty.org/library/print/ENGASA110072005.

16. http://www.af/nds/#1

17. Ministry of Women's Affairs. (2005). *Statistical compilation on gender issues in Afghanistan: Background study for a gender policy framework.* Kabul: Ministry of Women's Affairs, UNIFEM.

18. Amnesty International. (2005). Afghanistan: Women still under attack — A systematic failure to protect. http://web.amnesty.org/library/print/ENGASA110072005.

19. Ministry of Women's Affairs. (2005). *Statistical compilation on gender issues in Afghanistan: Background study for a gender policy framework.* Kabul: Ministry of Women's Affairs, UNIFEM.

20. Women's Commission for Refugee Women and Children. (2006). *Displaced women and girls at risk: Risk factors, protection solutions and resource tools.* New York: Women's Commission for Refugee Women and Children, p. 16.

21. U. Narayan. (1997). *Dislocating cultures: Identities, traditions, and third world feminism.* New York: Routledge.

22. *Ibid.*

23. UN S/2002/1154

24. J. Barry. (2005). *Rising up in response: Women's rights activism in conflict.* Boulder, CO: Urgent Action Fund for Women's Human Rights, p. 70.

25. C. Moser & C. McIlwaine. (2001). *Violence in a post-conflict context: Urban poor perceptions from Guatemala.* Washington, D.C.: The World Bank, p. 41.

26. United Nations Development Programme & Islamic Republic of Afghanistan. (2004). *Afghanistan national human development report 2004: Security with a human face: Challenges and responsibilities.* Kabul: United Nations Development Programme, p. 56.

27. IRIN (2004). Our bodies — Their battle ground: Gender-based violence in conflict zones. *IRIN web special.* From http://www.irinnews.org, p.18.

28. S. Turner. (2000). Vindicating masculinity: The fate of promoting gender equality. *Forced Migration Review,* (9), 8.

29. *Ibid.*

30. R. Perez. (2002). Practising theory through women's bodies: Public violence and women's strategies of power and place. In K. Saunders (Ed.). *Feminist post-development thought: Rethinking modernity, post-colonialism and representation.* London: Zed Books, p. 32.

31. E. Enarson. (2005). Women and girls last? Averting the second post–Katrina disaster. *Affilia: Journal of Women and Social Work*, 22(1), 2.

32. United Nations Research Institute for Social Development. (2005). Gender equality: Striving for justice in an unequal world. Geneva: United Nations Research Institute for Social Development, p. 233.

33. N. H. Dupree. (1996). *The women of Afghanistan*. Stockholm: Swedish Committee for Afghanistan, p. 6.

34. This email was sent to a select distribution list, of which I am a member, on 6 May 2005.

35. *Daily Outlook: Afghanistan's Leading Independent Newspaper*, 53. (2005, May 11).

36. *Soundless Cries* by Nadia Anjuman was translated by Abdul S. Shayek and can be found at http://www.pulpmovies.com/gagwatch/2005/11/lethal-poetry/.

37. S. Schutte. (2004). Urban vulnerability in Afghanistan: Case studies from three cities. *Working Paper Series*. Kabul: Afghanistan Research and Evaluation Unit, p. 23.

38. For further information, see L. Abirafeh. (2005, November). From Afghanistan to Sudan: How peace risks marginalizing women. *Forced Migration Review*, 24, 46–47.

39. F. Pickup, S. Williams, & C. Sweetman. (2001). *Ending violence against women: A challenge for development and humanitarian work*. Oxford: Oxfam Great Britain.

40. Women and Children Legal Research Foundation. (2005). *Report on women political participation in Afghanistan*. Kabul: Open Society Institute.

41. F. Pickup, S. Williams, & C. Sweetman. (2001). *Ending violence against women: A challenge for development and humanitarian work*. Oxford: Oxfam Great Britain.

42. T. Bouta, G. Frerks, & I. Bannon. (2005). *Gender, conflict, and development*. Washington, D.C.: International Bank for Reconstruction and Development, p. 55.

Chapter 9

1. D. Mosse. (2005). *Cultivating development: An ethnography of aid policy and practice*. London: Pluto Press.

2. A full analysis of lessons learned — or not — can be found in L Abirafeh. (2005). Lessons from gender-focused international aid in post-conflict Afghanistan … learned? In A. Wieland-Karimi. *Gender in international cooperation*. Bonn: Friedrich-Ebert-Stiftung.

3. S. Shah. (2003). *The storyteller's daughter*. London: Penguin, p. 200.

4. S. Barakat & G. Wardell (2004). Exploited by whom? An alternative perspective on humanitarian assistance to Afghan women. In S. Barakat (Ed.). *Reconstructing war-torn societies: Afghanistan*. Hampshire, Eng.: Palgrave Macmillan, p. 110–111.

5. D. Kandiyoti. (2003). *Integrating gender analysis into socio-economic needs assessment in Afghanistan*. Kabul: United Nations Development Fund for Women, p. 4–5.

6. R. Skaine. (2002). *The women of Afghanistan under the Taliban*. Jefferson: McFarland and Co., p. 102.

7. For example, in the 1980s, aid to Afghanistan was tied to Cold War alliances, and in the mid-1990s the agenda switched to promote peace. For more information, see C. Johnson & J. Leslie. (2004). *Afghanistan: The mirage of peace*. London: Zed Books.

8. N. H. Dupree. (1990). A socio-cultural dimension: Afghan women refugees in Pakistan. In E. W. Anderson & N. H. Dupree. *The cultural basis of Afghan nationalism*. London: Pinter Publishers, p. 131.

9. M. Weiner & A. Banuazizi (Eds.). (1994). *The politics of social transformation in Afghanistan, Iran, and Pakistan*. Syracuse: Syracuse University Press, p. 24–25.

10. C. Johnson & J. Leslie. (2004). *Afghanistan: The mirage of peace*. London: Zed Books, p. 25.

11. E. Rostami-Povey. (2007). *Afghan women: Identity and invasion*. London: Zed Books.

12. *Ibid.*, p. 19.

13. Rabbani is a Tajik leader who founded Jamiat-i-Islami as an offshoot of the Muslim Brotherhood in the late 1960s and played a key role in the Afghan *jihad*, or holy war.

14. M. Bhadrakumar. (2006, 3 June). Kabul riots a turning point for Afghanistan, Karzai. *Asia Times Online*. Retrieved 3 June 2006, from http://www.atimes.com/atimes/South_Asia/HF03Df04.html.

15. Afghanistan in print. (2005, May 11–17). *Kabul Weekly*, 168.

16. R. Morarjee. (2006, May 30). Riots breach Kabul "Island." *Christian Science Monitor*.

17. R. Morarjee. What has Afghans so angry. *Time World: Web Exclusive*. Retrieved 30 May 2006, from http://www.time.com/time/world/article/0,8599,1199254,00.html.

18. This information was compiled through Human Rights Watch, the Afghanistan NGO Security Office, and Patronus Analytical.

19. D. Loyn (Director). (2006). Afghanistan: Losing the aid game [Television broadcast]. *BBC Special Report*, 35 minutes.

20. P. Hensher. (2006, July 6). It's deja vu in Afghanistan. From http://www.SeattlePI.com.

21. International Crisis Group (2003). Afghanistan: Women and reconstruction. *ICG Asia Report No 48*. Kabul: International Crisis Group, p. 23.

22. World Bank. (2002). The conflict analysis framework (CAF): Identifying conflict-related obstacles to development. *Dissemination notes*. Social Development Department: Conflict Prevention and Reconstruction Unit. Washington, D.C.: World Bank, p. 2.

23. United Nations Development Programme & Islamic Republic of Afghanistan. (2004). *Afghanistan national human development report 2004: Security with a human face: Challenges and responsibilities*. Kabul: United Nations Development Programme, p. 228–236.

24. N. Long & A. Long (Eds.). (1992). *Battlefields of knowledge: The interlocking of theory and practice in social research and development*. London: Routledge, p. 37.

25. J. Ferguson. (1994). *The anti-politics machine: "Development," depoliticization, and bureaucratic power in Lesotho*. Minneapolis: University of Minnesota Press.

26. S. Azarbaijani-Moghaddam. (2004). Afghan women on the margins of the twenty-first century. In A. Donini, N. Niland, & K. Wermester (Eds.). *Nation-building unraveled? Aid, peace and justice in Afghanistan*. Bloomfield, CT: Kumarian Press, p. 103.

27. L. Abu-Lughod. (2002). Do Muslim women really need saving? Anthropological reflections on cultural relativism and its others. *American Anthropologist, 104*(3), 783–790.

28. I. Delloye. (2003). *Women of Afghanistan*. Saint Paul: Ruminator Books, p. 158.

29. M. Centlivres-Demont. (1994). Afghan women in peace, war, and exile. In M. Weiner & A. Banuazizi (Eds.). *The politics of social transformation in Afghanistan, Iran, and Pakistan*. Syracuse, NY: Syracuse University Press.

30. N. Leader & M. H. Atmar. (2004). Political projects: Reform, aid, and the state in Afghanistan. In A. Donini, N. Niland, & K. Wermester (Eds.). *Nation-Building Unraveled?*

Aid, Peace and Justice in Afghanistan. Bloomfield, CT: Kumarian Press, p. 181.

31. M. A. Nawabi. (2003). Women's rights in the new constitution of Afghanistan, p. 7. Retrieved from http://www.cic.nyu.edu/peacebuilding/oldpdfs/E22Womens%20RightsFullVersionNawabi.pdf.

32. United Nations Development Programme & Islamic Republic of Afghanistan. (2004). *Afghanistan national human development report 2004: Security with a human face: Challenges and responsibilities*. Kabul: United Nations Development Programme, p. 18.

33. B. R. Rubin. (1994). Redistribution and the state in Afghanistan: The red revolution turns green. In M. Weiner & A. Banuazizi. *The politics of social transformation in Afghanistan, Iran, and Pakistan*. Syracuse: Syracuse University Press, p. 216–217.

34. J. Ferguson. (1994). *The anti-politics machine: "Development," depoliticization, and bureaucratic power in Lesotho*. Minneapolis: University of Minnesota Press, p. 226.

35. "The Personal is Political" is a feminist approbation of an anarchist notion to democratize everyday life. The underlying concept is that power inequalities are rooted in social structures and therefore changing the institutions that shape personal life is a form of political activism. A. M. Jaggar. (2005). Arenas of citizenship: Civil society, state and the global order. *International Feminist Journal of Politics, 7*(1).

36. The magazine is named after the famed heroine Malalai, who is known for securing an Afghan victory in the Battle of Maiwand in 1880 during the second Anglo-Afghan war. Malalai used her veil as a banner to encourage Afghan soldiers. Her name has become part of Afghan legend and is used for many schools, hospitals, and so on.

37. J. Mujahed. (2002). Freedom for women: Only words. *Malalai*, 1.

38. Afghan Women's Resource Center, Afghan Women's Network, and Women for Women International (2003). *International Women's Day Statement: 8 March 2003*. Kabul: AWRC, AWN, WWI.

Bibliography

Abirafeh, L. (2003). The role of religion in the lives of women in the new Afghanistan. *Critical Half,* 1(1), 36–37.

Abirafeh, L. (2004, October). Burqa politics: The plights of women in Afghanistan. *Chronogram,* http://www.chronogram.com/issue/2004/10/news/burqa.php.

Abirafeh, L. (2005, November). From Afghanistan to Sudan: How peace risks marginalizing women. *Forced Migration Review,* 24, 46–47.

Abirafeh, L. (2005). Lessons from gender-focused international aid in post-conflict Afghanistan... learned? In A. Wieland-Karimi (Ed.). *Gender in international cooperation.* Bonn: Friedrich-Ebert-Stiftung.

Abirafeh, L. (2007a). Freedom is only won from the inside: Domestic violence in post-conflict Afghanistan. In M. Alkhateeb & S. E. Abugideiri (Eds.). *Change from within: Diverse perspectives on domestic violence in Muslim communities.* Washington, D.C.: Peaceful Families Project.

Abirafeh, L. (2007b). An opportunity lost? Engaging men in gendered interventions: Voices from Afghanistan. *Journal of Peacebuilding and Development,* 3(3).

Abirafeh, L. (2009). Afghanistan: Gendered interventions, identity, and the liberation agenda. In F. Shirazi (Ed.). *Images vs. realities: Muslim women in war and crisis: From reality to representation.* Austin, Texas: University of Texas Press.

Abirafeh, L. (forthcoming). Discourses on *chaddari* politics: Translating perceptions into policy and practice. In J. Heath & A. Zahedi (Eds.). *Women of Afghanistan in the post 9/11 era: Paths to empowerment.* California: University of California Press.

Abirafeh, L., & Skaine, R. (2008). Voices and images of Afghan people. In R. Skaine. *Women of Afghanistan in the Post-Taliban Era: How Lives Have Changed and Where They Stand Today.* (pp. 123–150). Jefferson, NC: McFarland and Co.

Abu-Lughod, L. (1989). Women as political actors. In L. Abu-Lughod (Ed.). *Remaking women: Feminism and modernity in the Middle East.* Princeton, CA: Princeton University Press.

Abu-Lughod, L. (2002). Do Muslim women really need saving? Anthropological reflections on cultural relativism and its others. *American Anthropologist,* 104(3), 783–790.

Acre, A. (2000). Creating or regulating development: Representing modernities through language and discourse. In A. Acre & N. Long (Eds.). *Anthropology, development and modernities: Exploring discourses, counter-tendencies and violence.* London: Routledge.

Afary, J., & Anderson, K. B. (2005). *Foucault and the Iranian revolution: Gender and the seductions of Islamism.* Chicago: University of Chicago Press.

Afghan lipstick liberation. (2002, 17 October). *BBC News Online: World Edition.* Retrieved 17 October 2002, from http://news.bbc.co.uk/2/hi/south_asia/2336303.stm.

Afghan Women's Resource Center, Afghan Women's Network and Women for Women International. (2003). *International Women's Day Statement: 8 March 2003.* Kabul: AWRC, AWN, WWI.

Afghanistan in print. (2005, May 11–17). *Kabul Weekly,* 168.

Afghanistan National Human Development Report 2004. (2004). Kabul: United Nations Development Programme Afghanistan, Islamic Republic of Afghanistan.

Afshar, H. (2004). Introduction: War and peace: What do women contribute? In H. Afshar & D. Eade (Eds.). *Development, women and war: Feminist perspectives*. Oxford: Oxfam.

Afshar, H., & Eade, D. (Eds.). (2004). *Development, women and war: Feminist perspectives*. Oxford: Oxfam.

Ahmed-Ghosh, H. (2003). A history of women in Afghanistan: Lessons learnt for the future *or* yesterdays and tomorrow: Women in Afghanistan. *Journal of International Women's Studies*, 4(3).

Ahmedi, F., & Ansary, T. (2005). *The story of my life: An Afghan girl on the other side of the sky*. New York: Simon & Schuster.

Afghan Independent Human Rights Commission–United Nations Assistance Mission in Afghanistan (2005a). Joint verification of political rights, first report, 19 April–3 June 2005. Kabul: Afghan Independent Human Rights Commission.

Afghan Independent Human Rights Commission–United Nations Assistance Mission in Afghanistan (2005b). Joint verification of political rights, second report, 4 June–16 August 2005. Kabul: Afghan Independent Human Rights Commission.

Afghan Independent Human Rights Commission–United Nations Assistance Mission in Afghanistan (2005c). Joint verification of political rights, third report, 17 August–13 September 2005. Kabul: Afghan Independent Human Rights Commission.

Alvarez, S. E. (1990). *Engendering democracy in Brazil: Women's movements in politics*. Princeton, CA: Princeton University Press.

Amnesty International (2005). Afghanistan: Women still under attack — A systematic failure to protect. http://web.amnesty.org/library/print/ENGASA110072005.

Anderson, M. B. (1999). *Do no harm: How aid can support peace — or war*. Boulder: Lynne Rienner Publishers.

Anderson, M. B., & Woodrow, P. J. (1998). *Rising from the ashes: Development strategies in times of disaster*. Paris: UNESCO.

Appadurai, A. (1990). Disjuncture and difference in the global cultural economy. *Public Culture*, 2(2).

Azarbaijani-Moghaddam, S. (2004). Afghan women on the margins of the twenty-first century. In A. Donini, N. Niland, & K. Wermester (Eds.). *Nation-building unraveled? Aid, peace and justice in Afghanistan*. Bloomfield, CT: Kumarian Press.

Azoy, W. G. (2003). *Buzkashi: Game and power in Afghanistan* (2nd ed.). Prospect Heights, Ill: Waveland Press.

Barakat, S. (2004). Setting the scene for Afghanistan's reconstruction: The challenges and critical dilemmas. In S. Barakat (Ed.). *Reconstructing war-torn societies: Afghanistan*. Hampshire, Eng.: Palgrave Macmillan.

Barakat, S., & Chard, M. (2004). Theories, rhetoric and practice: Recovering the capacities of war-torn societies. In S. Barakat (Ed.). *Reconstructing war-torn societies: Afghanistan*. Hampshire, Eng.: Palgrave Macmillan.

Barakat, S., & Wardell, G. (2001). Capitalizing on capacities of Afghan women: Women's role in Afghanistan's reconstruction and development. Infocus Programme on Crisis Response and Reconstruction series. Geneva: International Labour Organization.

Barakat, S., & Wardell, G. (2004). Exploited by whom? An alternative perspective on humanitarian assistance to Afghan women. In S. Barakat (Ed.). *Reconstructing war-torn societies: Afghanistan*. Hampshire, Eng.: Palgrave Macmillan.

Barry, J. (2005). *Rising up in response: Women's rights activism in conflict*. Boulder, CO: Urgent Action Fund for Women's Human Rights.

Beall, J. (1996). Urban governance: Why gender matters. Gender in Development Monographs series. New York: United Nations Development Programme (UNDP).

Beall, J. (1998a). The gender and poverty nexus in the DFID White Paper: Opportunity or constraint? *Journal of International Development*, 10, 235–246.

Beall, J. (1998b). Trickle-down or rising tide? Lessons on mainstreaming gender policy from Colombia and South Africa. *Social Policy and Administration*, 32(5), 513–534.

Beall, J., & Esser, D. (2005). Shaping urban futures: Challenges to governing and managing Afghan cities. Issues Paper Series. Kabul: Afghanistan Research and Evaluation Unit (AREU).

Beall, J., & Schutte, S. (2006). Urban livelihoods in Afghanistan. Issues Paper Series. Kabul: Afghanistan Research and Evaluation Unit.

Beneria, L. (2003). *Gender, development, and globalization: Economics as if people mattered.* New York: Routledge.

Benjamin, J. (2000). Afghanistan: Women survivors of war under the Taliban. In J. Mertus (Ed.). *War's offensive on women: The humanitarian challenge in Bosnia, Kosovo, and Afghanistan.* West Hartford, Eng.: Kumarian Press.

Bhadrakumar, M. (2006, June 3). Kabul riots a turning point for Afghanistan, Karzai. *Asia Times Online.* Retrieved 3 June 2006, from http://www.atimes.co m/atimes/South_Asia/HF03Df04.html.

Bill, H. (2002). Country without a state — Does it really make a difference for the women? In C. Noelle-Karimi, C. Schetter, & R. Schlangintweit (Eds.). *Afghanistan — A Country Without a State.* Frankfurt: IKO.

Biswas, S. (2005). Campaign climax in Afghanistan. *BBC News.* Kabul.

Boege, F. (2004). *Women and politics in Afghanistan: How to use the chance of the 25% quota for women.* Kabul: Friedrich-Ebert-Stiftung.

Boesen, I. (2004). *From subjects to citizens: Local participation in the national solidarity program (NSP).* Kabul: Afghanistan Research and Evaluation Unit (AREU).

Boesen, I. W. (1990). Honour in exile: Continuity and change among Afghan refugees. In E. W. Anderson & N. H. Dupree (Eds.). *The Cultural Basis of Afghan Nationalism.* London: Pinter Publishers.

Boserup, E. (1970). *Woman's role in economic development.* New York: St. Martin's Press.

Bouta, T., Frerks, G., & Bannon, I. (2005). *Gender, conflict, and development.* Washington, D.C.: International Bank for Reconstruction and Development.

Brittain, V. (2002). Women in war and crisis zones: One key to Africa's wars of underdevelopment. Crisis States Programme Working Papers. London: London School of Economics Development Research Centre.

Bryer, J. (2006). Those Heady Days — But Just Look at Us Now, Afghan Links.

Burke, J. (2006, June 25). Fear battles hope on the road to Kandahar. *Guardian Unlimited.* Retrieved 25 June 2006, from http://observer.guardian.co.uk/world/stor y/0,,1805334,00.html.

Burman, M. J., Batchelor, S. A., & Brown, J. A. (2001). Researching girls and violence: Facing the dilemmas of fieldwork. *British Journal of Criminology*, 41, 443–459.

Byrd, W. (2007). *Responding to Afghanistan's development challenges: An assessment of experience during 2002–2007 and issues and priorities for the future.* Kabul: World Bank.

CARE International in Afghanistan: Policy brief. (2003). Kabul: CARE International.

Carlin, A. (2005). *OTI Afghanistan program evaluation: Gender initiatives and impacts: October 2001 to June 2005.* Kabul: PACT/DevTech Systems.

Centlivres-Demont, M. (1994). Afghan women in peace, war, and exile. In M. Weiner & A. Banuazizi (Eds.). *The politics of social transformation in Afghanistan, Iran, and Pakistan.* Syracuse, NY: Syracuse University Press.

Charlesworth, H., & Chinkin, C. (2002). Sex, gender and September 11. *American Journal of International Law*, 96(3), 600–605.

Clark, K. (2004). The struggle for hearts and minds: The military, aid, and the media. In A. Donini, N. Niland, & K. Wermester (Eds.). *Nation-building unraveled? Aid, peace and justice in Afghanistan.* Bloomfield, CT: Kumarian Press.

Cleaver, F. (Ed.). (2002). *Masculinities mat-*

ter! Men, gender and development. London: Zed Books.

Cockburn, C. (2004). *The line: Women, partition and the gender order in Cyprus*. London: Zed Books.

Coghlan, T. (2005). Election hopes of Afghan women. *BBC News*. Qalat.

Cornwall, A., & Brock, K. (2005). Beyond buzzwords: "Poverty reduction," "participation" and "empowerment" in development policy. Overarching Concerns Programme Paper Number 10. Geneva: United Nations Research Institute for Social Development.

Cornwall, A., Harrison, E., & Whitehead, A. (Eds.). (2007). *Feminisms in development: Contradictions, contestations and challenges*. London: Zed Books.

Corrin, C. (2004). International and local interventions to reduce gender-based violence against women in post-conflict situations. From http://www.wider.unu.edu/conference/conference-2004-1/conference%202004-1-papers/Corrin-3105.pdf.

Costy, A. (2004). The dilemma of humanitarianism in the post–Taliban transition. In A. Donini, N. Niland, & K. Wermester (Eds.). *Nation-building unraveled? Aid, peace and justice in Afghanistan*. Bloomfield, CT: Kumarian Press.

Crisis States Programme (2001). *Crisis States Programme concepts and research agenda*. London: London School of Economics Development Research Center.

Daily Outlook: Afghanistan's Leading Independent Newspaper, 53. (2005, May 11).

de Vries, P. (1992). A research journey: On actors, concepts and the text. In A. Long & N. Long (Eds.). *Battlefields of knowledge: The interlocking of theory and practice in social research and development*. London: Routledge.

Delloye, I. (2003). *Women of Afghanistan*. Saint Paul: Ruminator Books.

Development Initiatives (2003). Afghanistan: How pledges are being turned into spending. *Afghanistan Update*. Somerset: Development Initiatives.

Donini, A. (2004). Principles, politics, and pragmatism in the international response

to the Afghan crisis. In A. Donini, N. Niland, & K. Wermester (Eds.). *Nation-building unraveled? Aid, peace and justice in Afghanistan*. Bloomfield, CT: Kumarian Press.

Donini, A., Niland, N., & Wermester, K. (Eds.). *Nation-building unraveled? Aid, peace and justice in Afghanistan*. Bloomfield, CT: Kumarian Press.

Dorronsoro, G. (2005). *Revolution unending: Afghanistan: 1979 to the present*. New York: Columbia University Press.

Doubleday, V. (2006). *Three women of Herat: A memoir of life, love and friendship in Afghanistan*. London: Tauris Parke.

Drinan, R. F., & Drinan, R. J. (2001). *The mobilization of shame: A world view of human rights*. Harrisonburg: Yale University Press.

Duffield, M. (2001). *Global governance and the new wars: The merging of development and security*. London: Zed Books.

Duffield, M. (2001). Governing the borderlands: Decoding the power of aid. *Disasters*, 25(4), 308–320.

Duffield, M. (2002). Politics vs. aid. *Insights*, 39.

Duffield, M. (2005). Human security: Linking development and security in an age of terror. *General Conference of the EADI*. Bonn, Ger.: n.p.

Dupree, L. (1980). *Afghanistan* (3rd ed.). Princeton: Princeton University Press.

Dupree, N. H. (1985). Women in Afghanistan: A brief 1985 update. In F. Rahimi (Ed.). *Women in Afghanistan*. Kabul: Paul Bucherer-Dietschi.

Dupree, N. H. (1990). A socio-cultural dimension: Afghan women refugees in Pakistan. In E. W. Anderson & N. H. Dupree. *The cultural basis of Afghan nationalism*. London: Pinter Publishers.

Dupree, N. H. (1996). *The women of Afghanistan*. Stockholm: Swedish Committee for Afghanistan.

Dupree, N. H. (1998). Afghan women under the Taliban. In W. Maley (Ed.). *Fundamentalism reborn? Afghanistan and the Taliban*. London: Hurst and Co.

Dupree, N. H. (2004). Cultural heritage

and national identity in Afghanistan. In S. Barakat (Ed.). *Reconstructing war-torn societies: Afghanistan.* Hampshire, Eng.: Palgrave Macmillan.

Dupree, N. H. (2004). The family during crisis in Afghanistan. *Journal of Comparative Family Studies*, 32(2), 311–332.

Eade, D. (2004). Introduction: Peace and reconstruction: Agency and agencies. In H. Afshar & D. Eade (Ed.). *Development, women and war: Feminist perspectives.* Oxford: Oxfam.

Edwards, R. & Ribbens, J. (1998). Living on the edges: Public knowledge, private lives, personal experience. In J. Ribbens & E. Rosalind (Eds.). *Feminist dilemmas in qualitative research: Public knowledge and private lives.* London: Sage.

Ehrenreich, B. (2003). Veiled threat. In A. Joseph & K. Sharma (Eds.) *Terror, counter-terror: Women speak out.* London: Zed Books.

Ellis, D. (2000). *Women of the Afghan war.* Westport, CT: Greenwood Press.

Emadi, H. (2002). *Repression, resistance, and women in Afghanistan.* Westport, CT: Praeger.

Enarson, E. (2007). Women and girls last? Averting the second post–Katrina disaster. *Affilia: Journal of Women and Social Work*, 22(1), 5–8.

Erturk, Y. (2005). Integration of the human rights of women and a gender perspective: Violence against women. New York: United Nations.

Evaluation report on general situation of women in Afghanistan. (2007). Kabul: Afghanistan Independent Human Rights Commission.

Faguet, J.-P. (2004). Democracy in the desert: Civil society, nation-building and empire. Crisis States Programme Discussion Paper. London: London School of Economics Development Research Centre.

Ferguson, J. (1994). *The anti-politics machine: "Development," depoliticization, and bureaucratic power in Lesotho.* Minneapolis: University of Minnesota Press.

Follain, J., & Cristofari, R. (2002). *Zoya's story: An Afghan woman's struggle for freedom.* New York: Harper Collins.

Gall, C. (2005). Afghan poet dies after beating by husband. *The New York Times*, 4.

Gardner, K., & Lewis, D. (2000). Dominant paradigms overturned or "business as usual"? Development discourse and the White Paper on international development. *Critique of Anthropology*, 20(1), 15–29.

Gasper, D., & Apthorpe, R. (1996). Discourse analysis and policy discourse. In D. Gasper & R. Apthorpe (Eds.). *Arguing development policy: Frames and discourses.* London: Frank Cass.

Geertz, C. (1983). *Local knowledge: Further essays in interpretive anthropology.* New York: Basic Books.

Giles, W., & Hyndman, J. (Eds.). (2004). *Sites of violence: Gender and conflict zones.* Berkeley: University of California Press.

Glatzer, B. (2002). *Conflict analysis: Afghanistan.* Kabul: Friedrich-Ebert-Stiftung, Gesellschaft fur Technische Zusammenarbeit (GTZ).

Goetz, A. M. (1997). Local heroes: Patterns of fieldwork discretion in implementing GAD policy in Bangladesh. In A. M. Goetz (Ed.) *Getting institutions right for women in development.* London: Zed Books.

Goodhand, J. (2002). Aiding violence or building peace? The role of international aid in Afghanistan. *Third World Quarterly*, 23(5), 837–859.

Goodhand, J., & Cramer, C. (2002). Try again, fail again, fail better? War, the state, and the "post-conflict" challenge in Afghanistan. *Development and Change*, 33(5), 885–909.

Goodwin, J. (2003). *Price of honor: Muslim women lift the veil of silence on the Islamic world.* New York: Plume.

Greenberg, M. E., & Zuckerman, E. (2006). The gender dimensions of post-conflict reconstruction: The challenges of development aid. Helsinki: UNU-WIDER.

Grillo, R., & Stirrat, R. (1997). *Discourses of development: Anthropological perspectives.* Oxford: Berg.

Gross, N. (2000a). Problems of the evolution of our Afghan national identity. In N. Gross (Ed.) *Steps of peace and our responsibility as Afghans.* Falls Church: Kabultec.

Gross, N. (2000b). The messy side of globalization: Women in Afghanistan. *Symposium on Globalization and Women in
Muslim Societies.* Washington, D.C.: Library of Congress.

Gupta, A. (1995). Blurred boundaries: The
discourse of corruption, the culture of
politics, and the imagined state. *American
Ethnologist, 22*(2), 375–402.

Hans, A. (2004). Escaping conflict: Afghan
women in transit. In W. Giles & J. Hyndman (Eds.). *Sites of violence: Gender and
conflict zones.* Berkeley: University of California Press.

Harcourt, W. (2005). The body politic in
global development discourse: A woman
and the politics of place perspective. In
W. Harcourt & A. Escobar (Eds.).
Women and the politics of place. Bloomfield, CT: Kumarian Press.

Hassan, R. (2002). Muslim women's rights:
A contemporary debate. In S. Mehta
(Ed.). *Women for Afghan women: Shatter-
ing myths and claiming the future.* New
York: Palgrave Macmillan.

Hensher, P. (2006, July 6). It's deja vu in
Afghanistan. From http://www.SeattlePI.
com.

Herold, M. W. (2006, June 4). Afghanistan
as an empty space. *Cursor.* Retrieved 4
June 2006, from http://www.cursor.org/
stories/emptyspace.html.

Heuvel, K. V. (2002). *A just response: The
nation on terrorism, democracy, and September 11, 2001.* New York: Avalon Publishing Group, Inc.

Hilhorst, D. (2003). *The real world of
NGOs: Discourses, diversity and development.* London: Zed Books.

Hosseini, K. (2003). *The kite runner.* New
York: Riverhead Books.

Human Rights Watch. (1999). *World report
1999.* New York: Human Rights Watch.

Human Rights Watch. (2004). *Between hope
and fear: Intimidation and attacks against
women in public life in Afghanistan.* New
York: Human Rights Watch.

Human Rights Watch. (2005). *Campaign-
ing against fear: Women's participation in
Afghanistan's 2005 elections.* New York:
Human Rights Watch.

Human Rights Watch. (2006). *Lessons in
terror: Attacks on education in Afghanistan.* Kabul: Human Rights Watch.

Hunt, K. (2002). The strategic co-optation
of women's rights: Discourse in the "war
on terrorism." *International Feminist
Journal of Politics, 4*(1), 116–121.

Hunte, P. (2004). *Some notes on the livelihoods of the urban poor in Kabul, Afghanistan.* Kabul: Afghanistan Research and
Evaluation Unit.

Hymowitz, K. S. (2003). Why feminism is
AWOL on Islam. *City Journal.*

International Crisis Group (2003). Afghan-
istan: Women and reconstruction. *ICG
Asia Report No 48.* Kabul: International
Crisis Group.

IRIN (2004). Our bodies — Their battle
ground: Gender-based violence in
conflict zones. *IRIN web special.* From
http://www.irinnews.org.

Islamic Republic of Afghanistan (2002).
*National development framework: Draft:
Version 2.* Kabul: Islamic Republic of
Afghanistan.

Islamic Republic of Afghanistan (2004). *Se-
curing Afghanistan's future: Accomplish-
ments and the strategic path forward.*
Kabul: A Government/International
Agency Report: Islamic Republic of
Afghanistan, Asian Development Bank,
United Nations Assistance Mission to
Afghanistan, United Nations Develop-
ment Program, The World Bank Group.

Islamic Republic of Afghanistan (2005).
National development strategy FAQ.
Kabul: Islamic Republic of Afghanistan.

Islamic Republic of Afghanistan (2005).
*Vision 2020—Afghanistan millennium de-
velopment goals report 2005.* Kabul:
United Nations Development Programme.

Islamic Republic of Afghanistan. (2006).
Afghanistan national development strategy.
Kabul: Islamic Republic of Afghanistan.

Islamic Republic of Afghanistan (2006). *In-
terim national action plan for the women of
Afghanistan: Executive summary.* Kabul:
Islamic Republic of Afghanistan.

Islamic Republic of Afghanistan. (2006).
The Afghanistan compact: Building on suc-

cess. The London Conference on Afghanistan. London: Islamic Republic of Afghanistan.

Islamic Republic of Afghanistan and UNDP. (2005). *Millennium development goals: Islamic Republic of Afghanistan country report 2005: Vision 2020.* Kabul: Islamic Republic of Afghanistan and UNDP.

Jacobson, R. (2000). Women and peace in Northern Ireland: A complicated relationship. In S. Jacobs, R. Jacobson, & J. Marchbank (Eds.). *States of conflict: Gender, violence and resistance.* London: Zed Books.

Jaggar, A. (1988a). *Feminist politics and human nature.* Totowa: Rowman and Littlefield.

Jaggar, A. M. (1998b). Globalizing feminist ethics. *Hypatia*, 13(2), 7–31.

Jaggar, A. M. (2004). Saving Amina. In *Global justice for women and intercultural dialogue.* Boulder, CO: University of Colorado.

Jaggar, A. M. (2005). Arenas of citizenship: Civil society, state and the global order. *International Feminist Journal of Politics*, 7(1).

Jalal, M. (2005, June 27). *Accelerating national peace and reconstruction by safeguarding women's rights and security.* Afghanistan: Ministry of Women's Affairs.

Johnson, C., & Leslie, J. (2004). *Afghanistan: The mirage of peace.* London: Zed Books.

Jonasdottir, A. G. (1988). On the concept of interest, women's interests, and the limitations of interest theory. In K. B. Jones & A. G. Jonasdottir (Eds.). *The political interests of gender: Developing theory and research with a feminist face.* London: Sage.

Jones, B. D. (2004). Aid, peace, and justice in a reordered world. In A. Donini, N. Niland, & K. Wermester. *Nation-Building Unraveled? Aid, Peace and Justice in Afghanistan.* Bloomfield, CT: Kumarian Press.

Jones, S. G. (2006). Averting failure in Afghanistan. *Survival*, 48, 111–128.

Kabeer, N. (1994). *Reversed realities: Gender hierarchies in development thought.* London: Verso.

Kamal, S. (2006). *Development communications strategies and domestic violence in Afghanistan.* Retrieved from Peaceful Families Project, http://www.peacefulfamilies.org/kamal.html.

Kamali, M. H. (2003). *Islam, pernicious custom, and women's rights in Afghanistan.* Malaysia: International Islamic University.

Kandiyoti, D. (1988). Bargaining with patriarchy. *Gender and society*, 2(3), 274–290.

Kandiyoti, D. (Ed.). (1991). *Women, Islam and the state.* Philadelphia: Temple.

Kandiyoti, D. (1998). Gender, power and contestation: Rethinking bargaining with patriarchy. In C. Jackson & R. Pearson (Ed.). *Feminist visions of development: Gender analysis and policy.* London: Routledge.

Kandiyoti, D. (2003). *Integrating gender analysis into socio-economic needs assessment in Afghanistan.* Kabul: United Nations Development Fund for Women.

Kandiyoti, D. (2005). The politics of gender and reconstruction in Afghanistan. *Occasional Paper.* Geneva: United Nations Research Institute for Social Development.

Kandiyoti, D. (2007). Political fiction meets gender myth: Post-conflict reconstruction, "democratization" and women's rights. In A. Cornwall, E. Harrison & A. Whitehead (Eds.). *Feminisms in Development: Contradictions, Contestations and Challenges.* London: Zed Books.

Karam, A. M. (2000). Islamisms and the decivilising processes of globalisation. In A. Acre & N. Long (Ed.). *Anthropology, development and modernities: Exploring discourses, counter-tendencies and violence.* London: Routledge.

Karzai, H., Japan, United States, European Union, & Saudi Arabia. (2002, January 21–22). Co-chairs' Summary of conclusions: The international conference on reconstruction assistance to Afghanistan. *Bonn agreement.* Tokyo, Japan.

Kazem, H. (2005). Afghans decry violence against women. *Los Angeles Times.*

Kelly, L. (2000). Wars against women: Sexual violence, sexual politics and the militarized State. In S. Jacobs, R. Jacobson, & J. Marchbank. *States of conflict: Gender, violence and resistance*. London: Zed Books.

Kensinger, L. (2003). Plugged in praxis: Critical reflections on U.S. feminism, internet activism, and solidarity with women in Afghanistan. *Journal of International Women's Studies*, 5(1).

Khadra, Y. (2004). *The swallows of Kabul*. New York: Anchor Books.

Khan, S. (2001). Between here and there: Feminist solidarity and Afghan women. *Genders*, 33.

Kunder, J. P. (2006). *USAID's progress in helping the people of Afghanistan: Statement to committee on armed services at the US House of Representatives*. Washington, D.C.: United States Agency for International Development.

Latifa. (2001). *My forbidden face: Growing up under the Taliban: A young woman's story*. New York: Hyperion.

Leader, N., & Atmar, M. H. (2004). Political projects: Reform, aid, and the state in Afghanistan. In A. Donini, N. Niland, & K. Wermester (Eds.). *Nation-Building Unraveled? Aid, Peace and Justice in Afghanistan*. Bloomfield, CT: Kumarian Press.

Lederach, J. P. (1997). *Building peace: Sustainable reconciliation in divided societies*. Washington, D.C.: United States Institute of Peace Press.

LeVine, M., Mortensen, V., & Evans, J. (2003). *Twilight of empire: Responses to occupation*. Santa Monica, CA: Perceval Press.

Logan, H. (2002). *Unveiled: Voices of women in Afghanistan*. New York: Regan Books.

Long, N. (1977). *An introduction to the sociology of rural development*. London: Tavistock Publications.

Long, N. (1984). Creating space for change: A perspective on the sociology of development. *Sociologia Ruralis*, 24(3/4), 168–184.

Long, N. (2000). Exploring local/global transformations: A view from anthropology. In N. Long & A. Acre (Eds.). *Anthropology, development and modernities: Exploring discourses, counter-tendencies and violence*. London: Routledge.

Long, N., & Long, A. (Eds.). (1992). *Battlefields of knowledge: The interlocking of theory and practice in social research and development*. London: Routledge.

Loyn, D. (Director). (2006). Afghanistan: Losing the aid game [Television broadcast]. *BBC Special Report*, 35 minutes.

Macrae, J. (2002). Politics vs. aid: Is coherence the answer? *Insights*, 39.

Magnus, R. H., & Naby, E. (1998). *Afghanistan: Mullah, Marx, and Mujahid*. Boulder: Westview Press.

Majrouh, S. B. (1994). *Songs of love and war: Afghan women's poetry*. New York: Other Press.

Margesson, R. (2002). Afghanistan's path to reconstruction: Obstacles, challenges, and issues for Congress. Washington, D.C.: Congressional Research Service.

Marsden, P. (1998). *The Taliban: War, religion, and the new order in Afghanistan*. London: Zed Books.

McAllister, P. (1991). *This river of courage: Generations of women's resistance and action*. Philadelphia: New Society Publishers.

McCaffrey, B. (2006). *Academic report—Trip to Afghanistan and Pakistan*. New York: United States Military Academy, West Point.

Mehta, S., Ed. (2002). *Women for Afghan women: Shattering myths and claiming the future*. New York: Palgrave Macmillan.

Mehta, S., & Mamoor, H. (2002). Building community across difference. In S. Mehta (Ed.). *Women for Afghan women: Shattering myths and claiming the future*. New York: Palgrave Macmillan.

Meintjes, S., Turshen, M., & Pillay, A. (Eds.). (2001). *The aftermath: Women in post-conflict transformation*. London: Zed Books.

Mernissi, F. (1975). *Beyond the veil: Male-female dynamics in a modern Muslim society*. New York: John Wiley & Sons.

Mertus, J. (2000). *War's offensive on women: The humanitarian challenge in Bosnia,*

Kosovo, and Afghanistan. West Hartford, CT: Kumarian Press.

Miller, R. L., & Brewer, J. D. (Eds.). (2003). *The A-Z of social research.* London: Sage.

Ministry of Women's Affairs Proposed Framework for the Work of the CG Advisory Group on Gender. Kabul: Ministry of Women's Affairs.

Ministry of Women's Affairs. (2005). *Statistical compilation on gender issues in Afghanistan: Background study for a gender policy framework.* Kabul: Ministry of Women's Affairs, UNIFEM.

Miraki, D.M.D. (2006, April 30). Death made in America. *Rense.* Retrieved 30 April 2006, from http://www.rense.com/general70/deathmde.htm.

Moghadam, V. M. (1992). Patriarchy and the politics of gender in modernising societies: Iran, Pakistan and Afghanistan. *International Sociology,* 7(1), 35–53.

Moghadam, V. M. (1994). Reform, revolution, and reaction: The trajectory of the "woman question" in Afghanistan. In V. M. Moghadam (Ed.). *Gender and National Identity: Women and Politics in Muslim Societies.* London: Zed Books.

Moghadam, V. M. (1999). Revolution, religion, and gender politics: Iran and Afghanistan compared. *Journal of Women's History,* 10(4), 172–195.

Mohanty, C. T. (2003). *Feminism without borders: Decolonizing theory, practicing solidarity.* Durham: Duke University Press.

Molyneux, M. (1985). Mobilization without emancipation? Women's interests, the state, and revolution in Nicaragua. *Feminist Studies,* 11(2), 227–254.

Molyneux, M. (1991). The law, the state and socialist policies with regard to women; the case of the People's Democratic Republic of Yemen, 1967–1990. In D. Kandiyoti (Ed.). *Women, Islam and the state.* Philadelphia: Temple University Press.

Molyneux, M. (1998). Analysing women's movements. In C. Jackson & R. Pearson (Eds.). *Feminist visions of development: Gender analysis and policy.* London: Routledge.

Molyneux, M. (2007). The chimera of success: Gender ennui and the changed international policy environment. In A. Cornwall, E. Harrison, & A. Whitehead (Eds.). *Feminisms in development: Contradictions, contestations and challenges.* London: Zed Books.

Molyneux, M., & Lazar, S. (2003). *Doing the rights thing: Rights-based development and Latin American NGOs.* London: ITDG Publishing.

Molyneux, M., & Razavi, S. (Eds.). (2002). *Gender justice, development, and rights.* Oxford Studies in Democratization. Oxford: Oxford University Press.

Morarjee, R. (2006, May 30). Riots breach Kabul "Island." *Christian Science Monitor.*

Morarjee, R. (2006). What has Afghans so angry. *Time World: Web Exclusive.* Retrieved 30 May 2006, from http://www.time.com/time/world/article/0,8599,1199254,00.html.

Morris, D. (2004). *Off with their heads: Traitors, crooks, and obstructionists in American politics, media, and business.* New York: Regan Books.

Mosadiq, H. (2005). The new Afghan constitution: How women succeeded in ensuring certain rights and what challenges remain. *Critical Half,* summer.

Moser, C. & McIlwaine, C. (2001). *Violence in a post-conflict context: Urban poor perceptions from Guatemala.* Washington, D.C.: The World Bank.

Moser, C. O. N. (1993). *Gender planning and development: Theory, practice and training.* London: Routledge.

Moser, C. O. N., & Clark, F. C. (Eds.). (2001). *Victims, perpetrators or actors? Gender, armed conflict and political violence.* London: Zed Books.

Mosse, D. (2005). *Cultivating development: An ethnography of aid policy and practice.* London: Pluto Press.

Mujahed, J. (2002). Freedom for women: Only words. *Malalai,* 1.

Narayan, U. (1997). *Dislocating cultures: Identities, traditions, and third world feminism.* New York: Routledge.

Nassery, H. (2004). *The gender issue in Afghanistan.* Kabul: United Nations Development Programme.

National Center for Policy Research. (2004). *The database of women's projects in Afghanistan: December 2001 to August 2003.* Department of Social Sciences. Kabul: Kabul University.

Nawabi, M. A. (2003). Women's rights in the new constitution of Afghanistan. Retrieved from http://www.cic.nyu.edu/peacebuilding/oldpdfs/E22Womens%20RightsFullVersionNawabi.pdf.

Niland, N. (2004). Justice postponed: The marginalization of human rights in Afghanistan. In A. Donini, N. Niland, & K. Wermester (Eds.). *Nation-building unraveled? Aid, peace and justice in Afghanistan.* Bloomfield, CT: Kumarian Press.

Noory, L. S. (2006). Where have all the women gone? *The Examiner.* Retrieved 23 June 2006, from http://www.examiner.com/a-158037~Lida_Sahar_Noory_Where_have_all_the_women_gone_.html.

Nussbaum, B. (2001). Commentary: Liberation. *BusinessWeek.* Retrieved 3 December 2001, from http://www.businessweek.com/magazine/content/01_49/b3760701.htm.

Osman, A., & Loewen, A. (2005). *Real men keep their word: Tales from Kabul, Afghanistan: A selection of Akram Osman's Dari short stories.* Oxford: Oxford University Press.

OTI Afghanistan. (2005). *Evaluation of OTI's program in Afghanistan: Focus on gender: Scope of work, OTI.*

Oxfam. (2008). Afghanistan: Development and humanitarian priorities. Kabul: Oxfam International, Afghanistan.

Paci, P. (2002). *Gender in transition.* Washington, D.C.: World Bank.

Pankhurst, D. (1998). *Mainstreaming gender in peacebuilding: A framework for action.* London: International Alert.

Pankhurst, D. (2000). Women, gender and peacebuilding. *Department of Peace Studies Working Paper.* Bradford: University of Bradford.

Pankhurst, D. (2007). Gender issues in post-war contexts: A review of analysis and experience, and implications for policies. *Peace Studies Papers.* Bradford:

United Nations Research Institute for Social Development and University of Bradford.

Parpart, J. (2002). Lessons from the field: Rethinking empowerment, gender and development from a post-(post?)-development perspective. In K. Saunders (Ed.). *Feminist post-development thought: Rethinking modernity, post-colonialism and representation.* London: Zed Books.

Perez, R. (2002). Practising theory through women's bodies: Public violence and women's strategies of power and place. In K. Saunders (Ed.). *Feminist post-development thought: Rethinking modernity, post-colonialism and representation.* London: Zed Books.

Pickup, F., Williams, S., & Sweetman, C. (2001). *Ending violence against women: A challenge for development and humanitarian work.* Oxford: Oxfam Great Britain.

Pugh, M. (1998). Post-conflict rehabilitation: The humanitarian dimension. *Networking the Security Community in the Information Age.* Zurich: Swiss Interdepartmental Coordination Committee for Partnership for Peace.

Rahimi, F. (1977). *Women in Afghanistan.* Kabul: Paul Bucherer-Dietschi.

Ramachandra, V. (1999). *Faith in conflict: Christian integrity in a multicultural world.* Downers Grove, IL: InterVarsity Press.

Range, M. (2005, June 20). Gender equality as a driving force for achieving the MDGs. *Monday Developments.*

Rawi, M. (2004). Rule of the rapists. *The Guardian.* London.

Reynolds, A., Jones, L., & Wilder, A. (2005). *A guide to the parliamentary elections in Afghanistan.* Kabul: Afghanistan Research and Evaluation Unit.

Report on economic and social rights in Afghanistan. (2006). Kabul: Afghanistan Independent Human Rights Commission.

Rist, R. C. (1994). Influencing the policy process with qualitative research. In N. Denzin & Y. Lincoln. *Handbook of qualitative research.* Thousand Oaks, CA: Sage Publications.

Roashan, R. G. (2006, May 4). The compact is a contract with a conscience. *Institute for Afghan Studies.* Retrieved 4 May 2006, from http://www.institute-for-afghan-studies.org/Contributions/Commentaries/DRRoashanArch/2006/020406.htm.

Robichaud, C. (2006). Remember Afghanistan? A glass half full, on the *Titanic. World Policy Journal,* 23(1).

Robinson, J. (2002). *Development and Displacement.* Oxford: Oxford University Press.

Ross, J., Maxwell, S., & Buchanan-Smith, M. (1994). *Linking relief and development.* Brighton: Institute of Development Studies.

Rostami-Povey, E. (2004). Women in Afghanistan: Passive victims of the *borga* or active social participants? In H. Afshar & D. Eade (Eds.). *Development, women and war: Feminist perspectives.* Oxford: Oxfam.

Rostami-Povey, E. (2005). Women and work in Iran. *State of Nature,* Autumn.

Rostami-Povey, E. (2006). The reality of life in Afghanistan since the fall of the Taliban. *State of Nature,* Spring.

Rostami-Povey, E. (2007a). *Afghan women: Identity and invasion.* London: Zed Books.

Rostami-Povey, E. (2007b). Gender, agency and identity, the case of Afghan women in Afghanistan, Pakistan and Iran. *Journal of Development Studies,* 43(2), 294–311.

Rowlands, J. (1998). A word of the times, but what does it mean? Empowerment in the discourse and practice of development. In H. Afshar (Ed.). *Women and empowerment: Illustrations from the third world.* London: Macmillan.

Roy, O. (1994). The new political elite of Afghanistan. In M. Weiner & A. Banuazizi (Eds.). *The politics of social transformation in Afghanistan, Iran, and Pakistan.* Syracuse: Syracuse University Press.

Rubin, B. R. (1994). Redistribution and the state in Afghanistan: The red revolution turns green. In M. Weiner & A. Banuazizi. *The politics of social transformation in Afghanistan, Iran, and Pakistan.* Syracuse: Syracuse University Press.

Rubin, E. (2005). Women's work. *New York Times Magazine.*

Saeed, A. B. (2005). *Dangers of running for office in Afghanistan.* Kabul: Institute for War and Peace Reporting.

Safa, M. (2005, September 13). Women, defense and security. *Deputy Minister for Technical and Policy Concerns.* Afghanistan: Ministry of Women's Affairs.

Said, E. W. (1979). *Orientalism.* New York: Vintage.

Sayigh, R. (1996). Researching gender in a Palestinian camp: Political, theoretical and methodological issues. In D. Kandiyoti (Ed.). *Gendering the Middle East: Emerging perspectives.* London: I.B. Tauris & Co.

Schutte, S. (2004). Urban vulnerability in Afghanistan: Case studies from three cities. *Working Paper Series.* Kabul: Afghanistan Research and Evaluation Unit.

Schutte, S. (2006). Searching for security: Urban livelihoods in Kabul. *Case Study Series.* Kabul: Afghanistan Research and Evaluation Unit.

Security and Peace Initiative (2005). *American attitudes toward national security, foreign policy and the war on terror.* Washington, D.C.: Security and Peace Initiative.

Sen, A. (2006). *Identity and violence: The illusion of destiny.* London: Penguin Books.

Sen, P. (2002). In women's name? *Trouble and Strife,* 43(Summer).

Shah, S. (2003). *The storyteller's daughter.* London: Penguin.

Shapiro, A. (2004). Gender and the war on terror: Partnerships, security and women in Afghanistan. Symposium conducted at the 9th International Interdisciplinary Congress on Women, American University, Washington, D.C.

Sharoni, S. (2001). Rethinking women's struggles in Israel-Palestine and in the north of Ireland. In C. O. N. Moser & F. C. Clark (Eds.). *Victims, perpetrators or actors? Gender, armed conflict and political violence.* London: Zed Books.

Skaine, R. (2002). *The women of Afghanistan under the Taliban.* Jefferson: McFarland & Co.

Skaine, R. (2008). *Women of Afghanistan in the post–Taliban era: How lives have changed and where they stand today*. Jefferson: McFarland & Co.

Skjelsbæk, I., Barth, E. F., & Hostens, K. (2004). Gender aspects of conflict interventions: Intended and unintended consequences. *Report to the Norwegian Ministry of Foreign Affairs*. PRIO. Oslo: International Peace Research Institute.

Smillie, I., & Minear, L. (2004). *The charity of nations: Humanitarian action in a calculating world*. Bloomfield: Kumarian Press.

Stapleton, B. J. (2006). Security and reconstruction in Afghanistan: Shortcomings and mid-term prospects. Karachi: University of Karachi.

Staudt, K. (2002). Dismantling the master's house with the master's tools? Gender work in and with powerful bureaucracies. In K. Saunders (Ed.). *Feminist post-development thought: Rethinking modernity, post-colonialism and representation*. London: Zed Books.

Stockton, N. (2004). Afghanistan, war, aid, and international order. In A. Donini, N. Niland, & K. Wermester (Eds.). *Nation-building unraveled? Aid, peace and justice in Afghanistan*. Bloomfield: Kumarian Press.

Sultan, M. (2002). Hope in Afghanistan. In S. Mehta. *Women for Afghan women: Shattering myths and claiming the future*. New York: Palgrave Macmillan.

Sultan, M. (2005). *From rhetoric to reality: Afghan women on the agenda for peace*. Washington, D.C.: Women Waging Peace Policy Commission.

Swank, Jr., J. G. (2005). Success for females in Afghanistan. *Canada Free Press*, http://www.canadafreepress.com/2005/swank090205.htm.

Sweetman, C., Gell, F. et al. (2001). Editorial. In C. Sweetman (Ed.). *Gender, development, and humanitarian work*. Oxford: Oxfam Great Britain.

Tapper, N. (1991). *Bartered brides: Politics, gender and marriage in an Afghan tribal society*. Cambridge: Cambridge University Press.

Tarzi, A. (2006). Afghan president gets key cabinet picks, but at what price? Retrieved 21 April, 2006, from http://www.rferl.org/content/article/1067838.html.

Terre des Hommes (2003). *The nutrition capitalization report: TDH projects in Afghanistan*. Kabul: Terre des Hommes.

Tonkiss, F. (1988). Analysing discourse. In C. Seale (Ed.). *Researching society and culture*. Thousand Oaks, CA: Sage Publications.

Tortajada, A. (2004). *The silenced cry: One woman's diary of a journey to Afghanistan*. New York: St. Martin's Press.

Turner, S. (2000). Vindicating masculinity: The fate of promoting gender equality. *Forced Migration Review*, 9.

United Nations. (2003). *The situation of women and girls in Afghanistan: Report of the secretary-general*. Commission on the Status of Women. New York: United Nations Economic and Social Council.

United Nations. (2005). *The situation of women and girls in Afghanistan: Commission on the status of women*. New York: United Nations Economic and Social Council.

United Nations. (2005). *World population prospects: The 2004 revision — Highlights*. New York: Department of Economic and Social Affairs of the UN Secretariat.

United Nations. (2006). *The situation in Afghanistan and its implications for international peace and security: Emergency international assistance for peace, normalcy and reconstruction in war-stricken Afghanistan*. New York: United Nations General Assembly Security Council.

United Nations Agency for International Development. (2004). Afghanistan reborn: Building Afghan democracy. Kabul: United Nations Agency for International Development Afghanistan.

United Nations Agency for International Development. (2006). *International women's day special report*. Kabul: United Nations Agency for International Development Afghanistan.

United Nations Agency for International Development /OTI/Afghanistan (2005). *OTI grants benefitting women and girls, October 2001–April 2005*. OTI.

United Nations Development Fund for Women (UNIFEM). (2004). *Promoting women's empowerment and gender equality in Afghanistan: Strategic plan 2004–2007* (Draft: 28 April 2004). Kabul: United Nations Development Fund for Women.

United Nations Development Programme. (2003). *Executive board of the United Nations Development Programme and of the United Nations population fund, assistance to Afghanistan (2004–2005), note by administrator.* Kabul: United Nations Development Programme.

United Nations Development Programme. (2005). *Afghanistan: A country on the move.* Kabul: United Nations Development Programme.

United Nations Development Programme. (2005). *Human Development Report 2005: International cooperation at a crossroads: Aid, trade and security in an unequal world.* New York: United Nations Development Programme.

United Nations Development Programme & Islamic Republic of Afghanistan. (2004). *Afghanistan national human development report 2004: Security with a human face: Challenges and responsibilities.* Kabul: United Nations Development Programme.

United Nations Economic and Social Council. (2004). The situation of women and girls in Afghanistan: Report of the secretary-general. *Women 2000: Gender equality, development and peace for the twenty-first century.* Commission on the Status of Women. New York: United Nation.

United Nations Inter-Agency Network on Women and Gender Equality, OECD/DAC Network on Gender Equality, et al. (2003). Retrieved from http://www.un.org/womenwatch/ianwge/collaboration.htm.

United Nations Population Fund. (UNFPA). (2005). The promise of equality: Gender equity, reproductive health and the millennium development goals. *The state of world population report.* New York: United Nations Population Fund.

United Nations Research Institute for So-cial Development. (2005). Gender equality: Striving for justice in an unequal world. Geneva: United Nations Research Institute for Social Development.

United Nations Secretary General. (1997). *The situation in Afghanistan and its implications for international peace and security.* General Assembly Security Council. New York: United Nations.

United Nations Secretary General. (2002). *The situation in Afghanistan and its implications for international peace and security.* New York: United Nations General Assembly Security Council.

Villarreal, M. (1992). The Poverty of practice: Power, gender and intervention from an actor-oriented perspective. In A. Long & N. Long (Eds.). *Battlefields of knowledge: The interlocking of theory and practice in social research and development.* London: Routledge.

Wakefield, S. & Bauer, B. (2005). A place at the table: Afghan women, men and decision-making authority. *AREU Briefing Paper.* Kabul: Afghanistan Research and Evaluation Unit.

Walby, S. (1988). Gender politics and social theory. *Sociology, 22*(2), 215–232.

Walby, S. (1990). *Theorizing patriarchy.* Oxford: Blackwell.

Walby, S. (1997). *Gender transformations.* London: Routledge.

Walby, S. (2000). Analyzing social inequality in the twenty-first century: Globalization and modernity restructure inequality. *Contemporary Sociology, 29*(6), 813–818.

Walczak, L., Crock, S., & Balfour, F. (2001, December 3). Winning the peace. *BusinessWeek.*

Wali, S. (2002). Afghanistan: Truth and mythology. In S. Mehta (Ed.). *Women for Afghan women: Shattering myths and claiming the future.* New York: Palgrave Macmillan.

Ward, J. (2002). *If not now, when? Addressing gender-based violence in refugee, internally displaced, and post-conflict settings: A global overview.* New York: The Reproductive Health for Refugees Consortium.

Ware, V. (2006). *Info-war and the politics of*

feminist curiosity: Exploring new frame-works for feminist intercultural studies. London: Gender Institute, London School of Economics.

Watkins, M. B. (1963). *Afghanistan: Land in transition.* Princeton: D. Van Nostrand Co.

Weiner, M. & Banuazizi, A. (Eds.). (1994). *The politics of social transformation in Afghanistan, Iran, and Pakistan.* Syracuse: Syracuse University Press.

Weiss, T. G., & Collins, C. (2000). *Humanitarian challenges and intervention: World politics and the dilemmas of help.* Boulder: Westview Press.

Whitlock, G. (2005). The skin of the *bourka*: Recent life narratives from Afghanistan. *Biography,* 28(1).

Wieland-Karimi, A. (2005). *Afghanistan: Looking back on 2004, looking forward to 2005.* Kabul: Friedrich-Ebert-Stiftung.

Wieringa, S. (1994). Women's interests and empowerment: Gender planning reconsidered. *Development and change,* 25, 829–848.

Wilder, A. (2005). *A house divided? Analysing the 2005 Afghan elections.* Kabul: Afghanistan Research and Evaluation Unit.

Winthrop, R. (2003). Reflections on working in post-conflict Afghanistan: Local vs. international perspectives on gender relations. *Women's Studies Quarterly,* 31(3–4).

Women and Children Legal Research Foundation. (2004). *Impact of traditional practices on women.* Kabul: Afghan Women Leaders Connect.

Women and Children Legal Research Foundation. (2005). *Report on women political participation in Afghanistan.* Kabul: Open Society Institute.

Women in Afghanistan: Challenges and opportunities for women's organizations in Afghan civil society. (2005). Washington, D.C.: ActionAid International USA.

Women's Commission for Refugee Women and Children. (2005). *Masculinities: Male roles and male involvement in the promotion of gender equality.* New York: Women's Commission for Refugee Women and Children.

Women's Commission for Refugee Women and Children. (2006). *Displaced women and girls at risk: Risk factors, protection solutions and resource tools.* New York: Women's Commission for Refugee Women and Children.

World Bank. (2002). The conflict analysis framework (CAF): Identifying conflict-related obstacles to development. *Dissemination notes.* Social Development Department: Conflict Prevention and Reconstruction Unit. Washington, D.C.: World Bank.

World Bank. (2002). *Transitional support strategy: Afghanistan.* Washington, D.C.: World Bank.

World Bank. (2004). *Afghanistan: State building, sustaining growth, and reducing poverty: A country economic report.* Kabul: World Bank.

World Bank. (2005). *National reconstruction and poverty reduction: The role of women in Afghanistan's future.* Kabul: World Bank.

Yin, R. K. (1994). *Case study research: Design and methods.* London: Sage.

Young, K. (1993). *Planning development with women: Making a world of difference.* London: Macmillan Press, Ltd.

Index

ActionAid 170
Afghan National Police 144
Afghan Women Empowerment Act 27
Afghan Women Security and Freedom Act 27
Afghan Women's Bill of Rights 35
Afghan Women's NGOs 27
Afghanistan Compact 19
Afghanistan Independent Human Rights Commission 20, 27, 42, 43, 77, 145
Afghanistan: Losing the Aid Game 178
Afghanistan Maternal Mortality Ratio 21
Afghanistan's Millennium Development Goals Report 146
Afghanistan's National Development Strategy 147
afghaniyat 85, 86, 88, 92, 175
aftermath 2, 5, 6, 7, 9, 10, 11, 16, 23, 24, 26, 31, 32, 53, 56, 62, 65, 82, 85, 86, 87, 93, 96, 99, 106; definition 22
agency 6, 9, 11, 23–25, 27, 29, 30, 36, 37, 39, 44–49, 55, 59–61, 66, 68, 96, 106, 111, 112, 114–116, 132, 133, 135, 140, 161, 164, 182, 183, 185, 186, 188
aid apparatus 4, 5, 10, 17–20, 23, 28, 31, 32, 35–37, 39, 40, 42, 47, 50–53, 55, 57, 59, 60–65, 67, 69, 73–76, 81, 82, 87, 89, 91, 96, 99, 104–107, 115, 116, 118, 120–122, 130, 132, 145, 156, 158, 163, 171, 172, 175, 177, 179–181, 185, 187
aid community 11, 55, 62, 63, 142, 173
akl 108
Amanullah 13, 167
Angola 149
Anjuman, Nadia 158
anti-politics 10, 62, 64, 185
Attacks on Education in Afghanistan 82

bad 146, 147
badal 146, 147
Bashardost, Ramazan 118, 179
BBC 178, 179
Behind the Veil 110
bi-namoos 109
Bonn Agreement 17–19
Bonn Process 9, 18, 72–73

Bosnia 149
bourka 29, 35, 37–40, 42, 60, 61, 99, 112, 171, 172; *see also chaddari*; veil
bourka politics 60
Boxer, Barbara 27, 28
The Brains of the Family 111
Brandeis University 34
Bush, George 16, 37, 78, 172
Bush, Laura 78
Bush Administration *see* Bush, George; government, U.S.

chaddari 5, 11, 13, 15, 26, 32–45, 60, 75, 91, 99, 112, 126, 133, 134, 161, 182, 183
chador 134
civil society 85, 177, 181
cold war 214
community/communities 6, 22, 24, 46, 51, 55, 57, 61, 63, 67, 73, 80, 83, 84, 86, 87, 93, 96, 108, 114, 120, 141, 144, 150, 156, 159, 163, 164, 166, 170–172, 180, 187
constitution 14, 17, 35, 44, 72, 76, 142, 147
Convention on the Elimination of all Forms of Discrimination Against Women 17
couples 6, 95, 122, 124–127, 140
culture: Afghan 14, 37, 38, 40, 52, 54, 59, 61, 62, 71, 83, 84, 87, 91, 101, 106, 110, 111, 115, 118, 121, 124, 129, 131, 166–168, 171, 173, 175, 184, 187; general 28, 32, 36, 88, 94, 146, 148, 161

Daily Outlook 157
dar be dar 127–128
Dari 5, 52, 106, 108, 134, 152, 158, 177, 187
death 14, 21, 72, 81, 108, 111, 142, 147, 148, 158
The Deceptive Object 110
Declaration of Afghan Women's NGOs 157
democracy 6, 17, 27, 69, 71, 73, 75–77, 79–84, 100, 102, 119, 164
discrimination 15, 17, 21, 142, 145, 147, 152, 168
domestic violence 20, 22, 55–57, 68, 142, 146, 148–152, 158, 161
donors 17–19, 35, 51, 52, 60, 67, 72, 74, 86, 109, 135, 165, 166, 177

drugs 22, 41, 64, 149, 150, 164
Dupree, Louis 81
Dupree, Nancy Hatch 37, 86, 109, 142

economic opportunities 116, 128, 142, 149, 150, 169
education 20, 21, 43, 54, 57, 75, 76, 82–84, 89, 90, 92, 93, 95–97, 99, 101–105, 114–116, 124–127, 132, 133, 138, 140, 141, 146, 152, 180
election, parliamentary see parliamentary election
election, presidential see presidential election
employment 21, 46, 57, 66, 107, 109, 135, 153, 154
empowerment 23, 26–30, 48, 50–52, 54, 62, 65, 67–69, 148, 160, 161, 164, 167, 170, 171, 180, 185
Erturk, Yakin 146
ethnicity 34, 88–90, 92–94, 105, 108, 120, 134, 146, 181
Expatlordism 177
exploitation 21, 45

family 6, 14, 20, 24, 41, 42, 53, 55, 63, 67, 76, 78, 80, 86–91, 93–96, 101, 106, 107, 109–111, 117, 119, 120, 122, 123–129, 134, 137, 138, 140–142, 144, 146, 147, 149, 150, 152, 153, 158, 159, 166, 167, 171
female candidates 73, 76–81, 83, 101
female-headed households 22
femininity 24, 166
feminism 29, 35, 49, 186
Ferguson, James 10, 64, 185
finances 41, 75, 117, 149, 177
forced marriage 147
freedom 7, 9, 12, 27, 34, 37, 40–42, 57, 80, 89, 97, 100, 103, 104, 109–111, 115, 118, 119, 126, 130, 131, 139, 142, 147, 150, 164, 172, 176, 177, 187, 188
Freedom for Women: Only Words 187
From the Root of a Shrub 110
funding 11, 17, 19, 27, 35, 51, 65, 67, 76, 118, 170, 181

Gender and Development (GAD) 30
Gender Apartheid 18, 33, 36, 130
Gender Development Index 21
gender equality/inequality 3, 6, 18, 21, 32, 39, 53, 56, 69, 85, 88, 145, 147, 161, 183
gender-focused international aid 1, 3, 4, 5, 9, 10, 11, 31, 49, 61, 160, 171, 182, 183, 185
gender order 2, 3, 5, 9, 11, 23, 24, 25, 26, 30, 31, 56, 85, 87, 89, 91, 93, 95, 97, 99, 101, 103, 105, 122, 145, 146, 148, 159, 161, 176, 180, 181, 182, 183, 184, 187
gender relations 31, 45, 55, 65, 85, 86, 98,

99, 101, 102, 125, 127, 144, 146, 149, 154, 159, 162, 172
gender roles 6, 63, 86, 93, 97, 99, 100, 105, 106, 109, 111, 121, 144, 151, 159, 160
ghayrat 110
Global Peace Index 19, 148
government 14, 17, 34, 57, 72, 82, 99, 100, 102, 118, 127, 145, 147, 158, 164, 175, 177, 179, 181, 183–185; U.S. 27, 34, 64; see also Bush Administration
gozargah 187, 188
Grand Assembly 27, 199; see also Loya Jirga
Guatemala 149

harassment 18, 62, 73, 79, 81, 141, 142, 148
Hazara 120, 134
health 20, 21, 52
Herat 142, 147
history 5, 6, 9, 12, 14, 16, 19, 22, 24, 29, 32, 39, 55, 60, 69, 71, 72, 85, 86, 90, 92, 97, 99, 100, 102, 108, 109, 120, 127, 150, 160, 161, 166, 168, 171, 173–175, 178, 180, 184, 187
honor 6, 14, 15, 24, 66, 67, 68, 77, 84, 86, 92, 93, 96, 97, 106–111, 128, 129, 140, 144, 147, 154, 156
household 22, 41, 88, 96, 109, 122, 124, 149, 159
Human Development Index 21
Human Development Report 67, 73
human rights 17, 20, 27, 28, 34, 35, 42, 43, 45, 50, 64, 77, 82, 109, 141, 144, 145, 147, 173, 178, 186
Human Rights Department 42
Human Rights Watch 77, 82, 178
Human Rights Watch Report 82
hunger 35, 136, 140
Hurricane Katrina 150

identity 6, 17, 23–26, 28, 38, 56, 76, 85–91, 92–94, 105, 106, 121, 129, 132, 159, 175
illiteracy 21
imperialism 28, 30, 35, 145, 175, 176
income 21, 41, 66, 67, 117, 125, 151, 153, 154, 159, 172
inja Afghanistan ast 122
insecurity 3, 19, 82, 142, 146, 151, 170
instability 23, 144, 181, 182
interface 7, 27, 32, 33, 92, 175, 176, 181, 182
international community 15, 54, 61, 71, 80, 87, 153, 181
International Conference in Support of Afghanistan 19
International Women's Day 187
internet petition 34

jinsiyat 52
jirga see *Loya Jirga*; *Wolesi Jirga*

Joint Verification of Political Rights 77
justice/injustice 32, 34, 142, 147, 157, 186

Kabul City 13–16, 66, 73, 79, 93, 96, 98, 101, 116, 119, 120, 124, 129, 133, 137–139, 142, 152, 158, 175–177, 187
Kabul University 69
Kabul Weekly 158, 177
Kandahar 83
Karzai, Hamid 18, 27
kash-ma-kash 152
Khan, Daud Muhammad 111
kharab 42
kharijis 62, 71
khshoonat aley-he zanaan 152
khub musselman ast 94
Koran 80, 91

landay 110, 111
law 11, 16, 17, 21, 27, 39, 45, 72, 90, 91, 99, 131, 142, 146, 147, 149, 151, 152, 155, 179, 181, 183
leadership 74, 164, 167, 172, 183
liberation 5, 16, 17, 19, 26, 29, 33, 34, 36, 39, 41, 44, 46–49, 52, 59, 60, 64, 141, 164, 170, 185
literacy 14, 20, 21, 120
Loewen, Arley 110
London Conference 19
Loya Jirga 17, 18, 72, 73; *see also* Grand Assembly

maida 106
mainstreaming 44–46, 48, 50, 53, 86, 166, 170
Malalai 186
mamus 97
marda ra qawl 110
marriage 5, 86, 89, 92, 95–98, 101–103, 107, 114, 124, 125, 130, 132–134, 138, 139, 142, 145–147, 152, 154
masculinity 25, 56, 106, 107, 148, 149, 166
Mazar-i-Sharif 137
media 3, 5, 6, 15, 16, 19, 22, 23, 26, 32–37, 39, 45–48, 60, 74, 81, 96, 107, 115, 142, 166, 174, 180, 182, 183
Mexico 149
Minister of Women's Affairs 63, 80, 88, 141, 158
Ministry of Interior 42, 43
Ministry of Women's Affairs 10, 17, 19, 27, 44, 80, 147
modernization/modernity 1, 10, 13, 14, 120, 160, 175
money 19, 20, 28, 42, 45, 59, 63, 84, 117, 127, 128, 138, 139, 166, 169, 178
Mujaheddin 15, 172
Mullah 13, 75, 80, 91

Najibullah 167
namoos 96, 97, 108–109
nang 96, 97
nar shedza 109
National Action Plan for Women of Afghanistan 19
National Development Framework 18
neglect of men 56, 106, 116, 132, 167, 168, 182
nezaa 152
NGO 3, 6, 9, 27, 39, 40, 42, 50–54, 57, 59, 63, 64, 68, 69, 71, 73, 74, 78, 82, 87, 89, 117, 118, 130, 131, 145, 149, 150, 156, 157, 159, 164, 167, 168, 172, 173, 177–179, 182, 187
nufus-dar 93
Nuristani 120

occupation 7, 14, 20, 52, 91, 140, 145, 155, 163, 170, 173, 175, 176; Soviet 14, 97, 111
Open Letter to Expatriates in Afghanistan 177
opium 21; *see also* poppy
oppression 15, 18, 24, 28, 30, 34–38, 40, 44, 60, 68, 91, 96, 98, 108, 112, 114, 130, 141, 148, 158
Orientalism 29, 34
Osman, Akram 110

Pakistan 137, 138, 174, 181
parliamentary election 71, 73, 74, 77, 78, 80, 83
Pashto 5, 52, 111
Pashtun 37, 74, 108, 110, 111, 120, 133, 134
Pashtunwali 108
patriarchy 15, 21, 24, 60, 146, 180, 182
peace 19, 22, 23, 41, 64, 73, 85, 87, 100, 114–116, 137–141, 145, 148, 179
Peace Index *see* Global Peace Index
peacekeeper 20
police 43, 144
policy 2, 3, 5, 6, 9–11, 21, 31, 32, 40, 44, 46, 48, 61, 64, 68, 78, 138, 157, 163, 171, 175, 183, 185, 188; implementers 3, 32, 50, 55, 63, 69, 71, 74, 87, 135, 150, 151, 173, 174, 182; makers 3, 6, 9, 32, 50, 52, 69, 74, 87, 135, 144, 150, 151, 163, 173, 182
political interventions 5, 22, 30, 31, 65, 68, 182
political project 24, 65, 69, 85, 88, 108, 122, 183, 185
poppies 74; *see also* opium
post-conflict 19, 22, 23, 57, 148, 149, 151, 169, 170, 172, 178, 178
poverty 3, 20–22, 26, 30, 40, 42, 45, 46, 48, 50, 56, 61, 73, 75, 94, 98, 107, 129, 137, 139, 140–142, 145–147, 149, 151, 168, 179, 180

prayer 127, 189
presidential election 35, 71, 73
project 2, 10, 46, 48, 57, 61, 65–67, 166,
    172, 175, 177, 186, 187
Provincial Council 72
purdah 106–108

Qiam, Sanjar 177–178

Rabbani, Burhanuddin 176, 177
rape 156, 158
Real Men Keep Their Word 110
reconstruction 3, 17, 18, 19, 22, 85, 141,
    148, 158, 159, 162, 177, 187
recovery 3
reform 12–15, 106, 171, 180, 184, 186
refugees 15, 139, 149, 175
religion 54, 86, 90, 91, 94, 108, 115, 125,
    134, 173, 176
*Report of the UN Secretary General on the
    Situation of Women and Girls in Afghani-
    stan 2004* 142
revolution 12, 68, 150
The Revolutionary Association of the
    Women of Afghanistan (RAWA) 144,
    145, 167
Rozgaran 80
Rubin, Barnett 184, 185
Rwanda 149

The Saur (April) Revolution 14
school 21, 42, 72, 81–83, 117, 124, 126, 142,
    167, 171
Securing Afghanistan's Future 18
self-immolation 22, 147
September 11, 2001 10
Sex, Drugs, and Rock 'n' Roll 64
sexual identity 92, 93
sexual violence 62, 146–148
sexuality 52, 107
shabnam 82–84
Shah, Saira 110
sharia 77
social change 2, 10–12, 14, 15, 24–26, 31,
    32, 41, 45, 56, 61, 65, 85, 104, 115, 120,
    140, 160, 161, 168, 171, 173, 175, 176, 180,
    182, 184, 185
Soundless Cries 158
Special Advisor on Gender Issues and the
    Advancement of Women 37
The Storyteller's Daughter 110
Strategic Framework for Afghanistan 16, 17

Tajik 120, 134
Taliban 15, 16, 34–38, 41, 46, 47, 62, 82,
    84, 91, 99, 137–140, 145, 146, 154, 160,
    167, 172, 174, 177, 178, 186

Tanzania 149
tarsidah 152
tashadud 152
tashadud aley-he zanaan 152
technical interventions 5, 10, 11, 22, 23, 28,
    30–32, 45–48, 63–65, 67, 68, 76, 161,
    165, 180, 182, 185
technology 14, 21
terrorism 64, 114, 118
Tokyo Conference 18
transformation 3, 5, 9, 11, 22–28, 30–32,
    39, 48, 50, 54, 55, 62, 65, 69, 104, 159,
    160, 174, 181–187

unemployment 22, 41, 125, 145, 149, 181
United Nations 72, 73, 101, 103, 118, 184
United Nations Assistance Mission in
    Afghanistan 77
United Nations Development Fund for
    Women 147
United Nations Development Programme
    181
United Nations High Commissioner for
    Refugees 149
United Nations Research Institute for Social
    Development 150
*United Nations Secretary General Report on
    Women, Peace, and Security 2002* 148
United Nations Special Rapporteur on Vio-
    lence against Women 146
Universal Declaration of Human Rights 17
urban 14, 21, 22, 62, 114, 120, 132, 133, 142,
    149, 159, 171, 175, 176
Uzbek 120

veil 36, 182, 183
victim/victimization 15, 18, 29, 36, 37, 41,
    45, 48, 50, 60, 71, 83, 102, 112, 114, 116,
    130
vote 72, 74–80

Walby, Sylvia 25, 26, 48
War on Terror 19, 29
warlord 74, 81, 138, 164, 177
western feminism 19, 158
westernization 53, 110, 111, 151
widow 21, 93, 95, 117, 132, 133, 138, 139,
    158
Wolesi Jirga 72, 73, 80
Women in Development (WID) 30, 63
women's rights 14, 18, 20, 21, 27–29, 32,
    34, 35, 37–40, 42, 43, 57, 64, 67, 69,
    72, 80, 91, 98, 99, 100–103, 106, 112, 115,
    118–120, 124, 129, 131, 134, 139, 141, 142,
    144, 147, 150, 154, 155, 160–163, 165, 167,
    171, 172, 174–176
World Bank 20, 55, 180, 181